FOOLS and WISE MEN

The Rise and Fall of the One Big Union

FOOLS and WISE MEN

David J. Bercuson

McGRAW-HILL RYERSON LIMITED
Toronto Montreal New York St. Louis San Francisco
Auckland Beirut Bogotá Düsseldorf Johannesburg
Lisbon London Lucerne Madrid Mexico New Delhi
Panama Paris San Juan Saõ Paulo Singapore Sydney
Tokyo

Fools and Wise Men: The Rise and Fall of the One Big Union
Copyright © McGraw-Hill Ryerson Limited, 1978.

ISBN 0-07-082644-7 Trade edition
　　　0-07-082645-5 College edition

1 2 3 4 5 6 7 8 9 10 D 7 6 5 4 3 2 1 0 9 8

Printed and bound in Canada

Canadian Cataloguing in Publication Data

　Bercuson, David Jay, date
　　Fools and wise men

Bibliography: p.
ISBN 0-07-082644-7 bd. ISBN 0-07-082645-5 pa.

1. One Big Union—History. 2. Trade-unions—Canada—History. I.
Title.

HD8102.054B47　331.88'0971　C78-001132-5

Contents

For Mother and Dad and Cindy

Preface

This is the story of the One Big Union—the people who built it and those who tore it down. The tale is well known in its broad outlines to many people with an interest in Canadian history, but because it was a failure—and history is generally about winners—few have a clear idea of what the OBU was, why it was created and the reasons for its rapid demise. I have long believed the story should be told in full, because it carries with it an explanation of what happened to the spirit of radicalism and revolt that motivated many working people in the west prior to 1920. Sometimes the explanation of a failure is more revealing than the description of a success.

Many people and institutions gave their time and money to help me write this book. I am grateful to the Canada Council for two grants and to the University of Calgary for two. Craig Brown, Michael Bliss, William Rodney and Howard Palmer read chapters and commented critically on them. Terry Chapman, my research assistant, worked hard even after the money was gone to assure that the tedious task of newspaper scanning was complete.

I would like to thank Richard Berner at the University of Washington Library, Paul I. Chestnut at the Duke University Library, Jim Whitridge at the Canada Department of Labour Library, George Brandak at the University of British Columbia Library, Nancy Stunden at the Public Archives of Canada, Jean Van Raalte at the University of Calgary Library, Sheilagh Jameson at the Glenbow Institute, Allan Ridge at the Provincial Museum and Archives of Alberta, John Bovey and Barry Hyman at the Manitoba Provincial Archives. Thanks are also due to the staff of the State Historical Society at Madison, Wisconsin, and the Archives of Labor History and Urban Affairs at Wayne State University. Other people who helped in different ways are Lorry Felske, Tony Rasporich, Karyl Winn, E. C. Morgan, Robert Babcock, Anne Yandle, Ross McCormack, Ernie Forbes. I am grateful to my wife Cheryl for putting up with the inconveniences, for her research help on two trips, but most of all for her encouragement and strong support that sustained me through many a crisis.

I received much help, but my mistakes are my own.

Introduction

The Forgotten People

The worker's revolt which shook Canadian society to its roots in the months following World War I began when men first cut coastal fir, dug mines, or repaired railway cars and locomotives west of the Lakehead. This took place at various times—in the 1840s on Vancouver Island, the 1880s in the area which would become known as Lethbridge, the 1890s in the Crows Nest Pass or the 1890s, 1900s and 1910s in Calgary, Edmonton, Moose Jaw, Regina and Winnipeg. Whenever and wherever it occurred, a pattern of conflict, confrontation and revolt was established from the beginning.

The western industrial frontier was opened in the late 1840s with small-scale coal mining and lumbering on Vancouver Island. In the following decades, expanding markets on the California coast made these mining and logging operations attractive areas for capitalist enterprise. The gold mines which appeared in the Fraser, Thompson and Cariboo areas in the late 1850s were small, primitive extensions of individual placer mining efforts and had almost no lasting economic impact, although the hordes of non-British gold seekers they lured to the interior prompted the creation of a united British Columbia in 1858.

Resource extraction, transportation and construction were the three main activities of the western non-agricultural workforce. The extractive industry was based on coal mining, hardrock mining and logging. Transportation created a need for people to operate, service and repair the trains which were the veins and arteries of the west. Construction met the needs of hundreds of thousands of immigrants for houses and the demand of entrepreneurs for warehouses, office blocks, factories and, inevitably, industrial exchange buildings and private clubs. The story of these industries is as much a part of western history as the hardy peasant in his sheepskin coat.

The first western mining was for coal. The Hudson's Bay Company put the Nanaimo colliery on Vancouver Island into operation in 1851 (there had been some coal mining on the Island since 1849). The Island coal mines expanded as they passed from the Hudson's Bay Company to Robert Dunsmuir to Canadian Collieries Limited, under the ownership of William Mackenzie and Donald Mann. These collieries provided coal for the local and coastal market as far south as San Francisco. In the 1880s coal mines were opened in the Northwest Territories at Medicine Hat, Lethbridge and Canmore. The coals of eastern British Columbia, Alberta and Saskatchewan were usually of the soft, or bituminous variety, though lignite, the lowest grade coal, and small amounts of anthracite, the highest, were also produced. Western Canadian coal was "domestic," produced primarily for home heating in local and regional markets, and "steam" for the railways. In the 1890s the first mines were opened in the Crows Nest Pass and, by 1914, this was a major coal-producing area. The last significant coal mines in the west were opened at Drumheller in 1911 and west of Edmonton from 1909 to 1914. By the beginning of the First World War thousands of miners worked collieries from Lethbridge in the south, to Edmonton, Coalspur and Brulé in the north, and from Estevan and Bienfait in southern Saskatchewan, to Nanaimo on Vancouver Island.

Large-scale hardrock mining for lead, zinc, silver, gold and copper began along the British Columbia boundary with the United States in the early 1890s. The towns of Rossland, Slocan, Phoenix and Trail in the Kootenay mountains, near or on the shores of Lake Kootenay, developed alongside mines with colorful names such as Centre Star, War Eagle, Home Stake. Gold was the first object of this activity and discovery of a large deposit in 1893 at the LeRoi Mine brought a major influx of people and capital into the area. In 1892 the first lead-zinc-silver find was made in the Slocan Hills near the future site of Sandon. In the following decade smelters were established at Trail and Grand Forks and the foundations of a major mining industry were laid. The British Columbia ore deposits were the northernmost tip of a vast storehouse of precious and semi-precious metals which stretched from Denver, Colorado, to Virginia City, Nevada, and from the B.C. interior to Bisbee in southern Arizona.

By 1910 a complex, interrelated, industrial structure had developed based upon Kootenay metals. Smelters at Granby, Trail, Northport, Washington, and other locations refined the ore-bearing quartz. They used the higher grade bituminous coals of the Alberta and British Columbia Crows Nest Pass and Vancouver Island to provide energy for refining. As long as the smelters operated to meet world demand, the coal mines and the

hardrock mines which fed them ran smoothly and prof-
itably. Prior to 1913 the future looked bright. Investment money from banks, syndicates and railroads, from
central Canada, Britain and the United States, flowed
in. The region's hothouse economy, fueled by outside
demand and internal development, supported the
founding and growth of towns and railways. Few world
market price fluctuations had any serious impact on the
area during this period.

The logging industry on the Pacific Coast and in the
Thunder Bay, Ontario region bracketed the west.
Small-scale logging operations were started by the Hudson's Bay Company on Vancouver Island in the late
1840s. These efforts were intended to supply a market
for spars and masts in the San Francisco area. Later, in
the 1860s, more extensive logging was started at Bur-
rard Inlet, on the mainland, to compete in the international market for spars and sawn lumber on the Pacific
rim in places as far removed as San Francisco, Australia
and China. To the east, lumbering began in northwestern Ontario as an extension of the Minnesota logging
frontier in the 1880s.

These western industries employed tens of thousands
of workers, most of whom were immigrants. Some came
to escape political oppression, religious persecution and
economic deprivation. Others sought opportunity and
advancement. These were the forgotten people in the
saga of western settlement because every government
effort aimed at peopling the west was directed to farmers, not industrial workers. But they were essential to
western development. On the coast, British miners
worked alongside Americans and the hated Chinese. In
the interior, veterans of Idaho mining wars and the
struggles of the Nevada Comstock Lode worked the
hardrock mines with British immigrants and east Europeans. In the Crows Nest Pass and Alberta's domestic
coal fields, Italians, Slovaks and other Europeans min-

gled with the British and Canadians, many from the mining towns of Nova Scotia. In older mining districts, such as those on Vancouver Island, there were more native born workers, but in the new mining towns, almost everyone was from somewhere else (see Table 1).

The urban workforce was primarily a creature of the railways. Western cities were moulded by decisions made in railway board rooms. The yards and repair shops at Winnipeg, Moose Jaw and Calgary needed skilled workers who needed other workers to build their homes, stores, schools and churches. As the farming population grew they demanded implements, cloth, marketing facilities and banking services. The cities, with their wholesale and retail supply houses, express companies, slaughter houses, hospitals and funeral parlours, expanded accordingly. To these cities, from Britain, the United States and central Canada, came machinists, blacksmiths, boilermakers, electricians, plumbers, carpenters, bricklayers and stonemasons, as well as countless other workers in crafts from typesetting to bookbinding to tailoring. From eastern and southern Europe came the less skilled who laid track, carried bricks and boards or handed up the machinists' tools. In older communities such as Winnipeg, a thriving town by the 1880s, there was a larger native-born population to fill some of these jobs, but in the newer and smaller cities, immigrants were as necessary and as numerous as in the mining towns (see Table 2).

The pattern of immigration and industrialization was well established before the First World War. Thousands of workers built homes, offices and factories while thousands of others ran trains, moved freight, repaired cars and locomotives and tended waterworks, electrical lines and telephone networks. In Alberta and British Columbia valleys men dug coal or blasted quartz to extract lead, zinc, silver, copper and gold. In small logging camps in northwestern Ontario and among the tower-

TABLE 1

ORIGINS OF POPULATION IN SELECTED MINING AREAS
(BY PERCENTAGE) FROM DATA PRESENTED IN THE 1911
CENSUS OF CANADA

ORIGIN	KOOTENAY B.C.		NANAIMO B.C.		INVERNESS N.S.		CUMBERLAND N.S.	
	M	F	M	F	M	F	M	F
PROVINCE OF DOMICILE	11.20	22.70	21.94	36.28	91.57	95.81	81.37	83.40
REST OF CANADA	22.31	24.24	9.33	11.90	2.99	0.57	10.53	10.41
UNITED KINGDOM	24.28	25.56	37.32	38.83	1.59	1.67	4.62	3.58
CONTINENTAL EUROPE	24.95	13.59	8.88	4.00	2.56	0.99	1.47	0.71
ASIA	3.96	0.57	15.66	0.84	0.06	0.02	0.14	0.03
UNITED STATES	9.61	12.15	4.61	6.47	0.66	0.66	1.15	1.19

TABLE 2

ORIGINS OF POPULATION IN SELECTED CITIES (BY PERCENTAGE)
FROM DATA PRESENTED IN THE 1911 CENSUS OF CANADA

ORIGIN	HALIFAX N.S.		HAMILTON ONT.		WINNIPEG MAN.		CALGARY ALTA.		VANCOUVER B.C.	
	M	F	M	F	M	F	M	F	M	F
PROVINCE OF DOMICILE	87.80	88.93	58.72	67.37	20.50	26.54	10.24	15.82	12.25	18.55
REST OF CANADA	2.51	2.54	1.34	1.37	20.44	22.18	29.10	33.94	26.07	31.03
UNITED KINGDOM	8.45	4.09	27.72	25.27	31.69	25.88	32.75	27.92	33.08	30.23
CONTINENTAL EUROPE	0.61	0.36	7.51	3.28	19.37	18.65	12.20	7.49	8.53	3.97
ASIA	0.19	0.10	0.86	0.05	0.92	0.12	2.15	0.07	7.22	1.29
UNITED STATES	0.74	0.77	3.51	3.96	4.01	4.86	11.73	14.09	8.83	11.83

ing firs of the Pacific coast, an army of loggers cut millions of trees. This workforce numbered in the hundreds of thousands, a great but scattered and divided mass that soon began to mould itself into a force for the protection of its interests and the assertion of its rights. That moulding continued every day in the shops, mines and lumber camps of western Canada. Its eventual result—the workers' revolt—developed primarily out of the daily fight to survive.

Key

ACCL—All Canadian Congress of Labour
AFL—American Federation of Labor
APP—Alberta Provincial Police
B & O Plan—Baltimore and Ohio Plan
BCFL—British Columbia Federation of Labor
BESCO—British Empire Steel and Coal Corporation
CBRE—Canadian Brotherhood of Railway Employees
CCCL—Canadian and Catholic Confederation of
   Labour
CCL—Canadian Congress of Labour
CLC—Canadian Labour Congress
GWVA—Great War Veteran's Association
IAM—International Association of Machinists
ILA—International Longshoreman's Association
IMB—Imperial Munitions Board
IWW—Industrial Workers of the World
OBU—One Big Union
RNWMP—Royal North West Mounted Police
SPC—Socialist Party of Canada
TLC—Trades and Labour Congress
UMWA—United Mine Workers of America
WIUA—Workers Industrial Union of Australia

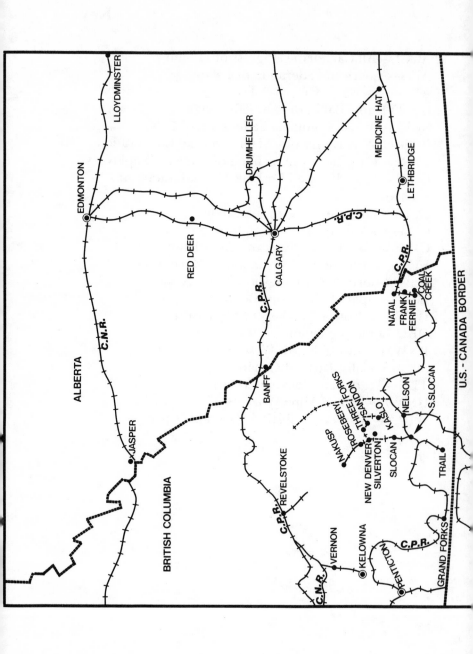

Only fools try to make revolutions,
Wise men conform to them.

—WILLIAM A. PRITCHARD, 1919.

Chapter 1

The Fight for Survival

A coal miner always knew it could happen to him; this day, any day, could be his last; he could die underground without ever again seeing the sun. This was a fact of life for the miners who worked the coal seams of the Canadian west. Perhaps they learned to live with death, not to think about it, as the man car, or the elevator, slipped into the gloom to take them to work. But it was always there, a stark reality that would never go away. On the morning of June 19, 1914, this reality was brought dramatically home to the little Alberta town of Hillcrest, 123 miles west of Medicine Hat, on the Crows

1

Fools and Wise Men

Nest Pass line of the Canadian Pacific Railway. At approximately 9:30 a.m., an explosion tore through the colliery where 235 men were working. Forty-six miners in Number 1 North level escaped unscathed. The rest, 189 men, were killed in Canada's worst mine disaster.

For a few brief days a shocked world focused on the Hillcrest tragedy. The King sent a message of condolence as the townspeople dug out the entombed remains of fathers, brothers and sons. Over one hundred of the miners left wives and children behind. The explosion was indiscriminate: fathers and sons, brothers, friends all died together. It killed many instantly and tore their bodies to pieces. As the hours passed, the grim task of recovering bodies, washing them and putting the proper arms and legs into the correct coffins, continued. On Sunday, June 21, 150 recovered bodies were laid to rest in the town cemetery.[1]

In June and July, 1914, a federal commission of inquiry examined the mine to determine what caused the explosion. They concluded that a pocket of methane gas, "firedamp," formed from fumes coming off the coal face, had ignited and had touched off another, more massive, explosion of coal dust lingering in the colliery. The United States Bureau of Mines had previously determined that the coal dust here was highly explosive but the commission concluded that the mine was not dusty and there was no evidence of faulty ventilation or an extraordinary gas build-up prior to the explosion. There was no way of knowing with any certainty what had touched off the gas.[2] A reasonably safe mine, kept in reasonably safe condition had killed 189 men.

Death was a way of life in the coal mines of western Canada—they were among the most dangerous in the world. In the decade ending 1918, 737 miners were killed in British Columbia and Alberta collieries.[3] On the British Columbia side of the Crows Nest Pass, coal dust was highly explosive and gas seepage was fifteen times greater than in comparable Pennsylvania mines.[4] Men working these pits were twice as likely to be killed as those in Nova Scotia or in the United States (see Table 3).

Serious accidents, which left maimed victims, were even more numerous than deaths. Just as there were countless ways to die in a coal mine—fire, explosion, rockfall, suffocation—there were innumerable ways to lose an eye or an arm. While gas explosions accounted for the most deaths, the ponderous movement of horses, mules or mine cars in the tricky dark of the collieries, accounted for most of the accidents. In the cramped space underground it was all too easy to have an arm or a leg crushed between mine cars or to have a foot run over. Sometimes the handling of the animals, which pulled the cars below ground in most mines, resulted in a hoof in the ribs or a crushed pelvis. The list was long and melancholy.

Some accidents could not be avoided; others were caused by poorly drawn or loosely enforced regulations, laxity in the inspection of mines for gas and coal dust, management negligence or the use of faulty equipment. At 10:20 p.m. on April 5, 1917, an explosion tore through No. 3 mine of the Coal Creek colliery in the Crows Nest Pass. The mine was owned by the Crows Nest Pass Coal Company and was known to contain high levels of gas. A neighbouring colliery, No. 2 mine, had been wracked by an explosion in 1902 with the loss of 130 lives. This time thirty-four men were killed. Later investigations revealed, among other things, that the ventilation system in the mine was inefficient and did not pull out enough gas to keep the air inside at a uniformly safe level. It was also found that government regulations requiring the evacuation of places inside the mine with dangerous levels of gas were loosely drawn and open to misinterpretation. Further, the mine was

3

TABLE 3
FATALITIES PER MILLION TONS OF COAL
MINED OVER ONE DECADE

	1907	1908	1909	1910	1911	1912	1913	1914	1915	1916	AVG.
B.C.	13.96	8.53	23.75	8.92	7.30	9.25	10.50	9.39	26.36	11.26	12.92
ALTA.	10.35	5.96	4.14	20.08	4.13	6.09	6.50	54.68	5.24	4.30	12.15
N.S.	5.61	6.09	5.82	5.05	5.18	4.46	5.95	4.72	5.74	3.99	5.26
U.S.	NA	5.97	5.73	5.62	5.35	4.53	4.89	4.78	4.27	3.77	4.99

Sources: Nova Scotia, *Annual Report on Mines 1940* (Halifax, 1941), p. 114; *Ibid.* (1944), p. 186; Alberta, *Annual Report of the Department of Public Works of Alberta 1916* (Edmonton, 1917), p. 110; British Columbia, *Annual Report of the Bureau of Mines 1910* (Victoria, 1911), p. 230; *Ibid.* (1920), p. 358.

too dusty and the watering system designed to keep the dust down was inadequate. While two inspectors refused to speculate on the ultimate cause of the explosion, a third blamed it on a faulty safety lamp and charged that lamp testing at this mine was inadequate. Later in the year a small explosion at No. 6 Mine, Comox Colliery, owned by Canadian Collieries (Dunsmuir) Limited, claimed four lives. This time the investigator pointed to a conscious contravention of regulations and the use of open flame, rather than safety lamps, as the cause.[5]

On the morning of February 9, 1915, at the South Wellington colliery on Vancouver Island, perhaps the sorriest wastage of human life occurred in an area where men went daily to their deaths. At approximately 11:30 a.m. miners working in No. 3 north level broke through into the Southfield mine, an abandoned and flooded colliery lying adjacent to the South Wellington mine. The water swirled five hundred feet up the mine slope, rising twenty-five vertical feet in minutes. Nineteen men were trapped and drowned. Though pumping operations were started that night, it took more than seventy days before the water had subsided enough to allow the bodies to be recovered.

The investigation by provincial chief inspector of mines Thomas Graham revealed incredible bungling and negligence by management. When the South Wellington colliery was planned, the company obtained blueprints of the adjacent, flooded colliery, drawn to a scale of 132 feet to the inch. The plans for their own mine were drawn on a smaller scale of 100 feet to the inch, standard for North America at that time. The company's draughtsman was aware of the difference in the two plans and scaled down the larger blueprint of the flooded mine to match the plans of the new colliery. The master blueprint thus showed a true picture of the relationship of the two mines. This was in 1908.

Fools and Wise Men

Over the years management personnel came and went and the master blueprint was somehow misplaced. When a new plan was drawn, the draughtsman overlooked the difference in scale of the two separate blueprints and drew the flooded mine 32% smaller than it really was. Its closest point to the new mine was represented as being 752 feet farther away. In the company's office lay yet another neglected set of master plans showing the two mines drawn to the same scale. Graham later discovered these during his investigation. He concluded that it was "difficult to understand how the information escaped the notice of the colliery staff" and did not see how the data could be "so overlooked or misapplied." Six days before the water rushed into the South Wellington colliery, a mine inspector was being conducted through the workings by manager Joseph Foy. When he remarked upon the unusual amount of water in the mine and asked if the seepage might be coming from the flooded colliery, Foy answered, "Have no fear about Old Southfield, we are from 500 to 600 feet below any workings of Southfield mine."[6]

Alberta and British Columbia had extensive coal mine acts on their statute books. These laws were intended to standardize and control safe mining practices and directed operators towards proper timbering, ventilating and testing of mines and equipment. The regulations were updated often and became more stringent through the years as governments, operators and miners learned more about their industry and about the causes of the high rate of deaths and injuries.[7] In British Columbia the law stipulated that a man had to be certified as having some knowledge of mining practices before he could go underground. This system was designed to separate the "practical" or professional miners from the fieldhands and harvest workers who drifted into the mining camps in the winter with no idea of how to dig coal. Because of their inexperience they had great

6

potential for causing accidents. The system rarely worked, but was better than in Alberta where there was no system at all. There the men tried, through their union, to determine who would go underground by establishing two systems of union dues, one for practical miners and the other for unskilled men.[8] Though laws and regulations were sometimes broken or ignored, the mines were usually as safe as current knowledge and practices could make them. Still, there were accidents, and the constant physical toll ground down the men's spirit.

On a February morning in 1912 two men were injured in a colliery in Michel in the Crows Nest Pass. Thomas Cunliffe, the fireboss, was loading sheet iron onto a mine car just outside the pithead when a miner came out and told him of the incident. Cunliffe grabbed a stretcher and followed the miner into the dark. When they reached the two men, they lifted one onto the stretcher and maneuvered it between some mine cars, carefully bringing the injured man up the slope. Cunliffe spoke to the man, who had been staring at him, and determined that he was still alive. The other man, who had suffered a smashed pelvis, was then placed on a stretcher and also removed. Cunliffe then fenced off the place where the injury had occurred.

As he walked back up the slope two miners blocked his way. "What are you doing here?" asked Cunliffe. "Two men have been killed," one miner answered. "No, there has none of them been killed, because I spoke to both of them." Cunliffe then told them to go back to work. They refused. One said that after hearing about the accident he didn't feel like working anymore that morning. Cunliffe passed the men and went out the entrance, following the stretchers. Outside, the two miners again approached him and were told to return to work. While Cunliffe was talking men stopped working and gathered around the fireboss and the two miners. Two men had been killed, some of then said, and they were going to go home.

By this time Cunliffe faced a minor rebellion. "Are you men going back to work?" he asked. One of the dissidents turned and spoke to the men: "Why can't you answer the man; what are you standing there for like a flock of sheep and nobody speaking?" Cunliffe stood his ground. "I want to know what you men are going to do; I don't want to keep these haulage men standing around. I want a decided answer . . . I think you had better go back to work." But the rebellion continued as the men decided to vote on returning to work. Cunliffe now realized he had a strike on his hands. He turned to walk to the mine office and growled, "Let every bloody man go home, then."[9]

Accidents like this were not the only cause of dissatisfaction. A main source of trouble was the contract system—a throwback to the days when the miner was, in theory at least, an individual entrepreneur who contracted to dig coal for the mine owner at a given rate per ton (or per yard if he was driving a tunnel to gain better access to the coal seam). Contract miners, as they were referred to, were different from, and higher in status than "company men" or day men, who were paid a daily rate. Contract miners were paid for the amount of coal dug, loaded onto mine cars and weighed at the scales located outside the colliery entrance. This was the standard system in the coal mines of Great Britain and the United States and was vulnerable to intentional or accidental abuses which cheated a miner out of his rightful wages.

A man was not necessarily paid for the coal he dug. Perhaps he worked in an area where the coal was hard or difficult to get at. This meant he or a fireboss had to loosen the coal with blasting powder (this was called firing a shot) before it could be shovelled into a car. In some mines blasting was not allowed because of the high gas content. In others a miner could not fire his own shots but had to wait for a fireboss, in still others all firing was done only between shifts. All these circumstances resulted in delays and less coal being loaded into the cars. Even when blasting could be done as needed it was sometimes counterproductive. The companies insisted that coal had to be of a certain minimum size to be marketable, and most coal was passed over a screen to separate the powder and small bits from the larger lumps. The miner was never paid for the waste. If the blasting charge was improperly placed or too strong, there was always a risk that the coal would be too pulverized.

Once the coal was loosened it had to be loaded. Miners complained continuously about car shortages. A man could dig many tons in a day but if he could not procure enough cars he would not get the coal to the surface and would not get paid for all of his work. Sometimes the daymen, who were responsible for providing the contract miner with enough rail to lay track right up to the coal face, were late or could not get any track from the surface. Then a miner might shovel the loosened coal forty or fifty feet to the car. This took a great deal of time and often meant that the coal had to be shovelled three or four times. Every time it was shovelled bits and pieces broke off, the lumps got smaller and the contract miner lost money. This materials problem also showed up when men were driving tunnels. If the timbering for shoring was not provided at the right place and on time there were delays and lower earnings.[10]

A major problem with the contract system was referred to in England as "abnormal places." This happened when a man was given a location in the mine where he could not earn a decent wage because of poor conditions. It might be wet, rocky, or too small to swing pick and shovel. In those western Canadian coal mines

9

where the men were represented by the United Mine Workers of America, the company undertook to pay a minimum wage for a full shift's work if the contract miner was unable to earn a stipulated minimum because of his workplace.

But this provision contained large loopholes. It was never quite clear whether a miner's earnings were to be calculated daily or over a period of time. If the latter, a man might earn less than the minimum on one day and make it up in a different location the next, but would still lose because he would not recover the wages lost from the first day. And who determined what an abnormal place was? If a group of men were ordered to drive a tunnel eight feet wide but decided to make it five feet because of conditions of the workplace, and thus earned less than the stipulated minimum, they would not recover their lost wages because they had not followed orders.[11] Nor was there any provision whatever for those men who were forced to leave a perfectly normal workplace because of gas. The contract system's easiest abuse to spot was also the easiest to remedy. The all-important scales were placed, by government order, in full view of the men outside the mine entrance, and were regularly inspected and watched over by a checkweighman, usually elected by the contract miners and paid for out of their wages.

The miners' difficulties did not end at the scales. Many miners, particularly those working in pits supplying heating coal to the domestic market, were unemployed for several months every year. It was difficult to store this coal because of its high moisture content and it was not unusual for these pits to close in April and remain shut until July. In the Crows Nest Pass and southern Alberta, miners faced other problems soon after the collieries reopened because of an annual influx of farmers or harvest workers into the mining camps looking for jobs.[12]

Coal mining was still considered a skilled occupation. The practical miner needed to know about gas and coal dust, explosives and timbering, ventilation, tracklaying, and the care and use of safety lamps. He needed to know how to work a coal seam to get the most mineral out of it to maximize his own earnings. His income and his life depended in large measure on his knowledge and skills. Miners generally worked in pairs and when the unskilled, seasonal workers came into the collieries they were put with practical miners who had to look out for the safety of both men and often earned less because of their unskilled partners.[13] Before the introduction of the compulsory checkoff in contracts between the operators and the union, the practical miners would periodically demand proof of union membership of new men coming into the mine and would try to keep out those who could not show a card. This was their only way of guarding against a flood of unskilled competition.[14]

Even under the best of circumstances a miner never kept all of the earnings he had coming. It was standard practice for the company to deduct a portion of the miners' wages for the checkweighman, medical facilities and doctor and blasting powder. This continued even after the miners were unionized and was written into the collective agreement. Miners in some parts of western Canada were paid in scrip, good only at the company store, as late as the First World War. This system was never as widespread in western Canada as in the United States but in the company towns where only one store was allowed, there was little real difference.

Western Canadian coal miners usually lived in "closed" or company towns adjacent to the mines. Even in areas where established towns existed independently of the coal industry—Fernie, Drumheller, Lethbridge—the mines were generally too far away to be easily accessible to the men forcing them to move to the small company camps. There, married men rented four or five

11

room houses while single men boarded in bunkhouses or "hotels," paid for their meals and usually supplied their own blankets. Living conditions in these camps varied. They were generally better on Vancouver Island, where years of bitter labour wars stimulated corporate paternalism, poorer in southern Alberta where newly-established coal companies saved every possible penny.[15]

Water supply in these towns was the company's responsibility and was haphazard at best. Running water was almost unknown. Water was either hauled to the shacks and bunkhouses by cart or was drawn from wells or streams by the miners and their families. It was not unknown for a company to levy a monthly charge for the water it distributed, but at least this was potable. In Wayne, Alberta, miners hauled their own alkali-ridden water from a shallow well that acted as a sump for every chicken coop and turkey run in the area. The town's creek was more polluted than the well water and generally killed the horse or dog unfortunate enough to drink from it.[16] In Cadomin, near Edson, Alberta, the company-dug well was too shallow and the residents were forced to draw water from a nearby river which sometimes ran dry and was frozen in the winter. Typhoid fever was common in many coal towns, and visits from the government health inspectors rare.

Sanitation was primitive. Refuse pits were allowed in the streets and garbage simply piled up outside the houses. Empty cans, peelings, ashes and slime created greasy and dirty drinking water when it was thrown near the wells. Inside toilets were unknown. Outhouses overflowed. Toilet pits were not dug often enough, while cesspools were located in the midst of residential areas and often backed up. In one town the single men's hotel was built on pilings above the cesspool. Sometimes no lye or ash was thrown into the pits for as long as a year and the stink hung heavily over the nearest living quarters. In the bunkhouses or "hotels" one pit might be shared by as many as ten people, while the blankets which the miners generally carried from camp to camp were usually ridden with lice.

Living quarters throughout the western mining camps were uniformly poor. Married men's houses were small frame structures of four or five rooms, each no larger than twelve to fifteen feet square. By the end of the First World War most of these shacks were equipped with electric lights but almost none had sanitary facilities or running water. A small kitchen with a single stove provided cooking and heating facilities. Ventilation was poor. At Lovatt, Alberta, some families lived in shacks which had been condemned and ordered torn down by the provincial health inspector. The company charged $6 per month for these derelicts in 1919.[17]

Accommodations for single men usually consisted of a wood frame bunkhouse that might sleep from thirty to sixty men. At Wayne, Alberta, each man was allotted fourteen square feet in the "chicken coops," as the miners referred to them. There was no space for anything but sleeping. The bunkhouses at Edson were typical of single men's quarters: each structure was approximately four hundred square feet and contained sixteen double bunks for thirty-two men. There were no partitions. The house had two wash basins, one water pail, one door, one stove and no ventilation in the roof. It was crowded, close and allowed no privacy. The food was expensive and poor in quality. The effect upon the men was summed up by one miner: "I know for a fact, . . . it's not exactly the money that counts so much, but if a man gets bad food and lodging, there's trouble going to follow."[16]

The difficulties faced by the hardrock miners of the British Columbia interior were different than those of the men who toiled in the collieries but were just as challenging to human survival. These mines were much deeper and hotter than the coal mines and the ore was embedded in quartz. Air drills and blasting loosened the quartz which was then loaded into mine cars and pulled to the surface by electric trains. There was no methane, no explosive coal dust and major disasters were rare. Death was more individual and personal, though it occurred no less often than in the collieries.

The death rate per thousand men toiling in these mines hovered around 4.3 to 4.4 per year. In 1915, seventeen miners were killed out of a total labour force of 4144.[19] Accidents involving explosives were common and the easiest way for a miner to die was to drill or pick into an unexploded charge that had misfired or had been left in the ore face by a previous shift. Other accidents occurred when explosives were stored above ground in the winter and had to be thawed in the mine. If steam heat was not used the results were usually disastrous. It was not until 1914 that most of the larger mines switched to a low-freezing powder at the urging of the government mine inspector.[20]

The hardrock mines were hellholes. Rockfalls, accidents involving mine trains, men slipping into ore shutes and open mine shafts accounted for hundreds of deaths over the years. Sometimes it was not known until days later how a fatal accident had occurred because the mangled corpse could not be recovered from the bottom of shafts or from underneath tons of ore. Miners occasionally discovered the decomposed remains of a worker who had killed himself in some dark corner of the mine to lay undiscovered and unburied for many days.[21]

Serious injuries were more common than deaths. If a man was not killed when he drove his pick into an unexploded powder charge, he might lose his hands and eyes in one brief explosion. If he was caught between two mine cars or between an electric engine and the mine wall, his limbs would be crushed. If he went too quickly into an area where a charge had just gone off, loosening the ore, he might be struck by falling rock. These were the more obvious forms of injury; occupational diseases were less conspicuous but widespread.

Most of the hardrock mines were deep, wet and hot. Miners worked stripped to the waist, often standing in pools of water that seeped through the rock. Many developed rheumatism. In the winter a man could be lifted in seconds from a deep hot level to the cold mountain air. Lungs deteriorated, joints were afflicted by arthritis and rheumatism, but these did not show up in annual statistics of the dead and injured. Nor did the creeping blindness that came after years of working in the gloom with nothing but a candle for light.[22]

When a miner was killed or seriously injured, he, or his widow or other dependents, was eligible for compensation of up to $1500 under a provincial law passed in 1902. In case of death the maximum sum was usually awarded but a claim had to be filed within six months. Since many of the miners were men with families in Britain or Europe this was often impossible. Those who were seriously injured were out of luck once the full amount was paid out, because no additional support was provided.[23] When Antonio Cervio had his right foot amputated after a rockfall in the Granby Mine at Phoenix, B.C. in March, 1909, he was awarded $1500 and no more. If he had lived in Alberta he would have received a weekly indemnity for the rest of his life.[24] In some cases the Compensation Board might decide that a death or injury had occurred because of the victim's serious or wilful misconduct and would refuse to make any award.[25] In 1916 the law was amended to allow more liberal benefits.

The situation was perfect for lawyers. A whole battery of compensation experts earned a significant portion of their incomes by suing the mining companies for compensation on behalf of injured workers or the estates of dead workers who had been denied an award by the Compensation Board.[26] The only way to collect was by proving that the company was at fault. The companies took the attitude that the men were always at fault. The Consolidated Mining and Smelting Company told its shift bosses in 1912 that most accidents were due "in part, if not entirely, to carelessness."[27] The collecting process was often long and expensive since the companies inevitably resisted such efforts with all the means at their disposal. Sometimes they used compensation as a weapon against union men. When two miners working together were killed by an explosion in the Granby Mine in the summer of 1912, the widow of the non-union man received $2000 from the company while the widow of the union member was forced to accept a $1500 award from the Compensation Board.[28]

Hardrock miners were paid according to the sliding scale or the contract system. Both contained pitfalls and would have been quickly abandoned in favour of a basic minimum wage if the miners could have forced their will on the managers. The sliding scale was adopted from the hardrock mines of the American Comstock and was based on the notion that a worker should share the fortunes and misfortunes of the company. The wage was pegged to the world market price of the metal and rose and fell as the price of the metal fluctuated. This system was prevalent in the B.C. metal mining industry except for a brief period during First World War when a basic daily minimum wage was paid by government order.[29] The sliding scale made no provision for increases in the cost of living.

The contract system was different from that of the coal mines. Here a miner was treated as an independent entrepreneur and signed, individually or with a group of other men, a contract to drive a specified length of tunnel or dig a specified number of tons at a given price. These miners received their pay when the job was completed and got only what they had signed for regardless of the time worked or fluctuations in the cost of living while the job was being done.[30] From 1901 on, when a strike was fought by the Western Federation of Miners in Rossland, British Columbia, and Northport, Washington, against the contract system[31] until the First World War, it and the sliding scale were two chief grievances of the hardrock miners.

Some of the communities of the British Columbia interior, like Sandon or Rossland, served a number of mines and smelters and were not true company towns. Here miners boarded in hotels which charged up to twenty-five percent of a man's daily wage for laundry, bed and meals. In one Moyie hotel, miners who earned $3.25 per day paid fifty cents of it for a private bath. The "free" tub sat in an open hallway, with dirty work clothes hanging all about. These establishments often depended on their bars; they earned more from liquor than from boarding charges. Customers were welcomed with signs that proclaimed "miners' cheques cashed here." One hotel owner explained that his free lunches kept the crowd: a teetotaler had a hard time getting fed in Moyie.[32] These towns were a northern extension of the communities of the western American mining frontier. July 4 and miners day parades featured stars and stripes flags and posters of American presidents alongside the Union Jack. No holiday was complete without a rock drilling contest. The sport first appeared in Nevada in the 1860s. One man swung a heavy hammer, striking a steel drill rod which another man held and twisted. The team with the deepest hole was the winner.

The towns were islands of settlement wholly dependent on the mines and smelters. There were hotels, bars, haberdashers, tobacconists, assayers, dry goods merchants and tailors. The merchants lived off the miners' trade but dared not defy the companies that ruled the region. When a handful of socialist members of the legislature began to pressure Conservative premier Richard McBride to pass an eight hour law for miners and smeltermen in 1905, the merchants of Trail supported the companies against it.[33] They charged whatever the traffic would bear and the miners constantly complained about high prices. Despite this, men who worked the year around could earn a healthy stake after several years. But few did. When a new tunnel crossed a subterranean water course, work stopped until water levels subsided. Miners with slight injury, or showing signs of aging, had trouble finding steady work. Some could not stand the working conditions for longer than six or seven months at a time.

Hardrock miners were gamblers. They wandered across the west searching for a chance to file their own claim, save enough to develop it and, perhaps, strike it rich. One man, a miner for thirty-five years who came to New Denver in 1896, put his case to a commission inquiring into a labour dispute: "we developed the country first, they [the large companies] did not share in our woes or wants at all . . . we have done the prospecting and carried our packs and they will not give us one cent for what we have done . . . without the miner and the prospector this country would be in its natural condition yet." This man, like many others, owned little more than the shirt on his back; everything he earned over the years he had put back "into the bowels of the earth." While the companies grew and prospered, the independent miner grew more bitter: "if we invested our money in the bank there would be no Slocan today, there would be no Clondyde, no place for you or the other men to build a smelter . . . it took my energy and that of the other miners . . . to pave the way and show that there was a country worth prospecting and that would induce the capitalists to come in."[34]

The mining towns were usually little different than mining towns all over the North American west. The men working for the Granby Consolidated Mining Company, with mines at Phoenix and Grand Forks, were probably both untypical and more fortunate. The Granby Company ran a closed town but tempered its rule with benevolent paternalism. Married miners were rented comfortable houses with light, running water and sanitary facilities. Single men lived in solidly-built and well-kept bunkhouses and ate at similarly maintained mess halls. The town had a recreation hall, meeting hall, tennis court, reading room, and baseball diamond. Moving pictures were regularly provided. But the men and their families were virtually serfs. Town authorities had standing orders to remove "dissidents." There was no town council or government of any sort. There was one company-owned store.[35] Their choice was to live with the heavy hand of Granby paternalism, or leave.

Life was much simpler in the logging camps. In fact, it was downright primitive. A logger's job was strenuous and dangerous whether he was a faller (one who cut the trees), a bucker (one who sectioned them on the ground), or a chokerman (one who attached cable to the logs so they could be hauled out of the woods). A huge tree might jump back as it fell taking the fallers with it. If the falling tree snagged an upright tree, a branch might be snapped off and come hurtling down with enough speed and power to kill a man. A bucker might complete his cut to have two sections of the log spring up and smash his limbs. The seven blasts of the donkey engine whistle signalling death or serious injury shrieked through the woods, as an average of twenty-five loggers a year was killed in the British Columbia forests.[36]

Sometimes a logger was so horribly injured he begged to die. Once, when a bucker's saw got stuck in a fallen tree, he jumped over the log to attack it from the other side. As he jumped, the log, about three feet in diameter, rolled onto his leg. The men around him tried to lift the tree off but it was too heavy. They began to cut it into pieces while the trapped man yelled in pain and begged to be hit over the head with a hammer. It took agonizing hours to free him and then he faced a long and painful journey to hospital in Vancouver.[37]

Logging camps were primitive affairs usually consisting of a stable, a combined cookhouse and messhall and a bunkhouse. The food was usually ample but with little variety. The logger paid for his own board and carried his blankets from camp to camp. The blankets were frequently ridden with lice while the bunks were infested with bedbugs. One camp was abandoned solely because of these insects.[38] A logger's bunk usually consisted of a pile of straw or pine boughs on a wooden platform. Some loggers never slept under anything thicker than "P.I. blankets"—the Seattle *Post-Intelligencer* carried by some American loggers into the B.C. woods to use as blankets or pillows. The bunks themselves were always double and were usually "muzzle-loaders," so called because the only way into them was from the end. Inside, the bunkhouses were crowded, damp, poorly lit and badly ventilated.[39]

Loggers sometimes came to their jobs via private employment agencies in cities such as Vancouver, Seattle or Victoria. These fly-by-night operations advertised jobs in the bush and promised wages that existed only in someone's imagination. Sometimes a man had to pay simply for the privilege of scanning the list of openings, though this was more often free. Even so, the logger needed money to get to the location (loaned by the company against his wages) and never knew until he arrived what he would be doing, at what wages and under what conditions.[40] The work was always hard, low paying and long. The ten hour day, sixty hour week was common before the First World War. Wages averaged about thirty dollars a month out of which board had to be paid, and a further deduction was made for medical expenses. By the end of the war a logger could expect about twice this amount, but the daily wage system was dropped in favour of hourly wages so that a man would earn nothing if he was forced to stay in camp because of weather.[41]

Throughout these years the urban workforce in western Canada was growing rapidly and becoming more sophisticated. Jobs ranged from skilled typesetting, bricklaying and locomotive repair and operation to tracklaying, sewer digging and garbage collection. The most highly skilled earned relatively good wages under satisfactory working conditions. Those with few or no skills lived in slums, without plumbing or inside toilets and worked for low wages in dark and cramped shops or on dangerous open air job sites. Western urban workers were, for the most part, no worse off than their counterparts in Toronto or Montreal, but they were no better off either. For most of them the west was not a new land of opportunity with unbounded horizons; it was merely a change of scenery.

In western Canada shop and factory regulation was primitive, narrow and often loosely enforced in the years before the First World War. In machine shops leather belts strung from spinning shafts near the ceiling provided power for lathes and other machine tools and could fling an unwary or careless worker through crushing wheels and pulleys. On building sites scaffolding collapsed too often, while hundreds of accidents occurred in freight sheds, on loading docks or in railway yards. When a boy in Winnipeg slid off a pile of material in a mattress factory and was killed in a pounding machine, the local labour newspaper pointed out that there was not a single factory inspector in the province to enforce the already poor Shops Regulation Act.[42]

Fools and Wise Men

Wages were generally on the increase, but so were prices. Some groups of skilled workers stayed ahead of the rising cost of living, but others were not so fortunate. Uncertainty stalked the lives of almost all workers, since unemployment, sickness or injury invariably meant a serious loss of wages. Employers sometimes added to these difficulties by paying their workers with cheques that bounced or making deductions for services, such as medical insurance, which did not exist. Those who had pensions, usually railway workers, lost them if they dared strike. For most workers a lifetime of toil and risk brought them no closer to security and status than when they started out.

The depressions which periodically wracked the western Canadian economy drove home many of these bitter facts of life. In 1907-08 and again in 1913-15, thousands of jobless walked the streets of the cities. Only Calgary was relatively unaffected in 1907 because of the large number of public works projects then under construction.[43] For others, however, these depressions, particularly that of 1913-15, were marked by wage cuts, unemployment and the indignity of charity. Private relief agencies offered little protection and municipal efforts were confined to make-work projects such as the street, lane and lot cleaning offered in Edmonton and Winnipeg.[44] For most workers there was no work, little relief and almost no sympathy from civic officials. Skilled tradesmen such as construction or railway shop craft workers could find no jobs for months on end, as unemployment in some of these trades reached 90%.

Immigration was always a sore point. Workers in British Columbia were convinced that Chinese, Japanese and East Indians were threatening their livelihoods by working longer hours, for less pay, under poorer conditions, than whites. They fell victim to the anti-oriental paranoia that gripped the west coast's white population with lurid stories of opium dens, white slavery, secret societies and Asian plots to destroy Christian civilization. But they also saw Asiatics hired by the bosses to go down into the mines to dig coal, or into the forests to cut trees, breaking strikes for union recognition or safer conditions. The presence of a large force of potential strike-breakers was reason enough for white workers' hatred and they and their unions were always in the forefront of efforts to restrict Asiatics' freedoms, block their immigration and deny them the vote. The "oriental question" was always a major issue amongst coastal workers.[45] In other western centres European immigrants created intense competition for unskilled jobs and Anglo-Saxon workers reacted by calling for entry to Canada to be restricted to agricultural workers or farmers. During depressions immigration of any kind was denounced. But these complaints went unheeded, partly because the government was sympathetic to manufacturers' pleas for large pools of unskilled labour from which they could draw their workforce.

In more normal times working conditions varied according to skill and place of employment. Railway machinists at the CPR shops in Winnipeg worked a six day week until one group took it upon themselves to blow the shop whistle at noon on Saturdays to enjoy an afternoon of football.[46] These highly skilled, well paid men had cause to worry about the effect of technological innovations on their jobs. Replacing the headers on a locomotive, a task that once called for a journeyman with metallurgical skills to work with hammer and chisel for days, could be done in hours by an unskilled helper with a new oxy-acetylene torch. But their difficulties paled compared to those endured by less skilled workers. Waitresses in Calgary worked long hours in dirty conditions and often slept in restaurant basements. Packinghouse workers in Edmonton laboured ten hours a day in an industry notorious for its high labour turnover. Winnipeg policemen were on the job seven days a week. Motor-

men and conductors worked in prairie winters in un-
heated cars without even the small protection of double-
paned glass windows and demanded to have sanding
devices installed to cut down accidents. Chinese cannery
employees in British Columbia worked until they
dropped from exhaustion. Women telephone operators
in Winnipeg sat without breaks for long hours in unven-
tilated rooms for five and a half days a week. Waterworks employees in Calgary slept in 400 square foot
tents, with twenty-four men sharing double bunks and
ate their meals crowded around a single stove sitting on
boxes of dynamite.

These workers lived according to their means, and
the poor amongst them fared badly. In Calgary they
lived in tent towns in Hillhurst or near the Centre Street
Bridge. In Edmonton they crowded into frame shacks
along the Grand Trunk Pacific main line, near the
Calder Yards or east of Mill Creek. In Vancouver they
jammed into tenements along the waterfront, to the
southeast of Stanley Park. In Port Arthur and Fort William they ended up in the crowded squalor and filth of
the Coal Docks section. In Winnipeg they poured into
the tenements and hovels of the North End. East European immigrants lived in the poorest conditions. In the
North End of Winnipeg, overcrowding, lack of toilets
and the almost total absence of an adequate fresh water
supply created one of the highest rates of infant mortal-
ity and deaths per thousand persons on the continent.[47]
Unskilled Anglo-Saxon workers were only slightly better off; skilled Anglo-Saxons—train crew workers, machinists, bricklayers, etc.—did the best of all. They had
hope for improvement in their standards and status and
barring periodic losses of earnings, could aspire to a
middle-class life style. They built modest houses on
small lots in Calgary's Mount Pleasant or Winnipeg's
Ward 4 near the Point Douglas yards. Some went into
business for themselves. Others were successful in local

politics. Nevertheless, they shared one common difficulty with the poorest Russian labourer, one from which most of their own problems ultimately stemmed—their powerlessness in the community. Western Canada's cities were tightly controlled by commercial elites who ran them like closed corporations.[48] In many important ways a worker had little more freedom or control over his life in Edmonton or Winnipeg than he did in a company town like Wayne, Alberta.

Western Canada's four largest cities, Vancouver, Calgary, Edmonton and Winnipeg, were dominated by the leading men of commerce. In Winnipeg and Edmonton, Boards of Trade effectively determined civic priorities. In Vancouver an alliance of real estate entrepreneurs, contractors and wholesalers maintained a tight grip on civic leadership, while Calgary was heavily influenced by merchants. In every case the ruling group never reflected, and rarely responded to, the aspirations of working people and often acted in direct contradiction to their interests because they were primarily oriented towards commerce and industry. This was nowhere more apparent than in Winnipeg, the largest western city.

It has been observed that "Winnipeg was established by businessmen, for business purposes, and businessmen were its first and natural leaders."[49] Only 21 workers were elected to city council out of 515 aldermen in the period 1874-1914 and only 2 or 3 directly represented labour's interests. By contrast, 419 businessmen were elected in the same period. In the powerful mayor's office, 37 businessmen and 4 professionals presided—not a single artisan. The basic reason for this lack of proportion was the franchise qualification. To vote in Winnipeg a person had to be male, over twenty-one, a British subject and either a property owner paying at least $100 a year in municipal taxes or a renter paying at least $200. In addition, a person could vote in every ward in which he met the qualification. The poor, and the non-Anglo-Saxon who could not yet qualify for citizenship, were barred from voting. In 1906 when Winnipeg contained over 100 000 persons, only 7784 were listed as municipal voters.[50]

This was particularly hard for workers. The city government was reluctant to spend money to improve facilities in the North End. It refused to force the privately owned but municipally chartered street railway to operate adequate services in working class areas. It would not pass improved health and building bylaws or minimum wage schedules. The imbalance of electoral power also assured the election to office of men such as Thomas Russell Deacon who, in the midst of the depression of 1913-15, opposed giving his policemen a day's rest in seven and told Winnipeg's unemployed to "hit the trail," while he struggled to obtain a municipal vote for property-owning corporations.[51]

Deacon, like many western entrepreneurs, was a self-made man. They were a special breed—intelligent, quick-witted, resourceful and tough, sometimes ruthless, towards competitors and employees. They had risen through their own efforts and abilities and believed anyone could do the same. Those who were left behind deserved their station. These men had an almost singleminded concept of industrial relations not far removed from feudalism. On Vancouver Island the largest collieries were run by the Dunsmuir dynasty who dealt with demands for higher wages by importing Chinese strikebreakers, and expelling miners from company towns. They were determined to rule their enterprise without interference, especially from unions. Robert Dunsmuir told a 1903 Royal Commission investigating labour troubles in British Columbia that the trouble in his mines arose from his refusal to let his employees join unions: "They can belong to the union if they like—I don't care", he said. "I have my rights. I can hire them if I like, and they can work if they like."[52] The message was crystal clear.

But Dunsmuir was only more visible than most. The manager of the Vancouver Employers Association told another Royal Commission in 1919 (attitudes hardly changed) that he had elevated himself from the shop through correspondence school: "Unless you have a sort of bull-dog tenacity, it is pretty hard to hang on, but the opportunity is there just the same. Any employee can become an employer if he has the personal initiative to do it. . . ."[53] This 'by-the-bootstraps' mentality generated paternalism. Deacon, who started as a poor Ontario farm boy, boasted that he knew all his workers by name. He stopped to chat with them during his many plant inspections, his wife brought them broth when they were ill and they each received a fine turkey every Christmas. Blythe Rogers, president of B.C. Sugar Refiners, dealt personally with grievances in his plant. His philosophy was straightforward: "When there is a grievance, I go and deal direct with the men, and I maintain that I do not and will not deal with men outside the plant; I do not recognize [their] authority to interfere with the management of the plant at all."[54]

Some employers, such as Pat Burns of Calgary, were benevolent enough to avoid ugly confrontations with their men, but others—Deacon, Dunsmuir, the Barrett brothers of Winnipeg's Vulcan Iron Works, Robert J. Hutchings of the Great West Saddlery Company—did not hesitate to take the velvet glove from the mailed fist when necessary. The west experienced many long and bitter strikes as militant workers challenged these and other rock-solid employers. Troops patrolled the streets of Winnipeg during a 1906 streetcar dispute and the towns and mines of Vancouver Island during a year-long coal strike in 1913 and 1914. Courts granted injunctions, workers dynamited mines, employers imported strikebreakers, in countless disputes in the largest cities and the smallest mining communities. Sometimes the ruthlessness of these 'frontier' employers was matched by the purposeful strength of powerful corporations such as Canadian Pacific. All bosses were not tyrants, as all workers were not militant, but a climate of class antagonism nevertheless began to develop early in many areas and this, in itself, helped fuel further antagonism between owner and workers. Out of these conditions and situations—the coal mines of the Crows Nest Pass, the logging camps of the coast, the hardrock mines of the west Kootenays, the slums of North Winnipeg—the western labour movement arose. The organization and growth of trade unions for self defense was natural and inevitable.

Chapter 2

The Unique Fermentation

Unionism grew earliest and most rapidly when workers were highly skilled and could risk the displeasure of their employers, or when they laboured in isolated regions where their bosses could not easily bring in union busters. Thus unions of literate and dexterous typographers grew alongside unions of skilled, bowler-hatted, British bricklayers and vested, pocket-watch-carrying railway conductors. While these skilled workers were organizing their Orders, Brotherhoods and Benevolent Societies, sooty men wearing miners' lamps, carrying picks and shovels, and greasy men, in coveralls, with calloused hands and fingernails blackened by the blows of hammer and wrench, organized their own International Unions, Federations and Associations. The first unions were organized in British Columbia in the late 1850s,[1] and, by the turn of the century, trades councils existed at Vancouver, Victoria, Nanaimo and New Westminster. Though Vancouver was a dynamic urban centre and attracted large numbers of British and American immigrants who emerged as important union and socialist leaders, labour was generally led, in this period, by the coal and hardrock miners. These were tough men whose beliefs were forged in the heat of the metal mines or the explosions of the collieries. They were strongly militant in their determination to improve their lives and earn what they considered a just share of the wealth they produced.

In Manitoba there was no resource extraction industry to speak of. The first unions were established by printers and other skilled workers in Winnipeg in the 1870s and 1880s. Winnipeg dominated the provincial labour movement after the Canadian Pacific and other major transcontinental railways located their western shops and yards there. The city's most highly organized workers were those in the building trades and transportation. Both groups found it relatively easy to organize, though recognition from a company such as the CPR was sometimes difficult. Locomotive engineers, firemen, conductors and brakemen were bargaining with Canadian Pacific by the turn of the century, but machinists lost a recognition strike in 1908. Success usually depended on how willing an employer was to sustain losses in his battle against labour.

The Winnipeg labour movement was moderate in its early years but was beginning to develop a distinctive sense of class awareness by 1911. The process was rooted in several bitter and prolonged strikes such as the streetcar strike of 1906 when the militia was called to quell rioting and set up a machine-gun post on Main Street.[2] It also hinged on a search for political alternatives such as the Single Tax of Henry George, the Nationalism of Edward Bellamy or the quasi-Marxism of the Canadian Socialist League. Winnipeg was a marketplace of ideas with colorful and eccentric vendors and a growing trade union movement as potential buyers.

There were two main focuses to the Alberta trade union movement: the craft unions of Edmonton and Calgary, dominated by building trades and artisans such as bricklayers and stonemasons, and the coal miners of the Crows Nest Pass and Lethbridge regions. The miners, like their brothers in British Columbia, were militant in their struggles for better living and working conditions. Their unions, first the Western Federation of Miners and later the United Mine Workers of America, were organized by industry and had been bloodied in the labour wars of Pennsylvania's anthracite fields or the Coeur d'Alenes in Idaho. The urban craft unions, on the other hand, were composed primarily of conservatively tempered artisans, jealous of their skills and position and somewhat contemptuous of the coal diggers, many of whom were Italians and Slavs, in the mining towns to the south.[3]

Saskatchewan labour was the last to be organized. Some local unions of railway workers were established in the 1880s and 1890s, but it was not until 1906 that urban organization really began, primarily in Regina and Moose Jaw, since Saskatoon was still a small town of slightly more than three thousand persons.[4] In the prewar years, and well into the twenties and thirties, the urban trade unions remained divided into three urban centres. This, and the basic rural nature of the province, determined the character of the labour movement. The militancy of resource extraction workers was confined to a small area in the south where coal was dug in the Bienfait and Estevan regions. The stimulating atmosphere of Winnipeg's marketplace of ideas was also absent because of the relative lack of immigration into the cities and their small importance in the province's society and economy. The Saskatchewan labour movement was quieter, tamer and more conservative because of its social and political weakness.[5]

Though unions soon became widespread, they did little to change basic living and working conditions. Wages were almost always higher in the west, but this was due largely to higher living costs and the constant demand for labour. The unions won wage increases and shorter hours, but the company towns, the restricted franchise, the bad housing and urban slums were still there. Workers who had come for opportunity and advancement found living and working conditions that equaled those of other societies in the throes of industrial development. For these people, choices were limited: they could work hard, save, send their children to school, in the hope that the next generation would prosper. Or they could fight, not only their employers, but the courts, laws and governments that supported those employers.

The west was a magnet attracting Irish, Scottish and English, Americans, Ontarians, Italians, Slavs, Russians, Ukrainians and others. The mix was unique in Canadian history and presented countless opportunities for ideas, principles, experiences and expectations from all over the world to come together. This fermentation made the Canadian west exciting and challenging to the traditional and the established and was an essential part of the emergence of labour radicalism. Though there were as many strains and roots to this radicalism as there were people supporting it, two main traditions can be discerned—the British and American—though important contributions were made by Ukrainians, Italians and others. British and American workers fit more easily than others into the Anglo-Saxon society of western

Canada. The physical proximity of the United States and the spiritual proximity of Great Britain were factors as well.

No country sent more of its sons and daughters to western Canada than Great Britain. This alone determined the tremendous impact that British events and personalities were to have on western trade unions. In many areas and industries the labour movement was created by British workers; the ranks of western trade unions were crowded with Britons. Most of these people came to Canada during a time when the British labour movement was casting about for new and more effective means of challenging the industrial power of their employers and the political power of their government. They brought anarchism, socialism, industrial unionism and other "isms" to Canada. More important, they brought a belief in the need for collective action whether in pursuit of moderate or revolutionary goals.

From the 1889 London Dock Strike to the First World War, industrial Britain seethed with unrest. The dockers closed the Port of London to gain a guaranteed hourly wage of 6d with overtime rates of 8d. After a long bitter struggle, aided by a gift of £30 000 from Australian workers, the strike was won. A group of unskilled and hitherto unorganized workers, ignored by the older, more established unions, triumphed.[6] This struggle symbolized the new ability and willingness of unskilled workers in mass industries to organize. The tendency created the "new unionism" which spread rapidly in the early 1890s amongst municipal employees, dock workers, shipyard workers, agricultural labourers and semi-skilled railway workers. These unions attempted to combine semi-skilled workers and unskilled or general workers into single organizations, though they eventually failed in their efforts on behalf of the general workers. But the "new unionism" remained important in the larger surviving unions of semi-skilled workers (such as gas workers) and their younger, more anti-establishment and socialist oriented leadership.[7]

The "new unionism" affected the old unions. Many began to engage in internal reform and democratization while some opened their doors to less skilled workers and increased their professional staff. This tendency was most pronounced in the Amalgamated Society of Engineers which also moved towards a policy of federating or amalgamating with other unions in the metal working industry such as the boilermakers and iron founders.[8] The Amalgamated was not alone in this. In 1899 a General Federation of Trade Unions was formed by organizations representing 300 000 workers to promote closer cooperation and mutual assistance amongst British unions. The Federation was not a success and eventually disbanded in 1915, but the very fact of its formation reflected a new interest in enhancing industrial strength through amalgamation.

After the turn of the century, and partially as a result of a court decision in the Taff Vale Railway case, an increasing number of workers turned towards Marxism and working-class political activity. The case resulted from a strike against the Taff Vale Railway in which management sued their workers' union for damages growing out of a strike and won. This convinced many that wholesale change of the political and court system was necessary if unions were to be saved. In the resulting move towards politics many parties vied for the workers' allegiance, from the moderate and still non-socialist fledgling Labour Party, to the revolutionary Socialist Labour Party. This involvement with politics, and particularly socialism, was not confined to a small elite but was increasingly pursued by a growing mass of British workers. When the students of Ruskin College, Oxford, a school established by an American philanthropist for the education of workers, were thwarted in their demands for a Marxist-oriented curriculum, they withdrew to form the Plebs League. The League aimed to spread Marxist doctrine amongst workers and grew rapidly, particularly in the South Wales coal fields and the Amalgamated Society of Railway Servants. Their converts pushed their unions into more aggressive tactics and one group of miners, the Unofficial Reform Committee of the South Wales Miners Federation, tried to shift their union to the support of revolutionary goals in 1912.[9]

A great variety of radical thought came bubbling to the surface in Britain. There was James Connolly (later executed by the British for his part in the 1916 Easter Rebellion in Dublin) and his espousal of revolutionary industrial unionism patterned after the ideas of the American Daniel De Leon and the United States-based Industrial Workers of the World. There was A. R. Orage and S. G. Hobson's Guild Socialism, which advocated establishment of a worker-controlled state through all-embracing national guilds. There was the anarchist thought of E. J. B. Allen. And there was the industrial syndicalism of Tom Mann.

In Europe and America syndicalist thought was maturing by 1910. It was different in each country but certain principles were common. Syndicalists believed class struggle was inevitable and the workers' only salvation was through revolution. They maintained all workers must come together into one massive union that would unite every wage earner—every member of the working class. They asserted that workers should organize themselves, within that one great union, to parallel the structure of modern capitalist society. Workers would thus prepare themselves and their unions for the day when they would take over society and the trade unions would become the basis for the new regime. Once the workers were completely organized, a great general strike would transfer power to them since they alone would determine what would function and who would eat.[10] By

1910 these theories were widespread and had become the guiding principle of the central congress of the French labour movement, the Confédération Général du Travail. Some of these ideas were present in Britain since the days of Robert Owen's Grand National Consolidated Trades Union of the 1830s[11] and William Benbow's Grand National Holiday and Congress of the Productive Classes—the general strike—in the 1830s and 1840s.[12]

The fall in real wages experienced throughout Britain after 1910 caused continuous industrial unrest. As workers struggled to maintain their living standards, they struck railways, coal mines, port cities, utilities and private industry with increased frequency. The strikes were usually long and began to involve troops. There were calls for general strikes, with much violence and imprisonment of strike leaders. It appeared to some that revolution was at hand. Tom Mann, an engineer prominent in the trade union movement since the 1889 dock strike, returned to Britain in 1910 after spending several years in Australia and New Zealand. He had been exposed to the ideas of De Leon and the IWW, which appeared in Australia soon after its founding in Chicago in 1905; Mann had been involved in a major coal strike at Broken Hill, Australia; here he first realized the importance of industrial unionism and syndicalism. Soon after his return he went to France to study French syndicalism and then established in Britain the Industrial Syndicalist Education League and a newspaper, the *Industrial Syndicalist*. Mann spent the following months organizing and speaking for his new cause. He tried to win the British labour movement to syndicalism by attracting workers to the League and organizing them into militant factions to capture their unions from within.[13] He was only partly successful since none of the major unions endorsed his aims. But his agitation, against the background of increasing industrial unrest, focused attention on the new importance of syndicalism amongst British workers. In June, 1914, Robert Smillie, a Scottish miner, proposed the formation of a Triple Alliance of coal miners, dockside workers and railway workers. The Alliance was not actually created until December, 1915, but seemed to portend the beginning of British working class revolution when combined with Mann's activities and the outright syndicalism espoused by the Unofficial Reform Committee of the South Wales Miners in a pamphlet, "The Miners' Next Step" issued in 1912.

It is impossible to estimate how many British workers in western Canada were directly touched by these events, but there must have been many. Most union leaders, moderate or radical, were British and some had been experienced in unionism before coming to Canada. These men, and the rank and file they led, were keen to follow news and developments of their home country. The important labour papers, such as the *Voice* of Winnipeg and the *British Columbia Federationist* of Vancouver, carried regular news in depth of trade unions and socialism in Britain. Tours were arranged for Tom Mann and Kier Hardie, the Scottish leader of the socialist Independent Labour Party. Pamphlets written by James Connolly and others were available through the Charles Kerr Company of Chicago and were avidly read.

The British influence was brought to the Canadian west by immigrants, the American influence was not. The only significant concentration of American workers was in the hardrock mines of British Columbia where as many as fifty percent of the workers were from the United States. There were many American loggers, but they did not begin to organize themselves effectively until the closing years of the First World War. In the coal fields, on the railways and in the cities, Americans were few.[14] Nevertheless, American ideas and attitudes had a strong influence on western Canadian trade unions. The militancy and radicalism of western American labour, and its struggles against the conservative craft unionism of the east, became part of the lore of western Canadian workers.

The labour movement in the United States was dominated by the American Federation of Labor and its leader, Samuel Gompers. At the turn of the century the AFL stood for exclusive craft unionism. It was a loose federation of unions, mostly skilled, which eschewed direct political action and scorned the "utopianist" ideas of socialists. The AFL and its member unions believed their role was to advance the worker's cause in capitalist society through higher wages, shorter hours and better working conditions won in direct negotiation with employers. They distrusted government, rejected most welfare proposals and ignored the unskilled or semi-skilled, particularly in mass industries. These doctrines were not suitable in much of the western United States where conditions were primitive and industry was based on resource extraction. The unions which developed there, such as the Western Federation of Miners which organized the hardrock miners, were militant and radical, reflecting the temper of their membership. At times the Western Federation of Miners was more dependent on the Winchester than the boycott or the strike. When these men tried to organize, and were met with rifle-toting private armies answering only to mine owners, they could surrender or shoot back, which they did most of the time.[15] These men had no patience for the principles of the AFL.

American labour radicals advocated industrial unionism—organization of all workers in one industry into one union rather than a series of craft unions—and socialism. The Western Federation of Miners was the largest and most prominent union representing these views. It launched or supported efforts to form an industrial union of railway workers—the United Brotherhood of Railway Employees—and two industrial union federations—the Western Labor Union and the American Labor Union. In the political arena Daniel De Leon's Socialist Trades and Labor Alliance and the Socialist Party of America tried to undermine the anti-socialist and non-political policies of the American Federation of Labor. These legacies were carried into the Canadian west by itinerant workers, mostly miners, who had laboured in the coal and metal mines of the western states. There was no border for these men. The fierce labour wars of the American Rocky Mountain mining frontier hardened their attitudes and prompted them to spread the message of socialism and class conflict into the southern interior of British Columbia in communities such as Trail, Nelson, Silverton, Sandon and Rossland. This radicalism was strengthened by American organizers working for the WFM or the American Labor Union. In 1901 the WFM fought the introduction of the contract system in southern B.C. with a strike of Rossland, B.C. miners and Northport, Washington smelter workers. The secretary of the Rossland Miners Union stated: "There is no 49th parallel of latitude in Unionism. The Canadian and American workingmen have joined hands across the Boundary line for a common cause against a common enemy."[16]

In the cities, particularly on the coast, the fluctuation of wages attracted artisans to one side of the border, then the other. One Victoria worker stated: "If I were to leave here and go to Frisco and Seattle, I have no trouble; I simply take my travelling card."[17] These men were "boomers," skilled workers with itchy feet who might work in Winnipeg, Calgary and Seattle in a single season, collecting stamps from different locals in their dues books. A Winnipeg stamp alongside a Regina stamp or a San Francisco stamp declared their independence to the world; for them there was only horizon to be reached.

As they travelled they carried news and impressions of far-away places, like roving minstrels in olden times, and often helped organize workers in the small towns they passed through.[18]

Though direct contact with American radicalism was greatest in B.C., workers in other parts of the west were also affected. American publications, such as the *Appeal to Reason* and the various pamphlets of the Charles Kerr Company, were essential reading. Most Canadian socialist organizations began as offshoots of American ones and slavishly followed the twisting and turning path of American socialism.[19] Vancouver was very much an extension of the American Pacific northwest and workers there followed events in Washington, Oregon and northern California. In Winnipeg the American impact was weakest, but even here the United Brotherhood of Railway Employees had an important, if fleeting, influence amongst yard and track workers in a 1902 strike.

The most dramatic result of American influence in western Canada was the appearance, shortly after its founding, of the Industrial Workers of the World. They brought a cohesive syndicalist doctrine founded upon work already done by the Western Federation of Miners and the American Labor Union. The IWW rejected political action as a sham and attacked the "collaborationist" policies of the AFL. It advocated the establishment of one big union of all workers organized into industrial "departments" or unions and sought, in classical syndicalist terms, to 'build the structure of the new society within the shell of the old.' In some ways the IWW was different from the syndicalist unions of Europe because it was born of conditions peculiar to class unionism in the American west. But its aims were essentially those of the French Confédération Général du Travail: the destruction of capitalism via the general strike and the creation of a worker's state to be administered by trade unions.[20]

By 1912 the IWW was a force of some consequence, particularly in British Columbia, with locals as far east as Winnipeg. It was highly visible and incurred the hatred of much of the press as well as politicians and conservative union leaders. The IWW conducted free speech fights in Victoria in late 1911 and in Vancouver a few months later, and tried to organize the logging camps of the coast and interior. It conducted a vigorous campaign on behalf of the unemployed in Edmonton in December, 1913 and January, 1914 and forced concessions from the municipal administration. Its most famous Canadian exploit was the strike of railroad construction workers on the Grand Trunk Pacific and Canadian Northern Railways in the summer of 1912. The strike was centred mainly around Yale, B.C., and stopped work in the Fraser River Canyon.[21] IWW leaders such as William "Big Bill" Haywood, Elizabeth Gurley Flynn and Frank Little carried the union's message to Canadians. IWW organizers worked both sides of the boundary and were harassed by provincial police and the Royal North West Mounted Police. Though the IWW began to decline in Canada by the outbreak of the First World War, it had had a measurable impact in British Columbia and in the coal fields of the Crows Nest Pass and southern Alberta.

A large minority of immigrant workers were Europeans and they also contributed to the development of radical traditions. They were never as prominent in union leadership as Britons, and tended to organize in ethnically-based groups of their own or to join organizations, such as the Socialist Party of Canada and later the Social Democratic Party, which were led by Anglo-Saxons. Nevertheless, they made a distinct impression in places such as the Alberta coal fields where Ukrainian socialists were working as early as 1907.[22] Here Ukrainian, Slavic and Italian miners proved fertile material for socialist organizers and ethnic organizations such as the

Ukrainian Social Democratic Federation. During the IWW strikes in the Fraser River Canyon in 1912, special efforts were directed towards Italian navvies through the use of Italian organizers and literature.[23] Most navvies were from rural peasant backgrounds and contributed little to the shaping of a radical ideology. But they sometimes provided support and impetus for the spread of immigrant radicalism.

The situation was different in the cities. Winnipeg was an important centre of radical immigrant activities. The Ukrainian community supported a regular labour newspaper and a workers' club. They were an important source of members for the Socialist Party of Canada and later the Social Democratic Party.[24] Jews also supported a workers' club and a labour newspaper and were active in socialist circles. When the German-British anarchist Rudolf Rocker visited the city in May, 1913, he found a Yiddish weekly sympathetic to his ideas and was pleased with the attendance at his meetings. He concluded there was "a good intelligent Jewish public in Winnipeg."[25] Farther east, in Fort William and Port Arthur, Ontario, (now Thunder Bay), Greek, Italian and Finnish workers were active in socialist politics and strongly supported a union of unskilled CPR freight handlers. These workers were perhaps the most militant in the country and their strikes against the CPR were bitter, protracted and accompanied by riots and killings. Such elements of European radicalism were increasingly wedded to dominant British and American traditions as allies were sought and alliances moulded in organizations such as the Social Democratic Party which, at its peak, counted over three thousand members, most of whom were Europeans organized into separate language locals supporting an overwhelmingly British leadership.

The profusion of ideas and traditions in prewar western Canada was reflected in the colorful characters who preached the gospel of socialism and labour radicalism. At busy downtown street corners, soapbox speakers for socialism vied with the Salvation Army to attract crowds. In Winnipeg one character stripped to the waist and broke ropes with his chest to attract bystanders before beginning speeches on socialism and the class struggle.[26] Another socialist evangelist, from the United States, mounted his soapbox and played a tune with a comb and a piece of tissue paper. When a small crowd gathered he began to sell combs, claiming they were unbreakable and could not be bought anywhere in the city. When several dozen were sold he stopped: "Do you know, you are an awful bunch of suckers. These are not unbreakable, there is no such thing as an unbreakable comb. But stop my friends, what I have done is nothing to the way in which you are robbed as workers. You are robbed at the point of production." Thus began a long speech on socialism.[27] Another worker, a machinist, caught the attention of younger workers by pointing to the rhythmic slapping noise of the leather belt which drove the lathe from a spinning shaft near the ceiling. "Just listen to that," he said, suggesting they pass the time by making up small verses to go with the rhythm. Verses like "The boss is robbing me, the boss is robbing me" or "you're being robbed you fool, you're being robbed you fool."[28]

One of the more colorful characters was a Manchester-born Jew, Moses Barretts, who had been a member of the Socialist Party of Great Britain. Barretts' special target was religion. One Sunday he attended a Winnipeg church meeting where a Chicago professor was talking about the life of Christ. "What evidence have you in profane literature that Jesus Christ ever lived?" Barretts asked from the audience. The professor was taken aback. He stammered that he would answer the question next Sunday. Barretts jumped up and said, "Here we are insulted. We bring a professor all the way up from Chicago to tell us about the man Jesus Christ and, Jesus Christ, he doesn't even know if he ever lived." He then launched a tirade which proved too much for the church-going audience who threw Moses out. That night he entertained a crowd at the Starland Theatre by telling them about the "Christian" treatment he had received in the afternoon.[29]

People from all over joined the socialist crusade. George Armstrong was born on a small Ontario farm where he learned the carpenter's trade. After he came west he fell in with a small group of radicals and joined the Socialist Party of Canada. He was a big man with a strong physical presence, considered by many as the SPC's most able speaker. Sarah and Joseph Knight always worked as a team. They lived in Edmonton, Joe coming from England, Sarah a native Canadian. Both were tireless Socialist Party workers while Joe, a carpenter, was prominent in the Edmonton Trades and Labour Council. Sarah was an exciting speaker. She smoked cigarettes in public (daring for a woman in those days) and stuck her hatpin in the butts when they were too small to hold. From the United States came another socialist lady who addressed her audience while she held her baby on her lap and puffed a cigar.

Trades council meetings, particularly in Winnipeg, were not dull business gatherings but forums for every conceivable approach to workers' problems from the Single Tax to syndicalism. Speakers who rose in council meetings were often self-educated experts and accomplished debaters. They had to be to survive the cross-fire. These meetings were sometimes the best show in town, featuring the stars of the labour world. They reflected the turmoil and mix of ideas in the Canadian west. The labour movement, drawing its support and membership from workers who had come in search of safer jobs, civilized living conditions and a greater share of the wealth they produced, leaned increasingly to radicalism and experimentation. Led by the Armstrongs, the Knights and other British radicals, workers began to question the narrowly exclusive, conservative and anti-socialist approach of their United States-based craft unions. Many concluded that capitalism itself was the greatest obstacle to their happiness. There thus developed a growing challenge to craft unionism, a rising socialist influence and increased enchantment with the idea of general strikes.

Western disaffection with craft unionism grew from numerical weakness. There were too few industrial workers in the west for them to keep their strength and unity while being divided into the over one hundred craft unions that made up the AFL and its Canadian affiliate, the Trades and Labour Congress. The Congress had been founded in Ontario in the 1880s to coordinate the political and organizing activities of unions in Canada. At first it was an all-inclusive centre which contained Knights of Labor assemblies, purely Canadian unions and United States-based 'international' unions. In the late 1890s these United States unions began to pressure Congress leaders to move closer to the AFL. Their numbers and their financial strength proved difficult to overcome. In 1899 fraternal delegates were exchanged by the two organizations and in 1902 the U.S. unions forced the Congress to expell all unions which were "dual" to those already in the AFL and which had headquarters and most of their members in the United States. This marked the start of AFL domination of the Trades Congress and made the Congress the champion of the Gompers craft union system in Canada. That system might have been best in Ontario, or the American northeast (though labour radicals denied this even in those places), but it was a handicap in Regina, Victoria or even Winnipeg. Coal and hardrock miners were organized into industrial unions and as the urban labour movement grew, an increasing number of skilled craftsmen concluded that they too should abandon craft organization or, at least, strengthen it through federation or amalgamation.

By the outbreak of the First World War, a variety of alternatives to craft unionism were under discussion. The most conservative was amalgamation. Its exponents wanted to unite kindred crafts into larger industrial unions and in some cases advocated one union per corporation, rather than per industry.[30] Pro-amalgamation feeling surfaced at the 1911 Trades and Labour Congress convention at Calgary when a resolution was passed, over the opposition of Congress Secretary P. M. Draper and other easterners, endorsing industrial unionism. This was not an indication of syndicalist influence, because most of the delegates who voted for it also supported a resolution that disavowed the methods and ideas of the IWW.[31] Westerners were interested in amalgamation and industrial unionism, but revolutionary industrial unionism was still unacceptable to most. They did not appear overly concerned when the 1912 TLC convention, at Guelph, Ontario, watered down the 1911 resolution and declared it to have been educational only and not a signpost of Congress policy. Western delegates believed the unity displayed at the Guelph meeting and the re-election of James Watters, a British Columbia social democrat who became TLC president the previous year, were cause for rejoicing. Their reports to the Winnipeg and Vancouver Trades and Labour Councils did not mention the industrial union question.[32]

Nonetheless, most westerners favoured industrial unionism. The founding convention of the British Columbia Federation of Labor in 1910 endorsed it as did the Vancouver Trades and Labour Council in 1912. The Vancouver council mounted a campaign to drum up support and succeeded in lining up the trades councils of Calgary, Nelson and Victoria.[33] But the issue was connected with the larger question of what direction western labour should move in and there was little consensus in the prewar years. Western workers were divided by geography, handicapped by ethnic and functional diversity and weak: prior to the First World War they lost almost every major fight on the industrial battlefield. Only the Railroad Brotherhoods, the unions of engineers, firemen, conductors and brakemen were able to beat the CPR in the 1890s to gain recognition. Western labour leaders, for all their color and passion, could not mount an effective campaign to change the basic policies of their craft unions. Some did not even believe this was necessary. Fewer still were prepared to secede from those unions to start a new labour movement of their own.

They did not have to secede to pursue socialism. Trade unionists had been fascinated with it since the early days of the western labour movement. There were other doctrines vying for the workers' support—the Single Tax of the American Henry George, which had been in vogue in Ontario in the 1880s, and the Nationalism of utopian novelist Edward Bellamy—but they received only fleeting attention and were favoured primarily by middle class progressives. Some unionists continued to support Liberal and Conservative parties, particularly the Liberals. Ralph Smith, a British Columbia miner, and president of the Trades and Labour Congress in 1898, won election to the provincial legislature as an independent progressive, but soon joined Liberal ranks and captured a seat in the federal parliament. But those who struggled for worker-oriented reform, and who believed industrial battles would only be won when workers controlled governments, usually gravitated to one of the socialist parties. By 1905 the Socialist Party of Canada emerged as the most influential and powerful of these organizations.

The Socialist Party of Canada prided itself on being

the country's only true exponent of pure Marxism. It rejected piecemeal reform and attacked trade unions for misleading workers. Led by American-born E. T. Kingsley, a sharp, uncompromising and doctrinaire intellectual, who had been crippled by an industrial accident, the SPC proclaimed that unions were not, and could not be, weapons in the class struggle because their only purpose was to raise the price of their members' labour. The SPC believed that revolution would come via the ballot box, but only if workers were educated in the principles of Marxism and knew what they were voting for. The Party was wedded to the belief that revolution was inevitable because of the immutable laws of Marxian economics. Though SPC members were always very active in pushing their cause, they believed that Marx's principles were "as absolute in their operation as the laws of gravitation or the laws which govern the growth of trees or icebergs."[34] The Party's anti-union attitude was most apparent in its early period when Kingsley's influence was greatest. In later years the Party's attitude softened. By 1919, the SPC was willing to admit that trade union struggle was an important means of educating workers to the inequities of capitalism and preparing them for revolution. But the emphasis was the same in 1919 as it had always been: "Education is, in the final analysis, all that any working class organization can consciously contribute toward the downfall of capitalism. And it is all that is necessary. For education means class consciousness, class consciousness creates class solidarity, class solidarity breeds militancy and it is out of these that the form and technique of revolution will take shape. . . ."[35]

Kingsley's anti-union attitude, shared by most of the early SPC leaders, did not scare away all unions or union members. There was always some disagreement in SPC ranks about the role and function of unions, and some union members looked to the SPC's brand of socialism as the only one with the rigor and discipline to deliver what they wanted. This was particularly true of the miners. Their attraction to the Party brought SPC election victories on Vancouver Island, in the mining communities of the B.C. interior and in southwestern Alberta. In October, 1906, a meeting of B.C. labour unions dominated by the Western Federation of Miners threw their support to the Socialist Party[36] while District 18 of the United Mine Workers of America, representing coal miners in the east Kootenays and Alberta, endorsed the SPC in its District constitution in February, 1914.[37] These victories were gained largely because of the growing radicalism of the miners and the strenuous efforts of SPC union members who rejected the doctrinaire approach of their leaders. But Socialist Party influence amongst the unions was weakened, in all but the most class-conscious areas, by anti-union SPC attitudes. When one leader of the United Mine Workers of America attempted to gain support for a miners' strike on Vancouver Island in 1912, Vancouver Local No. 1 of the SPC rejected his efforts, even though the Nanaimo SPC local backed the strike. One SPC member told him the miners needed to be clubbed over their heads to have some sense knocked into them.[38]

The SPC's importance to the western labour movement resulted from the rise of active SPC members through union ranks. Workers who believed that socialism and trade unionism did go together spread the message and were amongst the brightest and most hardworking union supporters. They were usually the best organizers and the most eloquent speakers, and were soon trusted and respected. After 1907 they were joined by members of the Social Democratic Party, which was founded in Vancouver by a group unhappy with the rigidity and the anti-unionism of the SPC. The Social Democratic Party accepted the tactical need to work for immediate reforms and believed election victories were

important. It considered the trade unions and the socialist movement to be allies in the battle against capitalism. Its flexibility attracted many workers who could not
warm to the austere doctrines of the Socialist Party of
Canada, and by 1912 it outnumbered the Socialist Party
and had attracted most of the former SPC members in
Ontario as well as the bulk of the SPC's non-Anglo-
Saxon supporters.

By the outbreak of war, Socialist Party or Social Democratic Party members were to be found throughout the
trade union leadership of the west. In Winnipeg, R. A.
Rigg, secretary of the trades council, was elected to city
council as a Social Democrat in 1912. Rigg had tremendous influence in the city's labour movement because of
his skill as trades council secretary and his uncanny ability to read the mood of his followers. He was an Englishman who had abandoned the Methodist ministry to
come to Canada and take up the bookbinding trade. He
was elected president of his own local in 1910, president
of the trades council in 1911 and secretary in 1912. He
was a strong socialist. In 1914, the Trades and Labour
Congress chose him to be their fraternal delegate to the
American Federation of Labor convention. Rigg had already reached the heights of leadership in 1914; Robert
Boyd Russell, another socialist, was just beginning to
emerge as a man to watch. Russell came to Winnipeg
from Glasgow in 1911 at the age of 22, familiar with
trade unionism and socialism. In Glasgow he had been a
member of the Amalgamated Society of Engineers, the
Independent Labour Party and the Clarion Scouts. In
Canada he joined the Socialist Party. When he took up
the machinist trade for the CPR in Winnipeg he joined
the International Association of Machinists and began
to write for the *Bulletin*, the Canadian IAM newspaper.
Russell liked to quote Edward Carpenter, a British socialist poet, and landed in trouble after the outbreak of
war because of his pacifist leanings. Russell and Rigg

were not the only important socialists in Winnipeg;
George Armstrong, Fred Tipping and John Queen
were three of the more prominent men who helped
move labour to the left.

In Saskatchewan, socialism was weak and divided, but
in Alberta most of the leaders of the coal miners supported it. In Edmonton, Sarah and Joe Knight carried
the Socialist Party banner aided by Carl Berg. Berg had
emigrated to the United States from his native Stock-
holm, Sweden, in 1904 at the age of 16. He was an agricultural labourer and hardrock miner in several states
before coming to Canada in 1906. He then worked as a
fruit picker in the Okanagan Valley in British Columbia
and a navvy on the Grand Trunk Pacific. Moving from
job to job, he tried his hand at homesteading, construction and road work before settling in Edmonton. Along
the way Berg joined the IWW and the Socialist Party of
Canada, and was a key figure in organizing the IWW
strikes in the Fraser River Canyon in 1912. He was secretary of Local 82 of the IWW in Edmonton and a
leader of the unskilled workers in that city.

In British Columbia, a whole galaxy of labour leaders
were socialist. Dave Rees, a Welshman from Fernie, rose
rapidly through UMWA ranks to become international
board member for District 18. Jack Kavanagh, a longshoreman who had emigrated to Vancouver from Li-
verpool in 1907, joined the Socialist Party almost on his
arrival and became a party organizer. Victor Midgley,
an Englishman with membership in the SPC, was secretary of the Vancouver trades council and an executive
member of the British Columbia Federation of Labor.
There were others: Joseph Naylor, a leader of the Cumberland coal miners and member of the Social Democratic Party, James Watters, elected president of the
Trades and Labour Congress in 1911 and a member of
the Social Democratic Party, and W. A. Pritchard, a
pugnacious Jack-of-many trades who came to Canada

51

from England in 1911 and joined the Socialist Party. Two union leaders in Vancouver, James McVety and R. P. Pettipiece, were also socialists and contested elections under the Socialist Party banner.

Though these individuals exerted a steady leftward pressure on the western labour movement prior to 1914, their influence was more apparent in the mining country than the cities where the conservative influence of the building crafts remained dominant. Socialist strength existed in the cities in that they held, or could be elected to, important positions, but often this was a result of personal popularity, not ideology. Workers in Vancouver rushed to the defense of the IWW when civic authorities tried to deny them the right to hold meetings in 1913, but this was a general matter of principle—those same workers did not join the IWW. In Vancouver, socialists were more influential than in other cities, but were not dominant and did not control. Throughout the west they shared power with moderates and conservatives like Calgary's Alex Ross, Edmonton's Alfred Farmilo and Winnipeg's Arthur W. Puttee.

Urban workers were more reticent about supporting radicalism, whether socialist or syndicalist, because the cities offered escape, amusement and diversion. Skilled workers could own property. Unskilled workers could find companionship. All found churches, libraries, social clubs, city mission workers and the Salvation Army. There was at least the illusion of mobility, opportunity and advancement. Until 1913, the west, particularly the cities, was a prosperous place. Expectations were high, rewards appeared to increase and there was optimism. The unskilled and the poor shared little of this, but they had no voice in the unions and no vote.

Hope began to fade with the onset of depression in 1913. This economic downturn, which lasted until 1915, wiped away much of the slow progress already made by the unions. Under these circumstances and against a background of British and American syndicalism, it did not take long before calls for general strikes were heard in union halls across the west.[39] There was no real general strike prior to the war, but there were many occasions when union members tried to resort to them to win ordinary industrial disputes. Even though some labour leaders were familiar with the importance of the general strike to syndicalist revolutionary theory, they viewed such strikes as a means to make it easier to win ordinary battles over wages, recognition and working conditions.[40]

Most of the preoccupation with general strikes was only talk, but in two instances, at both ends of the west, the talk was almost translated into action. In May, 1913, a long-smouldering dispute between street railwaymen and their employers in Port Arthur and Fort William erupted into a strike. The walk-out provided a focal point for much of the hatred and bitterness that had developed between labour and its enemies in the two cities for several years. Like so many other strikes at the lakehead, this one was soon marred by rioting, violence and death. After four days of disorder, sparked primarily by the use of strikebreakers, the trades councils of the two cities called upon their unions to vote on a sympathetic strike to back up the street railwaymen. The response from the locals was cool and the trades councils were forced to declare a "general holiday" for June 4, but most workers reported for work as usual on the designated day.[41]

In British Columbia, a coal mine dispute between District 28 of the UMWA and most of the Vancouver Island operators began in September, 1912 when 3 000 miners employed by Canadian Collieries at Cumberland and Ladysmith struck for a variety of reasons, including union recognition and claims that the company was violating provincial safety laws. The strike deepened in the following months with the union pulling out the pumpmen who kept the mines dry and the company evicting the miners from company towns and bringing in strike-breakers. By the spring of 1913 the company had brought its production up to two-thirds of pre-strike levels and the union responded with a strike of all the Island miners. In August the miners made a desperate attempt to halt production and strikebreakers' houses and mine equipment were dynamited and burned, while pitched battles, fought with clubs and shovels and punctuated by gunfire and dynamite explosions, broke out between union members and strikebreakers at South Wellington, Ladysmith, Nanaimo and Extension. The strike had become a war, and the province, led by Attorney General Bowser, intervened and sent in the militia. In the early morning of August 20, 1913 they surrounded a union meeting in Nanaimo and arrested seventy men. By the end of the month two hundred and fifty had been jailed, one of whom, Joseph Mairs, died in prison.[42]

At the February, 1914 convention of the British Columbia Federation of Labor, the question of a general strike was raised in response to events on the Island. The United Mine Workers, who had poured millions into this battle and were spending many more millions in a fight against the Rockefeller-owned Colorado Fuel and Iron Company in the United States, were losing their taste for the struggle and opposed the call for the province-wide strike.[43] But the miners' delegates broke with their international leaders and pressed for a special Federation convention to decide the issue. This was held in July and endorsed the rank and file miners' call for a general strike, but the move foundered on the opposition of the Vancouver and Victoria trades councils.[44] The general strike was never held. The failure of the two most serious attempts to bring about general strikes—at the Lakehead and in B.C.—did not destroy belief in the effectiveness of the tactic. Both fell flat because the depression had begun and would have seriously undermined them. The Vancouver trades council declined to support the general strike for that very reason.[45] The tactic thus remained in the never-never land of theory. It was an idea whose time had not yet come.

By 1914, a unique fermentation of ideas in the west provided direction for the growing numbers of radicals and their supporters in union ranks. The popularity of socialist and syndicalist ideas was a direct result of the influx of thousands of workers into the west who were forced to earn their livelihood in the class-polarized society of the cities or the closed, stifling, fiefdoms of the company towns. Once settled, workers had little chance for improvement of their lot. Many could not easily accept their change in status from migrants seeking opportunity to regulated industrial workers. The problem was intensified for those with rural backgrounds. Because there were more immigrants in the west than elsewhere, there were more potential radicals and more carriers of radical traditions. For every Scottish worker in Nova Scotia, there were ten or twenty in Alberta.

The miners were the first group to offer strong and consistent support to socialism because their living and working conditions were the poorest. Those who had worked the land in Europe, who had survived the mining wars of the American frontier, who escaped the turbulence, insecurity and polarization of British society, or the falling wages and lower productivity of the Welsh coal fields, had come to western Canada for a new start. This was the west, the frontier. But the mining communities were pockets of industrial feudalism as bad as in England or Wales. The cities rivalled those of the United Kingdom, or the northeastern United States, with their slums and 'upper' class rule. Some immigrants had come from places of such poverty and had been so destitute, that the west was indeed the heaven they sought. But others were bitterly disappointed. This frustration paved the way for the socialists and syndicalists who fought for radical social change and the abolition of "wage slavery." The freedom workers sought, but could not find, might be created in the "commonwealth of toil." Thus many turned to socialism or syndicalism as radical ideas became more popular and those who held them rose to positions of authority. Nevertheless, on the eve of war, the miners' radicalism, and that of a growing number of urban workers, was not yet focused or directed. In 1914, geographic, ethnic and ideological divisions still apparent among western workers made united action for reform or revolution impossible.

Chapter 3

War And Revolt

Canada experienced the shock of the First World War even though no armies churned up her fields and no bombs or shells shattered her cities. Over sixty thousand Canadians were killed in Europe while tens of thousands were wounded. In some areas of Canada, particularly in the west with its high proportion of British immigrants, entire communities suffered drastic reductions of their male populations. At the peak of battle in 1917 fully ten percent of the population of Manitoba was in uniform.[1] Every day those at home faced recruiting posters, censorship, victory loan drives, sermons exhorting sacrifice, commodity shortages and long lists of dead and wounded. The horror of mass death, the anguish of shattered families, and the pangs of self-denial left a permanent mark.

Prior to the war, organized labour, speaking through the Trades and Labour Congress, endorsed pacificism. As long as the world was at peace, conservatives, moderates and radicals shared a hatred for war. As soon as war began, however, the conservative and moderate majority in the labour movement endorsed the anti-Kaiser crusade. In the west most labour leaders and almost all radicals opposed the war—their enemy was the boss, not the German. Radicals believed that the war was a struggle between competing capitalists who would wage it from comfortable board rooms; working people would fight on bloody, shell-pocked battlefields. There was a strong conviction that whatever the outcome, workers would inevitably lose.

This was certainly true when tested in terms of real wages and earning power. From 1915 on, most Canadian workers experienced a drastic erosion in their living standards. Price increases, resulting from heavy demands placed on the economy by the war,[2] ran at from ten to twenty percent a year from the end of the depression in 1915 until 1919. An army of 600 000 men had to be fed, clothed and equipped. Millions of artillery shells, hundreds of ships, trucks, aircraft and thousands of rifles had to be produced. The peoples of Europe whose fields were scourged by war had to be fed. There was not enough of anything and the resulting shortages pushed prices of almost everything up. The federal government faced a problem never before tackled in Canada and was generally not equal to the task of regulating distribution. Though there was some small-scale rationing in the form of "heatless" and "meatless" days, it was barely enough to dent the runaway demand.[3] Workers rarely saw the problem as one of cold statistics. They charged they were the victims of "food pirates and price manipulators" and they demanded government action to improve the situation. The Trades Congress demanded the elimination of "gambling in foodstuffs by speculators" and suggested a comprehensive program of regulation and nationalization of cold storage plants, slaughterhouses, canneries, railroads and coalfields. Rising prices created pressure for higher wages. The Congress urged union workers in Canada to "use all the power at their command" to increase their wages and thereby avoid "serious depression of their standard of living."[4]

The eventual enlistment of over 600 000 Canadians in the armed forces created an acute manpower shortage at home. At first many thousands of volunteers came from the unemployed who were thrown out of work by the 1913 depression. By the end of 1915, however, war industries were being organized on a large scale, particularly in Ontario and Quebec, and the twin demands for manpower to run the machines of war production and for the machines of war created a labour shortage. The situation presented trade unions with golden opportunities to increase their power, while it threw a totally new problem across their path.

The number of organized workers in Canada increased by about one hundred percent during the war. This was due largely to drives and campaigns carried out by the unions themselves. There were few employers willing to recognize unions in those days, and fewer still who would grant closed shops. There were no laws to force employers to bargain collectively with their workers or to protect workers who joined unions from retaliation. The unions had to impress potential members with their strength and their ability to defend and advance their interests. The greater their achievements the better they looked, and this in itself created militancy. Many of the employers who opposed them were totally unscrupulous in their fight against organization and used every conceivable tactic, from espionage to dismissal, to keep them out. In these cases, there was little desire to compromise by either side. The manpower shortage also created problems for the unions. It took many years of apprenticeship to make a skilled journeyman. Those in charge of war plants did not have many years to find or train people to run lathes and other machine tools. One solution was to use unskilled labour, male or female, trained for one or two operations but lacking in the broad skills and knowledge of the journeyman. Naturally there was great employer resistance to paying high wages to these unskilled workers. The unions feared an erosion of their power as unskilled, low-paid workers, with temporary commitments to the work force, took the place of the full-fledged machinists, blacksmiths, boilermakers and others.

In the early years of the war the unions had to be cautious in their attempts to seek higher wages, attract new members and guard against erosion of living standards lest they be accused of putting their own interests ahead of the war effort. In 1916 the Trades Congress told prime minister Robert Laird Borden that his government had an obligation to "prevent employers from taking advantage of the war conditions to increase the exploitation of their employees" because patriotic obligations made it difficult for workers to strike.[5] The campaign to have fair wage clauses inserted in Canadian munitions contracts, for instance, was conducted solely by lobbying and persuasion. But such tactics were generally unsuccessful. The Borden government did little to help organized labour, rarely sought union advice and guidance and usually acted on labour matters without consulting the unions. When the unpopular Industrial Disputes Investigation Act, which provided compulsory conciliation and a "cooling off" period prior to any work stoppage, was extended to cover war industries in March, 1916, union leaders were unpleasantly surprised.[6] But such actions were all too common.

A large part of Canadian war production was directed by the Imperial Munitions Board, founded towards the end of 1916 to replace a scandal-plagued Shell Committee. The IMB was headed by Joseph Wesley Flavelle, general manager of the William Davies Packing Company, and was directly responsible to the British ministry of munitions. It placed contracts for shells, ships and other war material with Canadian manufacturers and eventually established "national factories" to turn out those products which private business could not produce. Flavelle was not sympathetic to organized labour and ran the IMB as if the unions did not exist. By the spring of 1917 the Trades Congress had a full list of complaints to present to the federal government concerning conditions in Board-controlled war industries. They charged that workers employed on camp and plant construction were being forced to live in unhealthy and unsanitary conditions. They claimed that wage standards were being undermined in war industries and that workers were being forced to labour from ten to sixteen hours a day. They accused the Imperial Munitions Board of deliberately snubbing union officials when drawing up wage and hour clauses in munitions contracts. They attacked the IMB for allowing "The unnecessary dilution of labor by the introduction of female labor" and the "substitution of cheap semi-skilled labor from rural districts . . . because of their willingness to accept less than Trade Union rates." They warned that the Board was forcing unions to "obtain reasonable conditions by use of their organized power instead of through negotiations . . ."[7]

By 1917 there was a significant growth of work stoppages throughout the nation. In Winnipeg, disputes involving packinghouse employees, store clerks and munitions workers in the spring and summer were stopped short by court injunctions and damage suits. The labour movement reacted with alarm. The use of such one-sided judicial instruments could strip the unions of their only effective weapon and stop the drives for organization, recognition and higher real wages. The Winnipeg trades council appealed to labour throughout the country and made special representations to the Trades Congress which brought the injunction issue to the attention of the federal government, but to no avail.[8]

Labour's political weakness was demonstrated by the struggle over conscription. In December, 1916 the federal government announced a program of registration designed to establish a national manpower inventory. The Trades Congress leadership opposed registration at first, but reversed its stand after it was assured by Borden that this was not intended as a first step towards compulsory military service. Labour was generally opposed to conscription because it represented compulsion and clashed with the ideal, still held by some despite the war, of a working class united across national boundaries. Conscription also represented a more direct threat: the prospect that it might lead to industrial conscription and put wage earners at the mercy of their employers by eliminating the right to strike or change jobs. Western union members, led by the trades councils of Victoria, Vancouver and Winnipeg, attacked registration, urged their members to defy registration laws, and accused Trades Congress leaders of knuckling under to the government. In May, Borden announced that conscription would be introduced and caught the Congress by surprise. Labour's ranks were forced together. Almost every union leader in Canada opposed the draft, their only differences centred around the best way to show that opposition. Western union leaders, for the most part, sought a national general strike, while those in central Canada and elsewhere opted for electoral action. At the September, 1917, Trades Congress convention, the westerners were blocked and it was decided to field candidates to oppose the Borden government in the forthcoming December, 1917 federal election. Every candidate was defeated.[9] Samuel Gompers openly opposed the Trades Congress by speaking in favour of conscription to the House of Commons and to a victory loan rally in Toronto in the fall of 1917.[10] After the victory of Borden's pro-conscription Unionist coalition, the Congress counselled its members to accept conscription as the law of the land. This re-opened the east-west split that first appeared over the registration issue.

Conscription was primarily a political battle, but other east-west splits developed in labour ranks in 1918. In late April 1918, Division 4 of the Railway Employees Department of the American Federation of Labor, encompassing over 50 000 shopcraft workers on all major Canadian railroads, began negotiations with the Canadian Railway War Board. The division was a bargaining federation created to face the Railway War Board, formed in October 1917 by major Canadian railways to promote more efficient rail transport during the war. The division was armed with a strike vote and pressed for a new schedule of higher wages to apply uniformly from coast to coast. The Board resisted at first, claiming they could not raise wages without increased freight rates. As negotiations dragged on, the government granted a freight rate increase and forced the railways to agree to the same wage schedule as contained in General Order 27 of the United States Railroad Administration under the chairmanship of William McAdoo. The workers refused to accept this and threatened to strike.

The Borden government had allowed this nation-wide bargaining to take place, but could not afford failure. It threatened to draft the shopmen and put them to work on army pay if they walked out, while American union leaders threatened to revoke and suspend charters.[11] Eastern representatives at the negotiations caved in; the westerners walked out in disgust.

The July, 1918 postal strike added to the division of Canadian labour. The postal workers had walked out after thwarted attempts, stretching back to early 1917, to win wage increases commensurate with increases in the cost of living. After a few days the eastern-dominated executive of the union ordered its men back to work following a vague government promise to investigate the matter. But western members refused to return. The government then promised that the Civil Service Commission would examine their grievances and granted them full pay for the time on strike. The westerners went back to work satisfied.[12]

East and west were drifting apart and the west's increased militancy was highlighted in the spring and summer of 1918 by a renewed call for general strikes. In Winnipeg a dispute between the city and three unions of civic employees degenerated into a strike on May 7. The city took a hard line and threatened to remove its workers' right to strike. The Winnipeg trades council responded with a call to its member unions to support the strikers, and workers all over the city, in public and private employ, started to leave their jobs in sympathy. The strike widened and almost became general but for the intervention, after three weeks, of Senator Gideon Robertson, acting as Borden's special representative. Robertson forced the city administration to settle on terms that were favourable to the three unions with substantial wage increases and guarantees of the right to bargain collectively. Trades council solicitor T. J. Murray concluded that without the sympathetic strike, the civic employees would have been defeated.[13] The sympathetic strike was without social or political objectives and was an expression of militancy and solidarity probably prompted by the injunctions of the previous year. It convinced some that workers could only win through similar tactics. The *Bulletin*, organ of the railway machinists, declared: "The ability of individual trade unions to enforce their economic demands is becoming less as the master class unite." The answer was to adopt industrial unionism, increasing the workers' unity and allowing them to "use their organized forces as a lever for [their] final emancipation . . . that is to say the abolition of the wage system."[14] R. J. Johns, a machinist member of the Socialist Party of Canada, praised the sympathetic strike as a fine example of class solidarity.

By mid-summer of 1918, the continous frustrations and defeats of the first three years of war forced many urban workers to become militant and to place the objective of winning the war on the shelf. In May and June, 1918, five thousand workers employed in Pacific coast shipyards, handling contracts for the Imperial Munitions Board, went on strike despite appeals to their patriotism. They were determined to win union recognition from the IMB and higher wages to keep up with cost of living increases. This strike was settled only through Senator Robertson's intervention and, though the unions did not achieve all they aimed for, they were satisfied with the results. Despite considerable public pressure, the shipyard workers remained united behind their leadership and returned to work only when an agreement was signed.[15] Victories, it was again demonstrated, came only through strike action or the very real threat of such action. This awareness prompted militants to move to radical positions and to support radicals whatever their own political views.

The new militancy of the urban labour movement was most apparent in the emergence of new leaders in Winnipeg and Calgary. In the foothills city, the building trades, personified by Alex Ross, were replaced by the railway shop crafts as leaders of the labour movement. Ross was a Scottish-born stone mason who had arrived in America in 1906 and had been a major leader of the

Calgary unions until his election to the legislature in 1917. His departure, together with the new wartime importance of the shopcrafts, brought socialists such as A. Broatch, R. J. Tallon and H. H. Sharples to the fore. Broatch was a strong supporter of industrial unionism while Tallon, elected president of the trades council in 1918, was a key figure in the national shopcraft negotiations.

In Winnipeg, the *Voice*, owned and edited by Arthur W. Puttee, ceased publication and was replaced by the *Western Labor News*. Puttee had served the cause of labour in Winnipeg since 1891 and had been elected to a four-year term in the House of Commons in a 1900 by-election. He was a moderate reformer who supported causes such as the single-tax and opposed the Socialist Party in election after election. He opposed the 1918 sympathetic strike and his opponents seized that opportunity to shove him aside and replace his newspaper with one owned by the trades council. It was edited by William Ivens, a Methodist Minister who left the church in June, 1918, because of his increasingly radical and pacifist views. R. B. Russell emerged as secretary of the Winnipeg Metal Trades Council and secretary-treasurer of Division 4. R. J. Johns, also of the Socialist Party, had been a member of the Division 4 negotiating team. William Hoop, another SPC member, became the trades council's first paid organizer in 1917 and was a leader of the 1918 postal strike. These radicals were not strong enough to gain election to any of the trades council's executive positions, but commanded enough support to push Fred Tipping out of the chairmanship in early September. Tipping, a socialist himself, fell from the radicals' favour when he signed a royal commission report highly critical of the Winnipeg Metal Trades Council, and, by direct implication, R. B. Russell.[16]

Difficulties arising out of the war were also creating

trouble among the coal miners. District 18's endorsement of the Socialist Party of Canada in 1914 had upset international president John P. White and an attempt was made at the district's 1915 convention to have the preamble of the constitution changed so that it reflected that of the international. Dave Rees of Fernie supported district president Phillips in his assertion that the SPC endorsement was unconstitutional because of UMWA rules and could not be allowed to stand since White opposed it. But the members rejected Phillips' ruling and refused to listen to Rees. They decided to stick by the Socialist Party regardless of the wishes of their officers.[17]

The disagreement foreshadowed a serious division between the miners and their leaders in the following year. From the spring of 1916 to the summer of 1917 there was a serious erosion in miner wages. The district executive, usually supported by president White in Indianapolis, tried to avoid strikes and consistently agreed to wage offers that were rejected by the members. On several occasions local strikes broke out in defiance of the union's leadership. During one stoppage in May of 1917 the men ignored two orders from White to return to work.[18] This strike was only settled through government intervention. W. H. Armstrong of Vancouver was appointed director of coal operations for Western Canada with the power to determine wages, working conditions and coal and coke prices. Armstrong quickly imposed a settlement which included a war bonus and a commission to adjust wages every four months in accordance with changes in the cost of living.[19] Though the men went back to work, they remained bitter towards their leaders. One sign of their mood was the rise to prominence of Phillip Martin Christophers.

Christophers had been born in Cornwall, England and came to Canada at the age of twenty-five. He settled in the Crows Nest Pass region and became a staunch

supporter of the United Mine Workers and the Socialist
Party of Canada. Christophers rarely minced words.
When the miners were discussing government intervention in the summer of 1917, he issued this challenge to
the government and labour minister T. W. Crothers: "I
defy the Canadian Government or any soldier to make
me work, they can put me into the cage and put me
down in the mine and they can make me stay there eight
hours, but I will be damned if they can make me dig coal
. . . So far as this damn Crothers coming around, all he
is doing is trying to peddle suck you for a vote . . . he is
just a damn peddler of bull-shit."[20]

Christophers was an angry man but so were thousands of other workers across the west. Defeats over injunctions, dilution, the high cost of living, union recognition, conscription and fair wage clauses convinced
many workers that society would give them nothing
they could not take themselves. In the cities, thousands
of skilled workers began to discover, by war's end, what
the miners already knew; that opportunity and mobility
were illusions and that their only real power was what
they generated through their unions. Under most circumstances, even this was not enough. They could win
recognition or higher wages through strikes—the more
massive, the more effective—but major victories were
still out of reach. This drove many to accept the leadership of socialists preaching Marxist ideas of class division and class struggle. Neither leaders nor followers
were philosophers—their Marxism was rarely pure—
but the message rang true and reflected their actual experiences. War conditions, therefore, allowed radicals
to assume leadership of the urban labour movement
and bring it closer in spirit to the miners. Westerners
were rejecting their institutional leaders in the east and
the United States, and were becoming more united.

The September, 1918 convention of the Trades and
Labour Congress, held at Quebec City, became the

focus for the emerging unity and radicalism of the western unions. This was the most contentious convention in many years and witnessed several determined western assaults upon the policies of international unionism in Canada. The Congress leadership, backed by a majority of central Canadian delegates, were determined to make the meeting a showcase of what they had succeeded in bringing about, cooperation between labour and government during the war. But the westerners, supported by some eastern radicals, strenuously objected. For the first time in years, the convention's committee on officers' reports split and the minority presented the convention with a scathing condemnation of the executive's relations with the government. They condemned their leaders for agreeing to registration, for asking the government to conscript workers from allied countries who were alleged to be stealing jobs from Canadians, and for arbitrarily choosing men to sit on boards and commissions rather than seeking nominations from trades councils and local unions.[21]

The minority report was overshadowed, however, by a long list of resolutions presented by western locals calling for restructuring of the Congress and redrafting of its policies. Every one of these resolutions, from those condemning the jailing of war opponents to those demanding the reorganization of the Congress into an industrial union, was defeated. There were only forty-five delegates present from the west out of over four hundred, and their weakness was all too apparent. In the elections for president the 'safe and sane' delegates finally had a chance to remove James Watters from office. Though he had been loyal to the 'win the war' policies pursued by Gompers and the international unions, he was still an outsider—a socialist miner from British Columbia. His successor, Tom Moore, was a man who could be counted on.

Moore epitomized the North American Dream, trade

union variety. He was a round-faced, prosperous-look-
ing labour statesman who came to Canada from Leeds,
England, in 1909 to spend his days washing dishes at the
Chateau Laurier Hotel in Ottawa. He was a carpenter
by trade and made his home in Niagara Falls, Ontario
where he joined the local carpenters' union and quickly
rose to become district business agent and then, in 1911,
general organizer for eastern Canada. Moore was an ad-
mirer of Sam Gompers and a firm believer in the principles of 'pure and simple' unionism. He, unlike Watters,
had demonstrated his loyalty to Gompers and international unionism by supporting conscription in 1917.
Western radicals shed no tears over Watters, they considered him a turncoat. He had received a rough reception on a speaking tour to Winnipeg several weeks prior
to the convention and was actually dressed down by the
man who introduced him. But Watters' defeat was sym-
bolic.

A new strategy was needed and a caucus of western
delegates, chaired by Dave Rees, decided to organize a
meeting of western union representatives to be held
prior to the next TLC convention. It was made clear
that no secession was intended by this move, and the
only outspoken opponent was Alex Ross. The western
delegates were particularly irked that western representation at TLC meetings was weak. They felt this was because conventions were held in the east, and they
wished to create an opportunity for the western voice to
be heard at a single gathering. A committee was struck,
chaired by Rees with Vancouver trades council secretary
Victor Midgley to handle correspondence.[22]

The federal government was worried about the increasing radicalism and militancy of the labour movement. On September 25, the cabinet issued an order-in-
council prohibiting the public use of fourteen languages
deemed to be 'enemy alien.' This was followed, three

days later, with another order declaring fourteen associations, including the IWW and the Social Democratic Party, illegal. Finally, on October 11, the government banned work stoppages and provided heavy penalties for violations.

Organized labour was incensed. Tom Moore lodged immediate and vigorous protests following all three orders. He pointed out that restrictions on languages would make the job of organizing foreign workers into unions difficult, but concentrated most of his fire on the strike ban. Moore challenged the government to explain its actions and to point to those it claimed were disrupting the war effort. He reviewed the many ways that the unions had cooperated with the government and reminded the government that it had, in turn, promised to return the cooperation on measures affecting labour. Instead, the government had issued three orders drastically curtailing the liberty of workers. He warned that the government could not take labour for granted. It should heed the obvious signs of the coming storm and remove some of the grievances before it was too late.[23]

Moore's reaction was calm compared to that of western union members. The orders were 'Prussianism at home' and were to be resisted with all possible strength. When a longstanding dispute involving CPR freighthandlers in Calgary erupted into a strike in early October, the labour movement in the city began to conduct a general strike vote in support of the strikers. On October 16 a federal government official, acting under authority of the five-day-old order-in-council banning strikes, arrested several of the CPR strike leaders. This sparked off another wave of fury as trades councils as far away as Winnipeg began to conduct a general strike ballot aimed at the order-in-council. The Calgary freighthandlers quickly became a *cause célèbre*. When the arrested men were freed by the courts without fines or imprisonment, it was taken as a government defeat brought about by the threat of general strikes in Calgary, Winnipeg and elsewhere.[24]

The orders-in-council were a tremendous blunder. They put the government directly across the path of the unions in an open and obvious fashion. The order-in-council banning strikes was, when combined with an earlier order outlawing 'idleness' on the part of healthy males of military age, nothing less than partial industrial conscription. Even Tom Moore was prompted to wonder aloud why the policy was adopted when the government must have had some word, so soon before the November 11 armistice, of Germany's desperate military situation. The orders also forced groups such as the Ukrainian Social Democratic Federation to cooperate much more closely with Anglo-Saxon radicals because they could not publish their own papers and turned to the English labour press instead. In Winnipeg the Ukrainian Labor Committee urged all its members to subscribe to the *Western Labor News* after the suppression of *Robotchy Narod,* their own newspaper.[25]

Against this backdrop, the committee appointed by the Quebec caucus to organize a Western Labor Conference began its work. Rees and Midgley decided on a January date in Calgary and approached the officers of the British Columbia Federation of Labor with the novel suggestion that they move their annual meeting there from Victoria. Calgary was a good central location and holding the BCFL meeting, and perhaps other provincial gatherings as well, just prior to the Western Labor Conference would save time and money. Midgley believed getting the Alberta Federation of Labor to follow would be easy,[26] but he was wrong. The apparently innocent problem of 'when and where' became a major bone of contention. Alex Ross, Alfred Farmilo and Frank Wheatley of the UMW believed that a gathering just prior to the 1919 TLC convention would tend to be nothing more than a strategy caucus, but a meeting in mid-winter in Calgary could easily be a launching pad for secession. In Alberta and in Winnipeg these reservations caused Rees and Midgley considerable trouble.

Though the executive of the B.C. Federation agreed to move their meeting to Calgary, after receiving overwhelming membership support, the leaders of the Alberta Federation, driven by Ross and Alfred Farmilo, did not. They set out to wreck the proposed Western Labor Conference if they could and to weaken Alberta support for it if they could not. In the first week of November they decided they would go ahead with their original plans to hold their own gathering in January at Medicine Hat. Instead of the proposed Calgary Western Labor Conference, they called for a small meeting of not more than four delegates from each province in Canada as well as the Congress executive to draw up a labour position on reconstruction. They could not, they maintained, "view with favor any sectional movement of wage workers on matters affecting us Dominion-wide until an opportunity is given organized workers of all provinces to be represented at a joint conference."[27] Rees contemptuously called them "Lloyd George coalitionists."[28]

But they would not be moved. Despite the actions of the B.C. Federation, the public pleading of Rees and the position taken by the Calgary trades council which attempted to rally the support of other councils in Alberta,[29] they stood firm. By this time an influenza epidemic had forced postponement of the Western Labor Conference until March, and provided the excuse that if they waited the extra three months they would miss the beginning of the legislative session in Edmonton and would be unable to make their annual pilgrimage to present convention resolutions to the government.[30]

Rees and Midgley had better luck in Winnipeg. The

Trades and Labor Council in the Manitoba capital was strongly influenced by radicals such as Russell and Johns, though its executive was composed of more cautious men. James Winning, president, Ernie Robinson, secretary, A. C. Hay, vice-president, and J. L. McBride, treasurer, had been swept along on the rising tide of radicalism but were, themselves, confirmed believers in international craft unionism. They would have no truck with secession. Towards the end of November they decided to ask Midgley if the proposed Western Labor Conference in Calgary could be replaced by a meeting in Port Arthur just prior to the 1919 TLC convention. They reasoned that events were moving so rapidly that decisions taken in the early part of the year might be irrelevant by September and would be "of little use as far as the Congress is concerned." There would also be financial problems created by sending delegates to one convention in Calgary and another, several months later, in Hamilton.[31]

Rees had an opportunity to size up the Winnipeg situation during a stopover on a trip east. He found Robinson to be "as bad as Wheatley or Alex Ross." Robinson not only continued to push the ideas he had set out to Midgley but wondered aloud if the whole matter could not be conducted by correspondence. McBride was not much of an improvement. But when Rees spoke to Russell he realized there were two distinct camps in the city and that Russell, Johns and Hoop would support the Western Labor Conference. Russell was "heart and soul" behind it and promised to write R. J. Tallon in Calgary and Joe Knight in Edmonton to try to get them to undermine the decision of the Alberta Federation executive. He also promised Rees to push the Conference at machinists' meetings in the city.[32]

Midgley and Rees were somewhat worried by developments in Winnipeg. Robinson was reminded that he had been present at the Quebec caucus and was "one of the parents" of the plan. But Robinson was not the key. When the matter came before the full trades council in early December, the executive was criticized for being delinquent on the matter and was instructed to make the necessary arrangements for the Western Labor Conference as soon as possible.[33] Unlike Alberta, Winnipeg lined up behind the Conference because here the radicals were powerful: "We have pretty nearly got control of the Trades and Labor Council" was Russell's assessment in January. "When we get it we will use it to our advantage."[34]

Suspicions that it was already being used were not unfounded. Members of the Socialist Party of Canada, the 'second generation' as A. R. McCormack has called them, were determined to seize the opportunities presented by the upcoming conventions to further their ambitions. These SPC members, Russell, Johns, W. A. Pritchard, Knight, Midgley and others, were confirmed union members who set out to weld labour radicalism to Socialist Party doctrine. They were, to a degree, successful. Chris Stephenson, secretary of the dominion executive committee of the Socialist Party of Canada, told Russell that the issues at stake were "too vital for our movement to stand aside impotently while all the resources of the bourgeois state are wielded ruthlessly to stamp it out . . . we must use what means we can and make the very best of them."[35]

There were many examples of workers around the world who were doing just what Stephenson had in mind: taking matters into their own hands and pressing their demands through direct action. "Revolution in Russia! Revolution in Austria! Revolution in Bulgaria! Revolution in that benighted country where we were told the tame slaves of the Kaiser would never revolt," trumpeted the *Western Labor News*. "Which country will be next? How far will the revolution spread? Can it be avoided in Canada?"[36] was the crucial question. The columns of the labor press overflowed with stories, editorials and feature articles about the strikes, riots and revolutions which seemed to be tottering the capitalist system in western Europe, Britain and the United States. Canadian radicals were inspired and heartened by these events, particularly the Russian revolution.

Their own reaction was heavily influenced by the traditions they had brought with them to Canada. But two new factors received attention in the last half of 1918. The rise of the Shop Stewards movement in Great Britain came under close scrutiny because it appeared to offer a new approach to industrial organization and the strengthening of working class political power. The movement was pre-war in origin and by late 1918 had spread throughout the engineering trades and was particularly strong in the Clyde shipyards. It began as an attempt to build the power and authority of the union shop steward on the factory floor but soon developed into a scheme for the "emancipation of the Wage-Slave" through the election of local stewards to district and national councils. The national bodies would unify the labour movement while abolishing craft and trade divisions which, it was asserted, weakened workers and made them incapable of dealing with modern capital. Proponents of the system wished to side-step the "cumbrous movement" of the "trade union machinery" to increase the workers' ability to take quick and effective direct action.[37]

Westerners were also becoming intrigued by the One Big Union movement coming to the fore in Australia. In that country syndicalism and industrial unionism had been important since the 1890's. The IWW had established itself there by 1907 and, though never large, became quite influential in certain industries, notably mining. The IWW was active in Australia's anti-conscription fight during the war and its opponents declared it to be a sabotage-oriented, pro-German organization. Eventually it was outlawed and its leaders jailed. This did not mark the end of organized attempts to convert the Australian union movement to syndicalism, however, since the Australian Workers Union, the dominant national labour congress, had endorsed the aim of One Big Union for all workers in 1915.[38] This ideal continued to remain important for many Australian workers and the only real disagreement arose over which organization would bring the dream of the One Big Union to reality.

In August, 1918, a conference of workers in New South Wales founded the Workers Industrial Union of Australia. This was to be the One Big Union and was intended to rival the AWU by eventually bringing all the organized workers of the Commonwealth into its fold. The WIUA pushed a plan of organization quite similar to that adopted by the IWW in Chicago in 1905, with an elaborate circular diagram outlining the various industrial departments, sections, and district and state councils that would make up the One Big Union.[39]

These events were followed with great interest in western Canada. There had always been links with Australia. Labour papers in Winnipeg and on the coast carried frequent articles about the southern dominion while workers such as Ernest Winch and George Hardy, both originally from Britain, crossed and recrossed the Pacific prior to settling in Canada. The *Western Labor News* reprinted both the preamble and the constitution of the Australian OBU since the matter was "of vital importance to the workers of Canada."[40] R. B. Russell told a national gathering of machinists in Winnipeg in late 1918: "the day of craft unionism is gone, and when we ... see that they are making this change in the Old Country, and from Australia we have word of the various Craft Unions all coming together into one big union ... it behooves us to give this question our most serious attention."[41]

Fools and Wise Men

SPC members were giving these matters serious consideration in the months following the September, 1918 TLC convention. They played the leading role in organizing the Western Labour Conference because they had become prominent in union ranks as leaders of strikes, organizing drives and anti-government and anti-AFL campaigns. They were popular and they were trusted. Everyone knew that R. B. Russell, or Sarah Knight or Victor Midgley had the best interests of the working class in mind. It was not long before they began to dominate the anti-TLC campaign and tried to steer the anger, frustration, militancy and radicalism of western labour on a course they would determine. As early as late November, Russell told Joe Knight that the Calgary meeting could be packed with 'reds' who could "no doubt start something."[42]

SPC members were strongly influential at the January, 1919 Alberta Federation of Labor meeting at Medicine Hat. Ross, Wheatley, Farmilo and their allies could not muzzle debate on the convention floor. Sarah and Joseph Knight, along with Carl Berg, went to the meeting from Edmonton and five SPC members were in attendance from Calgary. They, together with delegates from District 18 of the United Mine Workers, turned the meeting into a nightmare for Ross and his colleagues. Resolutions were passed by wide margins, often over the loud opposition of executive members, endorsing the proposed Calgary Western Labor Conference and calling for the establishment of a special provincial committee, composed of representatives from local unions, to conduct general strike votes when deemed necessary and to form part of an executive to carry on such strikes. Amalgamation of craft unions into industrial unions was endorsed.[43] The meeting also expressed itself in "full accord and sympathy with the aims and purposes of the Russian and German revolutions" and authorized the incoming executive to call a general strike if the Allies did not withdraw from Russia.

Sarah Knight was pleased. The radicals "gave the Bolsheviki the finest boost that has been accomplished for some time." She told R. B. Russell that Farmilo, "that arch traitor," and Ross were powerless to stop the resolutions. The lesson was obvious: "I think on the whole we did some fine work and excellent propaganda . . . with a big representation in Calgary in March we ought to make things hum." She pleaded with Russell to "get reds to be delegates" so that they "might be able to turn it into an S.P. Convention."[44] Russell did not need the prompting. He and Johns were selected to represent the Winnipeg trades council at Calgary and both worked to get "a number of Reds elected by the locals."[45]

By the end of January the move to Calgary was in high gear, but little had been heard from the coal miners. Their man on the Alberta Federation of Labor Executive, Frank Wheatley, had been lukewarm to the Western Labor Conference, even though he was a member of the Rees-Midgley committee. Then, in February, the annual convention of District 18 took place in Calgary. The ten day meeting opened with a morning-long attack from the convention floor against the *United Mine Workers Journal*. The delegates were angry that the international had set aside a special fund to finance the journal and was pushing a policy that would have every UMW member receive it. One delegate called it "more poisonous to the worker than any capitalist newspaper of Wall Street." The men were particularly upset by the *Journal*'s 'win the war at any cost' line and its constant castigation of those members who were less than enthusiastic about purchasing war bonds. At the end of the discussion, the convention passed an extraordinary motion to refuse to allow the *Journal* into District 18. Convention chairman Dave Irvine, international organizer of the UMW, observed: "It is only another point of variance between this district and the International."[46]

The debate over the *Journal* was somewhat quixotic, but many other resolutions were passed in the next few days aimed at the miners' living and working conditions as well as government policy. The delegates resolved to abolish the bunkhouse system, demand the release of political prisoners and seek the end of the ban on proscribed literature. Should the government not lift the literature ban, they declared themselves in favour of a national general strike through the TLC. They endorsed industrial unionism, use of general strikes as a last resort in industrial disputes and the six hour day to fight unemployment. They resolved to work with railway unions in an attempt to emulate the British Triple Alliance of coal, railway and dockside workers, and they elected P. M. Christophers as president.[47]

The high point of the convention was the debate on the contract system which followed introduction of a resolution from the Corbin local calling for its abolition. Many delegates were caught on the horns of a dilemma: work to abolish the contract system in line with their socialist beliefs or accept the system as part of the daily grind. District secretary Ed Browne probably reflected majority opinion when he pointed out that an abolition campaign would be folly because the market was glutted with coal: socialist theories were no use when "discussing an agreement with the other fellow." Both officials of the international, board member Robert Livett and Dave Irvine, strongly opposed the resolution. Irvine threatened, "If it goes forth from this convention that the miners of this district have abolished the contract system, there will be nothing but disruption." Alex Susnar, a district official from Brulé, Alberta, disagreed with Irvine and told the delegates they had followed 'Gompers types' for too long. Rees went along with Livett and Irvine: "you can call me a Sam Gompers if you like, but you will be wise if you will not act on the proposed resolution." Even though the newly-elected Christophers supported the resolution, it was defeated.

But even though the convention bowed to practicality, it went on record "opposed to the contract system" and pledged to work for its eventual overthrow.[48]

Dave Rees had been a leader of the drive to set up the Western Labor Conference along with Midgley, Russell and the Knights. But he was becoming uneasy about their motives. In a major speech he attacked those who were talking about industrial unionism, Triple Alliance, and the general strike. He criticized the delegates for "dallying and fussing" about whether they intended to meet the operators to negotiate a new working agreement. They must, he said, get their heads out of the clouds and face the real issues of the cost of living, wage negotiations and so on. It was foolish to keep up the discussion of general strikes because the unemployment situation and the coal market made such action irresponsible. Why, he asked, was the government building up its military forces in all the major cities in the country? It could only be to oppose the aspirations of the workers. If this was true, surely they must examine the situation carefully. He believed that governments throughout the world were trying mightily to get the workers to launch massive general strikes before they were ready: "What we are up against now is a peaceful or bloody revolution and it is only education that can prevent a bloody revolution from taking place."[49]

Rees was still a strong socialist. His speech challenged the miners to choose the peaceful path to revolution but not to abandon the quest. Nevertheless, his radicalism did not interfere with the more practical consideration of maintaining the strength of his union and defending the economic interests of the miners until the great day of revolution arrived. This reflected the overall pragmatism of the delegates who refused to let Susnar's arguments sway them into a useless and potentially disastrous attack on the contract system. Perhaps this belief, that the strength of the existing unions must be maintained and built upon, clashed with the increasingly visible evidence that Midgley and his allies were, in fact, out to disrupt the unions for purposes not yet apparent.

The fact that disruption was the aim clearly emerged at the Calgary gathering of the British Columbia Federation of Labor which met a few weeks after District 18. Every important radical leader in the province was there—W. A. Pritchard, Jack Kavanagh, Victor Midgley, A. S. Wells, and T. A. Grogan were particularly prominent. The tone was set early when a resolution committing the Federation to restructuring itself on "industrial lines" was debated and passed. There was a definite connection in many minds between "industrial unionism" and general strikes. The radical speakers, led by Kavanagh and Pritchard, believed unions should use their industrial strength for political purposes. They did not see the general strike as a weapon to topple the government, but rather as a means of enforcing political and economic demands.[50] This was because these two men were firm believers in the inevitability of revolution (they pointed out that it had already started in Europe) and saw no need to discuss tactics because the revolution would begin almost automatically.[51] There was also, however, a definite need to strengthen workers in their daily battles and prepare them for the day when the means of production would be in their hands. Kavanagh believed the ideal union to achieve all this would be "one industrial organization covering all lines [in which] the various crafts now in existence would simply all be members of the same organization." This was not craft amalgamation nor even industrial organization such as that of the coal and hardrock miners. The idea was not to "organize by industry as . . . the metal trades or the loggers"; it was to "organize into one big organization comprising all workers."[52]

The convention thus heard the first enunciation of an

SPC-influenced western Canadian syndicalism. These workers were not philosophers. They were, despite allegiance to some strange political theories, practical men, experienced in union work. The need for pure or consistent ideas was easily lost in the search to find strategies that worked. Nevertheless, a loose syndicalist theory emerged which bore a distinct resemblance to the ideas of French, British and American syndicalism, but which was also quite different. The radicals and their allies rejected the possibility that real changes could be brought about through electoral politics and advocated the formation of a universal, centralized union of all workers. They enunciated the inevitability of class struggle and advocated the use of direct action to force political and economic change. Unlike other syndicalists—notably the IWW and the French Confédération Génèral du Travail—they did not discuss sabotage and probably considered it somewhat irrelevant. They advocated general strikes to deal with industrial disputes and to force concessions from government, but not to topple the government and replace it with administration by trade unions. They never referred to reorganization of their unions as 'building the new society within the shell of the old.' Their job was to create a class union movement to defend them while the capitalist system still existed, to hasten the eventual triumph of the revolution and to help build the post-revolutionary society. They were unclear, however, about the shape of that society. The radicals looked to the Russians for inspiration but had no clear idea of what the Bolsheviks were really doing or what role Russian unions were assuming. A. S. Wells thought the unions were administering Soviet society—which they were not—and mixed up the Bolshevik system of workers and soldiers political soviets with the syndicalist notion of administration by trade unions.[53]

In three short days the B.C. delegates turned their

world upside down. Resolutions were passed condemning Allied intervention in Russia and censorship and jailing of political prisoners. The delegates decided to conduct a referendum on the reorganization of the federation into an industrial union, secession from the internationals, and the six hour day. Greetings were conveyed to the Bolsheviks and support registered for "industrial soviet control." The few, such as Trotter and McVety, who dared swim against the tide, were quickly overwhelmed.

Delegates from Winnipeg to the Rockies began to gather in Calgary as the British Columbia convention drew to a close. The *Western Labor News* proclaimed, "The more effete East is burdensome to the West and the slavish subservience of parliament to the interests of vested wealth has filled the cup of the West to overflowing."[54] These secessionist sentiments echoed the three conventions which had taken place since January and Dave Rees finally decided he could go along no longer. He opened the Western Labor Conference on Thursday, March 13, but soon left for a UMW board meeting in Indianapolis. R. J. Tallon took the gavel with Victor Midgley as secretary.

The B.C. convention had established the pattern for what followed. Kavanagh, Pritchard and R. J. Johns took control of the conference from the very beginning and kept it on the path laid out by the B.C. meeting. On the very first day, the B.C. resolutions against lobbying, for the abolition of capitalism, in favour of secession, and the formation of a new industrial union, were all introduced by Kavanagh, usually seconded by Pritchard, and passed.[55] A policy committee was then formed under the chairmanship of R. J. Johns, which reported back to the convention the morning of the second day, recommending secession from the AFL/TLC and the establishment of the One Big Union.

The Johns committee resolutions, and the resultant debate, fleshed out the essentials of the OBU. This was to be an organization of all workers in one union which would be more effective in calling and carrying on general strikes for specific, usually political purposes. The delegates actually decided to conduct a general strike vote aimed at a June 1 walkout to back demands for a six hour workday. A central committee and four provincial committees were established to spread propaganda on behalf of the new union and to organize a referendum on secession and formation of the OBU. Results of the vote were to be divided into those voting east and west of Fort William and those not voting were to be counted in the affirmative. The central committee was composed of Pritchard, Johns, Joe Knight, Midgley and J. Naylor, a Cumberland, B.C. miner. Provincial committee chairmen were Carl Berg (for Alberta), R. B. Russell (for Manitoba), Jack Kavanagh (for British Columbia) and R. Hazeltine (for Saskatchewan).[56] Hazeltine was the only one who was not a member of the Socialist Party of Canada. It was decided to wait until after the referendum results were in before a permanent structure was adopted, and therefore these men had no mandate to draft the organizational form of the One Big Union.

This meeting passed the standard resolutions expressing admiration for the European revolutionaries and condemnation of the Borden administration. But it also witnessed a debate which revealed an appreciation of what was necessary to wield power in politics and industry. On the final day, a Vancouver delegate moved that the referendum on secession and reorganization be conducted following the methods used by the B.C. Federation. This meant that on a vote to change the structure of an organization such as the Federation, a majority vote of the "vital trades" was necessary for passage. These were defined as those which "ceasing work compel others to cease by virtue of the fact they cannot carry on without them."[57]

The resolution sparked off a long, and sometimes bitter debate. Opponents viewed it as discrimination which ought not to be practised while embarking on a new venture into industrial unionism. But supporters, including Kavanagh, took a more realistic view. If transport workers, miners and the metal trades could be lined up, the others would be forced to follow. "Sure it is force, nothing but force in existence," he admitted, but "unless you are aggressive no other element counts."[58] The OBU could not be built on the backs of cooks and waiters. The motion passed with a heavy majority. This, along with the decision to divide the results into east and west meant that a heavy pro-OBU vote amongst western miners and railway workers would launch the new union.

Most of the resolutions passed at the Western Labor Conference received unanimous or near unanimous approval. The atmosphere was euphoric. The delegates were free of the influences of international officers and the votes of Ontario carpenters or Quebec plumbers. But opposition silence did not mean opposition approval. Rees' departure was a portent of things to come. Under the surface there was far less unity than pictured in the newspaper columns. Many Alberta delegates, especially those from Calgary, were disturbed by the anti-electoral bent of the meeting.[59] They wanted a new socialist political effort closely supported by the unions but were ridiculed by B.C. delegates fed up with lobbying and elections which appeared useless to them. Other workers, like Rees, would never support secession regardless of the aims. To compound the difficulties the country was in the grip of a wave of anti-Red panic and greeted this radical convention with hysteria. The Socialist Party members and their allies had succeeded in shoving western labour radicalism into their own mould, but how long could they keep it there?

Chapter 4

The Red Menace

The Western Labor Conference met during the time of the "Red Scare"[1] when many Canadians convinced themselves that radicals were laying the groundwork for violence, sabotage, murder, and revolution. The gathering confirmed many of their worst fears and provided an additional focal point for anti-Bolshevik hysteria. In this atmosphere the One Big Union was destined to face the police, military and judicial power of an aroused federal government.

Prior to the entry of the United States into the war in July, 1917, the Royal North West Mounted Police reported little likelihood of internal unrest in Canada. They believed, nevertheless, that enemy aliens "might throw all precautions aside and venture the most daring attempts," given the right incentive. After the U.S. entered the fray, police officials worried that groups such as the IWW would attempt cross border raids to disrupt the harvest in the Canadian west,[2] while the introduction of conscription prompted fears that "alien enemies," led by renegade Anglo-Saxon radicals, would try to disrupt draft enforcement. Military and police officials both advocated internment to deal with alien labour unrest, even when it involved something as simple as a labourers' strike on a water works project.[3] From here it was a simple step to proclaim that any strikes were treasonous. J. W. Flavell, chairman of the IMB, blamed the Pacific coast shipyards disputes on "the presence of dangerous men . . . actuated by pro-German motives."[4] Borden himself concluded that unrest among lumber workers in B.C. was due to IWW agitation and suggested that Canadians follow the example of a Washington state superpatriot, Col. Bryce Disque, in forming a Loyal Legion of Loggers and Lumbermen.[5]

Fear of radicals and revolutionaries grew alongside the budding awareness that Lenin's October, 1917 seizure of power in Russia could be a grave threat to the western democracies. Britain, the United States and their allies were angered by the Bolsheviks' conclusion of a separate peace with Germany and fearful of the revolutionary excesses they perceived in the new regime. The Bolsheviks were soon treated as enemies, and troops from Britain, Japan, Canada and the United States were sent to help Lenin's foes crush the revolution; Bolshevism and its exponents became hated and feared. Until November, 1918 the public's attention was focused on the western front, but after the armistice a veritable flood of stories and rumours concerning Bolshevism swept the Dominion. Canadians knew little about it, and their ignorance was compounded by the press. Newspapers labelled Lenin's followers "blood-thirsty hordes" who were more autocratic than the Czar and as destructive as anarchists. One observer, writing in the *Financial Post,* claimed that the United States and Canada were prime targets of Bolshevist activity because it was here that their foes lived: broadly, "people who wash regularly, have acquired some stake in the community and are reasonably satisfied with the government under which they are living."[6]

Some Canadians were willing to admit that Bolshevik sympathies in Canada had roots in real social grievances. The lieutenant-governor of Quebec, Sir Charles Fitzpatrick, called for the elimination of slums to fight the menace because urban blight increased the strength of "these fantastic ideas."[7] The *Calgary Herald* editorialized that Bolshevism was really an expression, "exaggerated, it is true," of "a class made mad through hopelessness of ever having its wrongs righted."[8] But some Canadians undoubtedly agreed with Reverend Cameron of Burnaby's Henderson Church who said of Bolshevism: "Its definite policy is destruction and it flourishes best in the soil of discontentment, irresponsibility and ignorance."[9]

In early 1919 Canadian newspapers warned their readers about the beginnings of Bolshevik activity in North America with headlines that proclaimed: "Red Bolshevism Declares War On World At Large," and "Lenin Agents Appear On This Side of Atlantic." In some reports New York city was pinpointed as having its own soviet located in "commodious quarters" on Fifteenth Street in Manhattan. A major network of groups such as the IWW, the Socialist Labor Party, the Workers International Industrial Union, the Russian Socialist Party and the Workers Defence Fund was alleged to be operating out of the city. At one meeting delegates from the United States and Canada, "most ... young men, some with long hair, some with short," demanded an end to allied intervention in Russia and pledged themselves to work towards the unification of all American wage earners.[10] But revolutionaries were to be found not only in New York—Brantford, Ontario was said to be Canadian Bolshevik headquarters, chosen because no one was likely to suspect that anything extraordinary could possibly happen there.[11] In St. Catherines, Bolshevik agents were blamed for distributing pamphlets calling on workers and soldiers to appoint delegates to revolutionary soviets.

The federal government was concerned about left-wing activities and had, in the fall of 1918, appointed a Montreal lawyer, C. H. Cahan, director of the Public Safety Branch of the Department of Justice. Cahan was charged with investigating the causes and extent of radical agitation in Canada and recommending action to deal with it. He quickly concluded that Bolshevik ideas and propaganda were strongly affecting Slavs, Russians, Austrians and Ukrainians and urged immediate action to make their activities illegal. The September 1918 orders-in-council, aimed at radical and alien enemy groups, were in part the result. After the armistice, when pressure from the unions mounted for a repeal of the orders, Cahan urged that they be kept and that Parliament enact laws to deal with radicalism on a more permanent basis.[12]

Many of the fears associated with the Red Scare, in Canada as elsewhere, centred on the thousands of returned soldiers demobilized after the armistice. These men arrived back to find old jobs filled and new jobs at a premium. There was plenty of sympathy, adulation and hero worship but little concrete in the way of reward for enduring the horror of European trenches. The government's Department of Soldiers Civil Re-Establishment oversaw campaigns to urge private business to hire veterans, while the government gave them preference in competitions for civil service jobs. A limited pension plan was established, veterans' hospitals were built and the Soldiers Land Settlement homestead scheme was put into operation. But these measures largely failed to solve the problem of what to do with, and for, over half a million veterans. Some of them, at least, must have been embittered at and discontented with the society that had held out so much and given so little. They were good material for the radicals to try to win over.

At first the returned soldiers were unlikely allies. Many trade unionists and most socialists had opposed the draft, and anti-conscription meetings throughout the country were mobbed or broken up by veterans. When Vancouver workers staged a general strike in August, 1918, to protest the killing of Albert 'Ginger' Goodwin, a union leader shot while evading the draft near Comox, B.C., soldiers rioted and broke into the labour temple. They forced Vic Midgley to kneel and kiss the Union Jack after they tried to shove him out a second story window. In Winnipeg, in January 1919, an open air socialist Party meeting called to honour the memory of Karl Liebknecht, a martyred German socialist leader, was broken up by veterans shouting "Fritzies are all the same to us." They beat up "alien" looking bystanders before ransacking the SPC hall on Smith Street and starting a bonfire with SPC literature.[13] In Halifax a newly returned officer declared confidently, "There is no Bolshevism among the Canadian Army."[14]

Government officials were not so sure. One Mounted Police officer told commissioner A. Bowen Perry that every effort had to be made to keep the veterans "on the right track" because anything was possible if they were not kept away from the Bolsheviks.[15] Perry agreed and wanted to use the Great War Veterans Association to do this. He believed that when sufficient officers returned

91

from overseas they would "exert a very great influence upon the Association."[16] Perry was worried about "the possibility of a successful revolution being accomplished by force" if a large number of veterans supported it. It was essential that veterans' grievances be quickly dealt with and that they be treated with sympathy and consideration, especially since there were already disturbing signs of a "pernicious propaganda" among returned men in Vancouver.[17]

Perry's fears were buttressed by a secret document, prepared by the assistant controller of the Mounted Police, which surveyed "revolutionary tendencies" in western Canada. The report claimed that "an appreciable number of people" were actively engaged in revolutionary activities with the avowed aim of setting up "a Soviet Government." They had a "clear idea of what they desire[d] to do and of the means whereby they expect[ed] to realize their wishes." The report stated that conditions and circumstances were possible "in which the designs of these people might prosper sufficiently to cause an attempt to be made at a bloody revolution by force of arms, with its accompaniments of bloodshed and destruction." This would not happen immediately. Revolutionary leaders were not well armed and were "deficient in physical courage and perhaps also in the fanatical devotion to the cause which usually has distinguished men who have pushed sedition to the point of violence." Nevertheless, the revolutionaries were alleged to be well organized, carrying on an "exceedingly formidable" propaganda, and maintaining a close association—"albeit of the parasitic nature"—with unions. They had the support of the IWW, enough money to carry on an "energetic agitation" and were building on a foundation of "general restlessness and dissatisfaction." One radical activity considered particularly dangerous was the attempt to befriend the returned soldiers.[18]

The Mounties believed the main Bolshevik concentrations in western Canada were Winnipeg, Vancouver and the Crows Nest Pass, with the remainder of the Alberta coal fields of secondary importance. They accordingly concentrated most of their anti-Bolshevik activities in these areas. Mounted Police, in uniform or undercover, engaged in work ranging from seizing 'prohibited' literature at the Esquimault naval dockyards to keeping tabs on the Russian Workers Union, "a revolutionary organization of the worst kind." Penetration of radical groups was accomplished by undercover operatives who worked their way into the ranks of the target organization by appearing to be helpful and eager members. One agent befriended Sava Karoba, Toronto organizer for the Russian Socialist Anarchist Party, and helped establish a secret west coast headquarters for the organization.[19] Another undercover man kept a close watch on Vancouver trade unions from the cover of the local branch of "Labor Defence" and was able to report in detail about the progress of the One Big Union referendum.[20]

In Alberta, the Mounted Police shared jurisdiction with the Alberta Provincial Police. The APP became concerned about overlapping secret operations, but the Mounties were not worried. Perry wrote Lt. Col. P. C. H. Primrose, commander of the Alberta force, that his secret police agents were "operating in every part of Alberta and especially in cities and industrial areas." These men were seldom known to district officers or to each other, and there was thus little danger of overlapping. In fact, conflicts with the Alberta Police could be beneficial. In the Crows Nest Pass an APP constable arrested an undercover Mounted Police agent. Perry believed that such arrests could "strengthen the agent's position and secure the confidence of the element he is investigating."[21]

By February, 1919, these and other anti-radical activities were in full swing. When the Western Labor Conference opened at Calgary in March, it appeared to some as if revolution was just around the corner. "Labor Convention Has Endorsed Soviet Rule As Most Efficient," warned the *Edmonton Journal*. "Western Labor Ready To Enter Class War," pronounced the Vancouver *Sun*. "One Big Union is also title for IWW Body," revealed the Regina *Morning Leader*. Which labour group was to prevail, asked the Vancouver *Daily World*, those who supported Bolshevism or those dedicated to the "orderly evolutionary development" of the "labour movement"?

Sir Thomas White, acting prime minister while Borden was at the Paris peace talks, was clearly worried by the apparent intensification of radical activity signalled by the Calgary meeting. His solution was to bring British military power to bear from the decks of a Royal Navy Cruiser. White feared it would be possible to find reliable troops in British Columbia in case of an emergency and told Borden, in Europe attending the peace talks, that a British cruiser from the China station would be a "steadying influence."[22] But Borden pointed out that the Dominion had been handling its own internal troubles as far back as the Northwest Rebellion of 1885 and suggested that perhaps the Mounties in B.C. be augmented. White insisted they were needed on the prairies and thought it would cause trouble to send them into the province. He continued to press the matter and Borden finally suggested that the British be invited to send a squadron to Halifax and Vancouver under the guise of showing Canada's appreciation for the Royal Navy's wartime service.[23]

On May 15, a general strike, called by the Winnipeg trades council in support of metal and building trades unions, began when over twelve thousand organized, and twelve to twenty thousand unorganized, workers tied up the city. The strike lasted until June 26 and set off a chain reaction of sympathetic strikes across the west in Vancouver, Edmonton, Calgary, Saskatoon, Brandon and several smaller centres. At its peak in early June over sixty thousand workers were engaged in these sympathetic strikes. Many local groups of business and professional people combined to form Citizens Committees to help municipal and provincial authorities battle the strikers, but the leading strikebreaker, lending moral, military, police and judicial aid, was the federal government, which feared the strikes were the beginning of a revolution. The government, represented in Winnipeg by Senator Gideon Robertson and acting minister of justice Arthur Meighen, acted on Robertson's belief that the One Big Union had been created to organize and coordinate these revolutionary activities,[24] notwithstanding the fact that in Winnipeg, at least, the general strike grew out of two ordinary disputes over higher wages and union recognition and that three of the five strike leaders—James Winning, Ernie Robinson and J. L. McBride—were faithful craft unionists.[25]

The strike epidemic became an additional ingredient in the Red Scare. The Toronto *Globe* claimed that "many avowed social revolutionists" stood behind the Winnipeg general strike and a threatened general strike in Toronto. Their object was not the improvement of working conditions, but "the destruction of the present social system and the introduction of the Marxian form of political and industrial organization." It was time, said the *Globe,* for trade unionism "to blow away the froth of Bolshevism."[26] The *Edmonton Journal* blamed the strikes on the One Big Union whose only chance for success was "to make it appear, as it has done in connection with the present general strike movement, that it is seeking to advance legitimate objects of labour."[27] The *Calgary Herald* was certain that the unrest sweeping the country had "much in common with the aims and object of Russian Bolshevism" and that there was "a central organization planning and directing" it.[28] When printers employed by the *Vancouver Daily Sun* walked out rather than set type for an anti-strike editorial, the *Sun* published the editorial in a leaflet and pronounced the Vancouver sympathetic strike "a demonstration by the 'Reds' who have taken Russia for their model and who hope to make their profit amid the general confusion and overturn of government."[29] The *Saskatchewan Cooperative Elevator Company News* claimed that strike leaders in Winnipeg "contemplated the complete overthrow of the present form of Government in Canada."[30] Almost every major newspaper, with the notable exception of the *Toronto Star*,[31] condemned the strikes and demanded government action.

But the editorials were meek compared to full-page advertisements sponsored by various Citizens Committees and other anti-strike groups. One Winnipeg Citizens Committee ad which ran in major dailies such as the *Calgary Herald* and the *Vancouver Sun,* claimed that the general strikes were "engineered by a group of anarchists and socialistic agitators for the purpose of destroying the Constitutional Government of Canada and introducing Bolshevist Government therefor." It warned that loyal Canadian workmen were being misled by alien agitators who had worked for Germany during the war and now aimed to tie up transportation to prevent foodstuffs from reaching market. It quoted F. B. Stanley, member of parliament for New Westminster, who stated in the House of Commons: "The One Great Thought in the west is whether the Union Jack shall float over Canadian cities or the Red Flag of Revolution."[32] Even more lurid were efforts of the Canada First Publicity Association. In Russia, they claimed, the revolutionaries had introduced starvation, destroyed religion, abolished liberty and the rule of law, transferred government into the hands of committees, confiscated property and "decreed that all women over eighteen must register at a bureau of free love, and there hold themselves subject to the will of any man." If Canada fell victim to revolution, they warned, she would not escape "The Frozen Breath of Bolshevism."[33] This group urged the elimination of alien influences in the workforce since Bolshevism was a "theory fomented by foreigners." Canadian workers were more sensible: "The Canadian laborer does not hate Millionaires. He may be a millionaire himself someday."[34] One ad pictured a deadly rattlesnake (Bolshevism) ready to strike at a muscular, clean-cut, lathe operator (Canadian labor) leaning unsuspectingly over his work.[35]

Bolshevism soon became a convenient scapegoat. N. G. Neil, manager of the Vancouver Employers Association, told the Royal Commission on Industrial Relations, headed by Justice T. G. Mathers, that much of the nation's industrial unrest was caused by Bolshevism. Some radical labour leaders were interested in revolution, not cooperation, and this justified special measures (which Neil did not spell out) to stop those intrigues which were preventing a "new era in industry."[36] T. R. Deacon, whose Manitoba Bridge and Iron Works was one of the original protagonists in the Winnipeg general strike, tried to get special favours for the city's iron works from the federal government as a reward for standing up to the local Bolsheviki: "these three iron-working shops in Winnipeg, have stood like a rock in a river of Bolshevism and sedition at enormous sacrifice to themselves . . . they have saved the situation in Canada."[37] Frontier College, which sent university students to work on track gangs and in bush camps to teach English and civics to immigrants after working hours, used the Bolshevik threat to good advantage. Superintendent Fitzpatrick told minister of immigration and colonization J. A. Calder that Bolshevik ideas were being openly expressed in the work camps where unskilled foreigners congregated. College instructors offset much of this "loose talk," he claimed, by their "conduct and influence." "The work of the College," he said, "was essentially patriotic."[38] More than one company president contributed to the College in the hope that its instructors would "preach some sense to these unionists,"[39] or in the belief that the education of "foreigners and rough fellows" would stop the spread of industrial trouble and IWW and Bolsheviki ideas in frontier areas.[40]

The stories of press, pulpit, educators and businessmen were no more fantastic than some of the information fed the government from its own secret sources. Commissioner Perry of the Mounted Police was concerned that the strike situation would make it necessary "to reconquer British Columbia, especially if it was cut off from Canada by the destruction, obviously an easy matter, of the railways and the telegraph lines."[41] The British warned they had learned that Bolsheviks might introduce a new weapon "employing ultra violet rays to cause blindness."[42] Another British report told of a secret Russian plan to finance the "revolutionary movement in Canada" by placing "two million Roubles [sic] in foreign money at the disposal of the Communistic sections at Ottawa, Calgary, Lethbridge, Regina, Victoria, Vancouver, Toronto and Montreal."[43]

Despite such dire warnings, prime minister Borden was at first reluctant to allow the government to get into the propaganda business lest it be accused of trying to strengthen "the position of the government and to better the political fortunes of its members."[44] But his attitude changed once he concluded that public support was necessary for an effective campaign "against the evil" and that the public wanted facts, not general allegations.[45] The result was a Department of Labour pamphlet which claimed to tell the story of Bolshevik and soviet activities in Canada. The piece relied heavily on material seized in raids on left wing organizations, union halls and private homes, but was full of errors. (It reproduced a phony OBU membership card distributed by an independent religious fanatic in Saskatchewan.)[46] Later, in early 1920, the government considered using motion pictures as propaganda. M. M. Mahoney, secretary of the Canadian War Mission in Washington, was asked to contact various American government agencies to find a suitable film. Mahoney found nothing, but discovered that the American secretary of the interior had persuaded leading motion picture producers, led by impressario Louis J. Selznick, to "join forces and begin a picture campaign to combat the spread of all disloyal ultra-radical tendencies in the United States." One product already on the market was "purely an Americanism propaganda picture," but Mahoney was sure he could pursuade Selznick to turn out similar movies for Canada.[47] The suggestion was apparently not acted on.

Throughout the Red Scare period there was considerable public pressure on the government to take an active and visible role in countering radical and Bolshevik activity. From some quarters there were hints that "something like the Ku Klux Klan in the Southern States would soon be necessary in Canada." But the government had no taste for lynch law. Borden told Cahan at the end of May, 1919, that many moderate men could be pushed to extremes if the government took "steps which they would regard as unjust."[48] In Canada, the campaign against radicalism and Bolshevism was initiated, orchestrated and executed by the federal government according to the laws on the books, or created especially for that purpose. The federal government never exceeded its legal authority, because it did not have to.

In April, 1919, the government introduced amendments to the Immigration Act giving them the power to seize and deport without trial, persons, except for the British-born, engaged in anarchistic or revolutionary activities. Because aliens were usually identified as the carriers of the revolutionary germ, deportation was an ideal way to destroy radical leadership. One supporter of the amendments claimed that many foreigners in Canada were easily misled by those who preached sedition and revolution, and it was necessary to have the power to remove the agitators from the country. But these amendments did not go far enough. Most of the evidence from the government's own agents pointed to Britons as the worst culprits. After the Winnipeg general strike began, many government officials begged the cabinet to do something about the British radicals. They were answered with the quick enactment into law of a further amendment giving immigration authorities the power to deport British-born radicals as well. The Trades Congress, which was unhappy about the general strike, gave its blessing to the amendment.[49] Robertson easily won P. M. Draper, TLC secretary, to support this move with an argument that this was really a blow at the OBU and therefore "in the best interest of organized labour as well as the state itself."[50]

By mid-June, 1919, immigration officials and Mounted Police officers began arresting known radicals, particularly those connected with the general strikes and alleged revolutionary organizations. In the best known of the raids conducted in Winnipeg in the early hours of June 17, seven Anglo-Saxon and four "alien" radicals were arrested, including strike leaders R. B. Russell, A. A. Heaps, R. J. Johns, William Ivens, R. E. Bray, John Queen and George Armstrong. In the days and weeks that followed police raids throughout western Canada netted others destined for internment camps and deportation. Most of the men arrested were identified by secret agents acting for the Mounted Police who were themselves given special powers to operate under the authorization of immigration officials.

The amendments to the Immigration Act and the use of Mounted Police officers vastly strengthened the immigration and colonization department's ability to act in the fight against the Reds. But deportations never became as methodical or regular as they were in the United States. No accurate figures are available of the total number of persons sent out of Canada for radical activities because they were generally grouped with military prisoners of war and Germans and Austrians interned during hostilities at camps in Vernon, B.C., Kapuskasing, Ontario, and Amherst, Nova Scotia.[51] Some of the "aliens" arrested in Winnipeg during the strike were secretly deported on the orders of Judge Hugh John Macdonald, but only one of the men arrested on June 17 was sent out of Canada and this was for illegal entry.[52] Not a single British subject was deported at any time.[53] In early 1920 a military man claimed that over a thousand Reds had been expelled, but this was clearly a gross exaggeration. Nevertheless, regardless of how widely the Act was used, it was a violation of the spirit of common justice. Persons seized under Section 41 were not entitled to bail and remained in custody until their fate was decided.[54]

Though the government had the power to deport the Anglo-Saxon strike leaders arrested in Winnipeg the night of June 16, 1919, there was a feeling, expressed by Senator Robertson, that public opinion would not stand for it.[55] After July 7, there was a possible alternative course. On that day, Section 98 of the Criminal Code was enacted into law which declared illegal any group which advocated force to bring about "governmental, industrial or economic change." Anyone who attended a meeting, or distributed the literature, of a proscribed group was held to be guilty of an offence "in the absence of proof to the contrary."[56] The law was retroactive in that persons who were associated with these proscribed groups prior to July 7 were still liable for prosecution. Nonetheless, the strike leaders were not charged with violations of Section 98 but were tried, instead, for seditious conspiracy. The government might well have believed that it could not prove that force had been specifically advocated by the strike committee and therefore the more general charge of sedition was more likely to bring convictions.

The strike leaders were joined by W. A. Pritchard, who had visited the city for the OBU central committee, taken part in mediation proceedings and was then seized at Calgary when returning to the coast, and Fred Dixon, who replaced William Ivens at the *Western Labor News* after the first arrests. The trials began in December, 1919, and dragged out for several months. The government introduced thousands of documents and letters seized during the arrests and in dominion-wide raids on June 30 to prove the men were engaged in a seditious conspiracy. The crown's basic case was that a revolutionary plan had been hatched at Calgary in March and that the general and sympathetic strikes, particularly the one at Winnipeg, were part of the overall campaign to overthrow the government. Heaps and Dixon were acquitted; the others were sent to prison for one year, except Russell who was sentenced to two years. In the appeal on the Russell case the following year, a Manitoba court upheld the conviction and decided that sympathetic strikes were themselves illegal.[57]

Though the Winnipeg general strike finally collapsed June 26, the government embarked on a program of strengthening the military in case of further domestic strife. This was undertaken by the department of militia and defence which had so efficiently arranged the quiet build-up of a heavily armed force of troops supported by machine guns, armoured cars and an observation plane in Winnipeg during the general strike.[58] They had a long history of intervention in labour disputes to "aid the civil power." The Militia Act assured that local authorities could call upon the armed forces if necessary and, in western Canada, this had occurred in 1906 during a streetcar strike in Winnipeg and in 1913 during the Vancouver Island coal strikes. After the Winnipeg general strike the militia played a leading role in shoring up the national defences against Bolshevism and laying plans to deal with trouble in all parts of Canada. In Winnipeg arms and ammunition were kept in ready and adequate supply, troops were sent into the area, continuous training was conducted and liaisons were established with local civic leaders.[59] In Vancouver, naval and air units were kept in reserve.[60] In April, 1921, militia headquarters in Ottawa took stock of the strength of units across the country fearing the likelihood of "serious disturbances or uprisings taking place in Canada due to the activities of the Sinn Feiners, Soviets, Red element, unemployed, etc."[61] The militia department also distributed information about the activities and organization of the Winnipeg Citizens Committee to help militia commanders set up close ties with such groups in other parts of the country.

Throughout Canada, the militia, the Mounties, provincial and municipal police, and other government agencies spied on unions, socialist parties, ethnic clubs and schools, and probably on each other. Canadians were placed under intense secret observation. Despite all this activity, all the manpower and money expended on spying, not a shred of evidence of real revolutionary preparation—arms stockpiling, secret drilling, illegal fundraising—was ever uncovered. In fact, very few of the groups kept under government surveillance were actually illegal under Section 98 of the Criminal Code— including the One Big Union. Towards the end of 1919 the justice department concluded the OBU was not illegal, notwithstanding Robertson's view that it aimed to "overthrow and destroy ... existing constitutional law."[62] Part of the campaign against the OBU and other left-wing organizations was undoubtedly self-serving— carried out by government agencies anxious to justify their existence and the sums spent to maintain them. Part was due to a gnawing public fear of Bolshevism. But part was also due to the government's determination to rescue the international craft unions from destruction and maintain the close relationships that had been established with the leadership of those unions during the war.

There were, of course, some anti-labour extremists in Borden's party. Senator Smeaton White, appointed to the 1919 Mathers Royal Commission on Industrial Relations as one of the 'employer' representatives, believed Tom Moore and the TLC leadership were dangerous radicals and disagreed with Robertson's support of them. But the men who counted—Borden, Meighen, Robertson, Thomas White—had become ardent Gompers supporters. When the AFL chief was injured in an auto accident in the spring of 1919, White wrote, "I feel I need not assure you of the deep appreciation of the kindly interest which you have always had in our welfare."[63] When the general strike broke out in Winnipeg, Robertson asked Gompers to tell the heads of the metal trades unions that this was a blow at their unions and "in support of what is known as the One Big Union."[64] During the strike at least one government minister declared his support for trade unions "as we have known them to exist,"[65] pointedly excluding the OBU. But whatever the motive, the anti-Bolshevik feeling of the Red Scare period assured that the government would never allow the OBU to become a potent force in Canadian life. All the necessary justification existed, real or imaginary, to crush it.

Chapter 5

Midgley and Co.

Victor R. Midgley had been a radical for a long time. He was a lather by trade but, since his involvement in the founding of the British Columbia Federation of Labor in 1910, increasingly earned his living as a paid union official. He was a staunch supporter of the Socialist Party of Canada and an active member of the British Columbia trade union movement. He had introduced the resolution favouring industrial unionism at the 1911 TLC convention in Calgary and leaned increasingly to syndicalism in the subsequent years. In 1917 he ran unsuccessfully for Parliament as an anti-conscriptionist labour candidate and, in 1918, barely escaped with his life when veterans attacked the Vancouver labour temple during the Ginger Goodwin general strike. Though pleasant looking, he was stiff and formal in business and personal relationships. By 1919, he was secretary of the Vancouver trades council and the B.C. Federation of Labor.

At the Quebec City TLC convention Midgley attended the caucus meetings of radical and western delegates and was chosen secretary for the committee elected to arrange the Western Labor Conference. At the Western Labor Conference he became secretary of the OBU central committee, and emerged as the central figure of a small group of dedicated activists determined to maintain the meeting's momentum. These men, along with thousands of other workers, were convinced the One Big Union would be the fulfillment of their dreams, and worked hard to bring it into being. There was W. A. Pritchard and Jack Kavanagh on the coast, Joe Knight and Carl Berg in Edmonton, and R. B. Russell and R. J. Johns in Winnipeg. They were by no means alone, but the OBU drive would have stalled without them.

At the Western Labor Conference the central committee was given responsibility for coordinating all OBU activity and conducting the referendum votes on secession and the six hour day. This placed a tremendous burden on Midgley. As committee secretary he was responsible for coordinating all committee activities including fund raising, communications and propaganda, and corresponding with other labour groups throughout the country, as well as his own writing and speaking. Midgley was given much help by Pritchard, who also wrote propaganda, edited leaflets and went on speaking tours, but the greatest burden fell on Midgley because he did most of the office work. In mid-May he was forced to seek a leave of absence from the Vancouver trades council, whose work he had continued to do as secretary.[1]

Midgley was primarily an office worker; Pritchard was a speaker second to none. He travelled up and down the coast to spread the OBU message. In April he went with Midgley to Seattle, Washington, and later he showed up in Butte, Montana, to deliver the May Day address to an OBU meeting organized by the local trades council. He contributed much time to the campaign in Vancouver itself where there was considerable demand from most of the union locals in the city for OBU speakers. Jack Kavanagh was also an effective campaigner and, as president of the B.C. Federation of Labor (he had been elected at the March convention), spoke at meetings from Prince Rupert to Tacoma, Washington. In late March and early April he spent two weeks on the road speaking for the OBU on a trip financed by the Federation.[2]

In Edmonton, Carl Berg and Joe Knight both worked tirelessly. Knight's talents were more inclined to the speaker's platform and he often went to Calgary, the coal camps in central Alberta and the Crows Nest Pass. Russell invited him to Winnipeg in early May to take part, with Johns and other speakers, at a giant OBU rally. Most of his travel was locally financed from monies raised by Carl Berg. Midgley wished there were "two or three Bergs in every province." He was well known in the northern and central coal fields and spent most of his time writing OBU correspondence and propaganda and raising money. He procured bundles of the *British Columbia Federationist* and the *Fernie District Ledger,* both strongly pro-OBU, for distribution in the coal fields and managed to write, edit and print an Edmonton *One Big Union Bulletin* which appeared before the end of March.

In Winnipeg Dick Johns and Bob Russell shared organizing and speaking responsibilities. Russell saved the

Fools and Wise Men

OBU hundreds of dollars by maneuvering the *Winnipeg Tribune* into printing the verbatim account of the Calgary Conference. OBU supporters in the city had been conducting an anti-*Tribune* boycott to protest the paper's attack on the Western Labor Conference. The loss of readership prompted the paper to offer to publish the Calgary proceedings in one of its issues if the boycott was ended. Russell agreed, provided they produced an additional 20 000 copies to be used as *Western Labor News* supplements.[3] Soon *Tribune*-printed bundles were sent to workers in all four western provinces. Russell also distributed OBU literature to Toronto, Cochrane, North Bay and Montreal, and wrote articles for Berg's newspaper. As secretary-treasurer of the Division 4 federation of railway shopcraft workers and editor of its organ, the *Bulletin*, he was able to push the OBU to the shopmen almost without interference.[4] *Bulletin* columns were crammed with OBU propaganda: "there is not much else worth writing about but the OBU, and regarding that we find ourselves in the position of Euclid when in trying to prove his first propositions in geometry he found them so simple that no proof was required, and called them axioms."[5] At the beginning of May the Manitoba Executive of the Trades Congress (the province didn't have a provincial federation) struck off a man to help Russell with his propaganda work. Dick Johns also wrote articles and pamphlets, but was more effective in speeches and debates. In late April, when he was sent to Montreal and other central Canadian centres as a Division 4 negotiator, he arranged several meetings on the way east. In Montreal, Toronto and Ottawa, he spoke to every conceivable group of workers about the OBU. Johns particularly relished the idea that this was paid for by the craft unions.[6]

These men spread a simple message: workers were organized into old-fashioned and obsolete craft unions which had outlived their usefulness. It was no longer possible for workers to arrange wages, hours of work, and general working conditions through their unions even when they worked together and were all part of the same industrial process because they were divided on the job. Should a dispute over matters such as the length of the work day arise, they could not take common action for the common good even when they all dealt with the same employer. Thus, One Big Union was needed. When they all became members of the same union, they could take "united action" along whatever lines were best suited to their own welfare.[7] What form this OBU was to take, however, was not made clear. The job at hand was to raise money, spread the message, sharpen the attack on the craft union system and count the votes; philosophy would wait.

In the first weeks after the Western Labor Conference results were quick and promising. Only in Edmonton did the OBU suffer an early and severe blow. Alfred Farmilo, secretary of the Edmonton Trades Council, was no lightweight and could hold his own despite the likes of Berg and Knight. Farmilo was a neat, fair-complexioned man, who had come to Canada in 1906 at the age of twenty-one from Nottingham, England and had settled in Edmonton two years later. He was a trade unionist, as his father had been before him, and, like Alex Ross of Calgary, was a skilled stonemason. Though he had vehemently opposed conscription, and allied himself with those who supported a general strike against it in 1917, he was also an organizer of the Edmonton Patriotic Fund. Farmilo was a married man with many interests, and he was tough.

The fight for control of the Edmonton labour movement began at the March 17 Edmonton trades council meeting when Farmilo delivered his report as council delegate to the Western Labor Conference. He vigorously attacked the meeting and its Chairman, R. J.

Tallon, for refusing to deal with the questions originally agreed upon at Quebec and taking up the question of secession. Tallon, charged Farmilo, showed open bias to those favouring secession and gave them a virtual monopoly of the floor. The Western Labor Conference was not representative of western feeling, he cautioned, and had been railroaded. Farmilo warned that council delegates should take care not to lose what they already had in adopting something new.

The attack sparked off a vigorous debate in which Berg, Knight and other OBU supporters squared off against Farmilo, trades council president McCreath and others. A motion was proposed and seconded to "repudiate the action of the Western Inter-Provincial Convention." The meeting then degenerated into a shouting match with delegates jumping up and demanding the floor, shouting down opponents and yelling insults across the room. One motion to adjourn, put by OBU supporters, lost, while another, to extend the debate, supported by Farmilo, passed. But when the chairman called for a vote on the original motion, many delegates didn't know what they were being asked to vote on. About half were on their feet yelling at the top of their voices when the motion passed by a large majority.[8] Sarah Knight was angry and vowed that the matter was far from over, but Joe had a more realistic view: "Edmonton will be the hardest district to move in Alberta."[9]

Subsequent events proved him right. OBU opponents had a clear majority in the Edmonton trades council and used it to keep the OBU in the cold. Protests from several locals over the actions of the March 17 meeting were ignored. When council delegates had just taken their seats for the meeting of April 21, President McCreath read a notice from the executive committee which ordered immediate expulsion of "all delegates voting and active in the interests and formation of the

One Big Union." When a machinist asked if he was included since his lodge had instructed him to vote for the
OBU, McCreath replied that it did. The expulsion affected four locals and was immediately endorsed. Berg
then asked those delegates affected by the ruling to
move to another room to hold their own meeting. Later
in the evening the council passed another motion to
conduct a "counter vote" on the two questions being
submitted to a referendum by the OBU central committee.[10]

The OBU men were in trouble. Berg urgently wired
Russell in Winnipeg to come to Edmonton to speak at a
mass meeting,[11] but he was unable to attend because of
prior commitments. The *Western Labor News* called the
Edmonton trades council "the most reactionary of the
trades councils in western Canada" and its president
"better fitted for a chaplain of a ladies aid society."[12] But
this was futile; the craft union men clearly ruled the
roost in Edmonton. Efforts to disenfranchise OBU supporters in the locals continued along with attempts to
stop the voting on the secession and six hour day resolutions. Workers were threatened with loss of membership for voting OBU and were told they would be fired
from their jobs. "It is no easy matter to hold the workers
together," Berg told Midgley.[13] When the street railwaymen told the council they would withdraw their delegates until the pro-OBU representatives were re-in-
stated, the council cooly accepted their resignation and
ruled they would have to pay back all per capita before
being re-admitted.[14]

The fight in Edmonton was effectively over before it
had begun, but in other larger centres it was all the
other way. Many Calgary radicals, such as alderman A.
G. Broatch, had been bitterly disappointed that the
Western Labor Conference rejected their bid for a new
political initiative and also fought strenuously against the
'vital trades' concept of weighted referendum voting.

But they continued to back the secessionist effort—at least in the first months. Some observers thought Calgary would be a difficult victory for the OBU, particularly because it was the home of Alex Ross and Alberta Federation of Labor secretary Walter Smitten. One unidentified labour man told the *Calgary Herald* that the Western Labor Conference had been "too radical" and did not provide the "sane constructive policy" needed by the labour movement. The paper concluded that "there is not a very rosy outlook for 'The One Big Union' being a pronounced success in Calgary."[15]

This, at first, looked accurate. When the Calgary trades council considered the OBU matter on March 19, they decided to postpone action until they received official printed copies of the Western Labor Conference resolutions. The issue was examined again the following week after copies of the *Federationist*, containing published versions of the resolutions, were distributed by Council Chairman Hooley. A long and bitter debate followed introduction of a resolution calling for a secession referendum. Alex Ross jumped to the attack. He claimed there were only 35 000 union members in western Canada who would, if they followed the OBU, be separating themselves from everyone else: "and you have the audacity to call it 'The One Big Union' . . . I call it a dinky little union . . . when we compare it to the total number of workers on the North American continent. It is simply an I.W.W. movement . . . Why put up another I.W.W.? Why not fall in with the present I.W.W. and make it a real 'big' organization?" Speakers for and against followed Ross, but the council ran out of time before voting on the resolution, and put the debate over to its April 11 meeting.[16]

This time Broatch and the other OBU supporters took no chances and called Joe Knight down from Edmonton to take part. Alex Ross was not to be intimidated. He warned that workers who refused to support the OBU would stay with their charters and the result would be dual unionism in western Canada. But Ross, Smitten and their allies were overwhelmed by Knight, Hooley, Broatch and Ed Browne of the miners. All hammered home the argument that the international unions were undemocratic, unresponsive and handicapped by archaic structures. Knight and Broatch stressed that the first main OBU objective was to finish the referendum before taking other action. The craft union forces were defeated, 46 to 25.[17] The following week council voted to grant the OBU central committee's request for a two cent per member levy to finance propaganda and referendum activity.

The council thus placed itself on record favouring secession, but there were qualms about counting those workers who did not cast ballots in the affirmative. The council complained to Midgley, who replied that he was obliged to carry out Conference wishes and could not change the voting rules. He pointed out that the OBU would never succeed anyway unless it had the support of most workers over a wide area. The referendum was only an expression of opinion. Unions would not be asked to take any definite action until the vote results were known.[18] This went to the heart of the matter. The vote was only an expression of opinion and was not binding on anyone, while the resolutions of bodies such as the Edmonton or Calgary trades councils bound only themselves and not their member locals. The important point would only arrive after the referendum results were known and the OBU officially launched. Only then would locals, councils, federations and individual members be called upon to tear up their AFL/TLC charters and membership cards and join the One Big Union. For the moment there was still no OBU to join, only a central committee and four provincial committees conducting a propaganda campaign and a referendum, which was itself nothing more than another propaganda instrument. Nevertheless, the approval of secession by bodies such as the Calgary trades council was an important moral victory.

In the other major area of union strength in Alberta—the coal fields—the OBU was very popular. Both Robert Livett and Dave Rees threw their weight against the secession movement but they were bucking majority sentiment. P. M. Christophers and District 18 secretary, Ed Browne, both favoured the OBU. Browne told the Calgary trades council that "the miners are going to carry the OBU by a large majority; they are sick and tired of the system of international unionism as it exists to-day."[19] There were no trades councils in the coal fields to demonstrate this support but large cash contributions flowing in to Berg in Edmonton and Midgley in Vancouver attested to the truth of Browne's statement.

In Winnipeg the OBU was very popular. The trades council, in a packed meeting, unanimously adopted Russell's report of the Western Labor Conference and voted to contribute to the two cent levy. Later the council empowered its executive and educational committees to hold OBU propaganda meetings.[20] In Saskatchewan, the Moose Jaw and Regina trades councils quickly voted to endorse the Western Labor Conference, but in Saskatoon the OBU ran into considerable opposition. Despite the support of council president Walter Mill, the secessionist movement made almost no headway and was given no council funds or encouragement. Mill thought the workers were "all scared of it" and did his best to avoid a repetition of the Edmonton events.[21]

The B.C. Federation of Labor had opted for secession at its convention, and support for the OBU continued to be strong on the coast. In Vancouver, trades council president Ernest Winch of the B.C. Loggers Union told a council meeting: "Capital [is] no longer necessary to human progress [and] will be eliminated. The workers, being absolutely essential, will . . . be the dominant fac-

tor in society."[22] The Mounted Police considered Winch
a dangerous radical and monitored his activities. He was
the driving force behind the B.C. Loggers Union and
had arrived in British Columbia by a circuitous route
that took him from England to Canada, twice to Australia, back to England and finally to B.C. in 1910. Soon
after settling he began to attend socialist meetings and,
in 1912, supported the IWW in its struggle for the right
to hold open meetings at Vancouver's Powell Street
grounds. From here it was into the Socialist Party of
Canada and active union work. When the B.C. Loggers
Union was organized in early 1919, Winch became secretary. His support of the OBU at the Vancouver trades
council, along with that of Pritchard, Midgley, and
others, allowed the OBU to sail through. Because of
constitutional difficulties the trades council did not immediately vote to contribute funds to the OBU, but this
was done at the following meeting.[23] The Victoria
trades council also backed the OBU by a wide margin
and within one month of the end of the Calgary convention it appeared as if the OBU would sweep the west.

But problems began to crop up. Money, in large
amounts, was vitally necessary if the leaflets, bulletins
and pamphlets were to be printed, postage paid for, organizers and speakers put on the road and the referendum successfully completed by June. Though rumours
abounded that the OBU was financed by Bolshevik
agents, no evidence was ever uncovered to prove the
charge. The central committee's hope for funds lay with
the existing craft unions and a campaign to get them to
underwrite the OBU began soon after the Western
Labor Conference ended. After a slow start, money
began to trickle in to Midgley by mid-April. Never in
large quantities, the funds were only enough to finance
pamphlets and keep speakers on the road—$10.80
from the Prince Rupert trades council, $225 from Ma-
chinists Lodge 122 in Winnipeg, $53.00 from a miners'

local in Edmonton. The money was usually channeled to Midgley via the OBU provincial executives, but some came directly to Vancouver. In some cases anti-OBU union leaders held up the contributions. The Winnipeg trades council voted to give financial support to the OBU in March, and re-affirmed its decision at least once,[24] but secretary Ernie Robinson had still not sent any money by the end of April. By this time Russell was conducting individual appeals which eventually netted about $1200.[25]

The coal mines were the most important source of funding.[26] P. F. Lawson, editor of the *Fernie District Ledger,* and Carl Berg were particularly active in raising cash and several hundred dollars was received from individuals and locals by the middle of April. Many miners were eastern Europeans and Italians who gave as much as the Anglo-Saxons. On one list of contributors published in the *Ledger,* only two out of thirty-six names were English.[27] Thirty-eight out of the fifty-three members of UMWA Local 4070, which contributed one dollar per member, were eastern European or Italian.[28]

It was evident quite early that legal obstacles might prevent craft union lodges from contributing to the OBU. Midgley advised Russell and other OBU supporters to secure legal advice before transferring funds from their own lodges to the One Big Union central committee. At the end of April, machinists Lodge 777 in Vancouver voted to donate $400 to the OBU and J. H. McVety, local president, and Percy Bengough, local business agent, revoked the charter and went to the courts to seize the union's assets. One member beat McVety and Bengough to the bank and transferred the money to another institution, but before the $400 was completely paid out, the money was discovered and the local was enjoined from handling any more funds. The lodge then seceded from the International Association of Machinists and set itself up as Machinists Local #1 of the City of Vancouver.[29] In Winnipeg, Russell and his allies tried to avoid such problems by setting up a bogus benevolent fund and having the different craft lodges who wished to contribute to the OBU pay money into it. These payments were then entered on union books as gifts to a special benefit fund.[30]

Lodges which pledged to support or donate money to the OBU, such as the Vancouver painters and boiler-makers, rapidly found themselves expelled from their international unions and their funds seized through the courts. Midgley suggested that OBU supporters advise local unions favouring the OBU to put their funds in "some place of safe keeping," which did not include "chartered banks and safety deposit boxes."[31] He also urged Russell to get "some good legal advice" as to whether his "benevolent fund" was really secure. The whole question of who owned union funds was very complicated. Many months of legal battles lay ahead before any authoritative court decisions were handed down and those funds in dispute freed.

The OBU was primarily a western creation, but the Western Labor Conference also generated interest east of the Lakehead. The man who spread the OBU message in northern Ontario was Tom Cassidy, an Irish machinist and Socialist Party of Canada member who lived in Montreal and was temporarily based in North Bay. Cassidy was a handsome, debonair fellow who began his letters to Russell with "mon cher Robert," laced them with jaunty, flourishing language and was, in Russell's words, "the most influential platform speaker you could ever meet." In Toronto, OBU work was carried out by members of the Socialist Party of North America as well as visitors such as Dick Johns. Referendum returns were sparse from this part of the country but one machinists local in the city voted 147 to 11 in favour of the OBU. Johns touched many points on his Division 4-financed trip and was aided by Lewis Moore, a prominent Toronto machinist. The *Ontario Labor News* backed their efforts and asserted, "no one can deny that the present form of organization is obsolete and cumbersome and our respective Grand Lodges will have to sooner or later wake up to the changing psychology of the workers or go out of business."[32]

In Montreal, machinists working in the CPR Angus and Point St. Charles shops gave strong support, led by Cassidy, John Houston and the ailing Dick Kerrigan. Kerrigan was a lively man who had attended the IWW's founding convention in Chicago in 1905 and knew many leading figures in the needle trades including Sydney Hillman, president of the Amalgamated Clothing Workers of America, whom he introduced to Johns. Hillman was quite interested in western radical activities and asked to be informed about the progress of the OBU. He told Johns he would try to attend the founding convention or send a representative. Johns was excited about the prospects of attracting Hillman's support and urged Midgley to send him information and invite him to the founding meeting.[33] Kerrigan was convinced there were thousands of discontented workers in the needle trades who would support the OBU: "the little Jewish tailor has sat and wondered when the guys would get wise and instead of you seeking him, he will see you coming."[34]

There was much unwarranted optimism about the chances of a quick breakthrough in the east. Rose Henderson, a socialist on the fringes of the needle trades, thought French Canadian workers were ready to embrace the One Big Union,[35] while Johns believed three weeks of concentrated work would mean a tremendous difference in gaining eastern support. He considered Montreal the key—if the workers there could be won over, Ontario would more easily fall into line.[36] He urged Midgley not to ignore or abandon the east because of the encouraging reception he received, but he forgot that expressions of sentiment aired at so-called mass meetings were highly unreliable. All over Canada workers were in a rebellious mood, and interest in the OBU was expressed in Nova Scotia as well as Montreal and Toronto. Amherst, Nova Scotia, which witnessed a general strike in late May, was a strong pro-OBU centre. The Nova Scotia Federation of Labor demonstrated OBU tendencies and its president, Frank Burke, championed the OBU idea.[37] Whether this kind of sentiment would lead to revolt and secession was another matter.

Far to the west, in the Kootenay country, a series of strikes in some of the hardrock mines complicated the job of OBU organizers. The mine owners, supported by the local Great War Veterans Association, used mob rule and vigilante violence to keep the area free of radical influences. In mid-April a crowd of veterans chased Joseph Naylor, a Vancouver Island coal miner working for the OBU, out of Trail and Silverton. In Cranbrook, veterans robbed Alex Mackenzie, an organizer for the B.C. Loggers Union, of union funds and threw him out of town. Veterans called George F. Stirling, organizer for the mild Federated Labor Party, an "undesirable citizen," stopped him from speaking in Nakusp and Silverton and warned he would get no police protection. Three times veterans threatened Tommy Roberts, secretary of the Silverton Miners Union, and an active OBU supporter, to leave Silverton and gave him until April 21 to do so. When the veterans were marching through the small interior mining towns, several mine officials marched with them and the Mounted Police stayed on the sidelines to watch. The Mounted Police commander in B.C., F. J. Horrigan, thought GWVA members had "done a good deal in some of the outlying districts to frustrate the extremists from holding their meetings."[38] With this kind of police connivance, Roberts was forced to find his own protection. "The time

119

has arrived," he wrote, "when a working man [needs] a body guard as well as a King."[39]

The police attitude reflected government policy. Senator Robertson told the press that the Trades and Labor Congress had done all it could to cooperate with the government, assist the war effort and maintain industrial peace. But in the west, "unwise and radical leaders" were trying to cut labour bodies away from the TLC to establish unconstitutional and revolutionary policies. His department, he warned, would refuse to recognize any such organization as representing the sentiments of Canadian organized labour, and would continue to cooperate with "organizations which were promoting constructive and not destructive policies."[40] This attitude was, if possible, hardened by the general and sympathetic strikes of May and June as Robertson snuggled even closer to the international craft unions with his plea to Gompers to intervene and his stand that the strikes were attacks on international unionism as well as attempted revolution.[41] He claimed that socialism through the OBU sought to destroy trades unionism, "an impassable bar to its revolutionary program."[42]

Both the Trades and Labour Congress and the American Federation of Labor reacted sharply to the Western Labor Conference. The TLC warned its directly chartered locals, trades councils and federations to take no action that would conflict with their obligations under the laws of Congress,[43] while the AFL linked the OBU with the Knights of Labor, the American Railway Union of Eugene V. Debs and the American Labor Union. This was the latest "subtle and pernicious plea again resorted to for the purpose of severing the wage earners from their orderly and pratical course of action."[44] During these months Sam Gompers was absent from his office in Washington recuperating from an automobile accident, and Frank Morrison, AFL executive secretary, took charge of the opening counterattack in western Canada.

Morrison was a good and faithful servant of the AFL chief and the aims of international craft unionism. He was Canadian-born and had taken a more than passing interest in Canadian trade union developments for several years. At first, he was caught napping by the Calgary meeting (he called it the "Midgley conference") but as soon as he heard of it, he contacted TLC president Tom Moore and asked for the names of the provinces represented there and any other information available so that he could inform the AFL's affiliates.[45] He concluded that quick action was necessary in the person of one and preferably two special organizers. Moore recommended Farmilo, and Morrison immediately contacted him by wire, offered him a position as an AFL organizer at $42.00 a week and expenses, and told him to begin work at once.[46]

Morrison acted quickly because he was worried. He reported to AFL treasurer Daniel J. Tobin that he was holding up an additional mortgage payment on the AFL headquarters building because of the extra expenses of the AFL peace mission to Europe coming just when the One Big Union in Canada and the IWW in the United States were becoming active. "It was the part of wisdom," he told Tobin, "to have a considerable fund available for special organizing work."[47] Several days later Morrison began looking for a second man to fight the OBU in the west. Moore and P. M. Draper suggested J. T. Gunn of the Toronto electricians who declined to take the position, but gave Morrison the name of William Varley, a member of the Street Railway Employees' union in the city. Varley was hired. He is a figure who remains clouded in obscurity but there can be no doubt of his allegiance to craft unionism and his distaste for the radicalism that was welling up in the ranks of organized labour. He told Morrison that "the Trade Union movement is being made vulnerable to those who have an ulterior motive in view . . . It is absolutely necessary that the international Offices of the different crafts

. . take this phase of the situation in hand."[48] The evening of May 14, 1919, Varley boarded a train for the Lakehead. Within days both Varley and Farmilo began to investigate the situation and file reports with Morrison which then went to the rest of the AFL Executive Council.

The AFL knew exactly what it was fighting against, but did the OBU supporters know what they were working for aside from secession? Was the OBU to be syndicalist and anti-political? Was it to be an industrial union? Was it to have a structure like the IWW? Though Midgley and the other leaders of the OBU campaign did not intend to discuss policy matters until the founding meeting, scheduled for late May or early June, such debate was inevitable. Workers wanted to know what they were being asked to support. The discussion went on not only within the ranks of OBU supporters, but in the western labour movement in general. The issues were complicated and confusing. Alex Ross may have been called a "barnacle" because he opposed secession and the One Big Union, but he was no orthodox Gompersist and would have been considered progressive elsewhere. He believed in independent labour politics, called for a thorough examination of the craft union system and urged western labour to consider adopting the Duncan Plan for reorganization of the AFL.[49] This plan, drawn up by James A. Duncan, secretary of the Seattle Central Labor Council, proposed the transformation of the AFL into a federation of industrial unions by amalgamating kindred craft unions into industrial unions. The idea was popular in the United States northwest and was circulated by the Seattle Central Labor Council to AFL affiliates throughout North America. Gompers and the AFL hierarchy strongly opposed it. In the Canadian west Farmilo and the Edmonton trades council, like Alex Ross, supported the Duncan Plan as a way to solve the problems of the craft union system.[50]

There was talk of "industrial unionism," but what was it supposed to mean? P. M. Christophers said, after the District 18 convention in February, that it did not mean IWW but rather "a consolidation of labor forces without any cleavage from the present international bodies."[51] By May he had changed his tune. Rees spoke not of one big union, but of "the United Big Organizations." He was totally opposed to secession and regretted the actions of the Western Labor Conference. He advocated a "more progressive policy" for Canadian labour through the combined action of westerners and eastern progressives within the Trades Congress. He looked to the British Triple Alliance for inspiration.[52] Rees was certainly no conservative following Gompers' policies, and neither was Robert Livett, who advocated craft union consolidation and industrial unionism like that of the UMWA. He believed industrial unionism should start with the organization and amalgamation of the different crafts and trades within each industry.[53] None of the more prominent western opponents of the OBU were Gompersists. In Winnipeg, George Armstrong was a member of the Socialist Party of Canada, R. A. Rigg and Ernie Robinson of the Social Democratic Party. In Vancouver, McVety, W. R. Trotter and J. W. Wilkinson were all members of the Federated Labor Party. Both R. P. Pettipiece and E. T. Kingsley, guiding spirits of the SPC, opposed the OBU. These men were radicals or progressives who refused to sanction the OBU revolt, not because they deeply believed in the sanctity of craft unionism, or that labour had no partisan role to play in politics, but out of conviction that the One Big Union would undermine existing union strength or sidetrack more effective political efforts.

Midgley and the other secessionist leaders made no effort to enter public debate on these issues. Some were unsure of their own positions while others were divided into those leaning to true syndicalism and those who could not shake off the chiliasm of the Socialist Party of Canada. The indecision and division was glossed over with the excuse that the central committee had been charged with conducting a referendum, not drawing up policies.[54] Midgley told one Ontario worker that the secessionists intended to work within the existing unions by establishing a common membership card and having the workers themselves attend to the amalgamation of their scattered unions. Beyond this he would say nothing until the OBU preamble and constitution were drawn up.[55] Towards the end of March he and Pritchard issued a leaflet which stated that OBU supporters should take no definite steps toward secession until the rank and file had decided, by vote, that they wished industrial organization. Industrial unionism was defined as organization according to industry with union members divided according to trades for discussing, and voting on, common problems. The craft was being wiped out by the machine and workers would have to cast themselves into the same mould as the industrial system in which they lived and worked.[56]

But this was not enough. When the IWW was born it had broadcast the organizational diagram known as "Father Haggerty's Wheel of Fortune" after Father Thomas Haggerty who had drawn it up. In a scientific age this carefully divided wheel, with its spokes representing different groups and subgroups of industry and with a general administration at the hub, appealed to those who styled themselves scientifically minded. When the Australian OBU movement began to emerge, it produced a similar plan. Many also expected this of the Canadian OBU. Despite a desire to "guard against the tendency of the new move towards utopianism," in the words of SPC secretary Chris Stephenson,[57] the secessionists felt called upon to play around with such diagrams.

The exercise began with the publication, in the *West-*

ern Labor News, of the Australian One Big Union outline. Russell did not think much of the plan but made
arrangements to publish the IWW diagram which he received from Rose Henderson in Montreal and which he
mistakenly identified as one drawn up by American socialist Daniel De Leon in 1910 and used by Lenin "in
planning his Soviet Organization."[58] When this appeared in the *Western Labor News,* it was labelled "The
Russian Soviet System" and readers were told the *News*
had "the only copy on the American continent."[59] Russell was somewhat dubious about the whole business and
did not think it possible to draw up a form of organization to wrap around the new movement "like a suit of
clothes." But he thought the exercise would help edu-
cate the workers and clear the atmosphere for the time
when a Canadian plan would be needed.[60] When the
News was finished with the cuts of the two diagrams,
they were sent to Vancouver. Pritchard and Midgley
were even less enthusiastic about them than Russell.
They were afraid a publicly proposed plan would be
criticized and wanted to avoid splits on philosophical
questions. At one point they tried to draw their own diagram, but eventually gave it up, fearing that OBU enemies would "use [it] . . . to pick holes in the proposed organization."[61]

Midgley and Pritchard had good reason to fear dissension within OBU ranks because ideological divisions
were beginning to appear. In an early edition of the Edmonton *One Big Union Bulletin,* Carl Berg published an
article which Midgley and Pritchard condemned as
"I.W.W. sabotage philosophy."[62] Berg reacted sharply
and Midgley was forced to soothe his ruffled feathers.
But the disagreement underlined a major difference between Berg and those termed "political friends," in obvious reference to Socialist Party of Canada members:
Berg deeply mistrusted the motives of the SPC activists.
He wrote a friend in early May: "there is only one In-

dustrial Unionism and I for my part do not want to see the O.B.U. used as a cloak for any political purposes." He did not believe that all the SPC people had "turned industrialist over night." One of those he resented was Joe Knight whom he accused of pushing SPC-brand socialism rather than the OBU.[63] As the weeks dragged by, Berg felt increasingly isolated from the central committee and thought they would not invite him to the founding meeting.

While Berg and Midgley were arguing, the votes continued to roll in. There was no systematic method of balloting and, for the most part, the provincial executives conducted the vote in their jurisdictions. Some unions were issued individual ballots, others printed their own, still others filled out forms supplied by the central or provincial committee. Returns from east of Port Arthur were scattered and mostly negative, but those from the west were heavily in favour of the OBU, though not so strongly in favour of the six hour day.[64] By the beginning of June, 24 230 out of approximately 45 000 union members in the west had voted for secession and 6 147 against, but the ballots of about 10 000 of Winnipeg's organized workers were tied up in the mails by the general and sympathetic strikes of late May and early June. On May 16 the central committee, anticipating the final result of the vote, called the OBU founding meeting for June 4 in Calgary.

The general and sympathetic strikes were "not exactly to the liking of the One Big Union" in Midgley's words,[65] because they affected both attendance and mood of the Calgary meeting. Late arriving delegates forced a three-day delay and, in contrast to the March meeting, only twenty-five, mostly central committee and provincial executive members, attended. There was considerable trouble getting delegates from Winnipeg, one of the strongest OBU centres, and neither Russell nor Johns was able to attend. Those in attendance were probably more cautious in planning the meeting than they might have been. Sessions were held behind closed doors, no representatives of the press were present and no information was released until the meeting was over. In fact, no record of the discussions has ever emerged, but it is clear from Berg's disgust with the proceedings, that he found himself isolated and defeated on almost every point of contention.

The key decisions of the OBU founding convention were made at closed meetings of the central and executive committees which were dominated by active Socialist Party members—19 men designed the One Big Union to their own specifications, the other delegates were excluded.[66] The preamble and constitution they produced was a victory for the SPC and reflected most of the views expressed by Pritchard and Kavanagh at the B.C. Federation of Labor Convention and the Western Labor Conference of February and March. The document announced the inevitability of class struggle and called upon workers to prepare themselves "for the day when production for profit [would] be replaced by production for use." The OBU was to be democratic with provision for a recall, a common membership card and a nominal initiation fee. Procedures for the use of general strikes in industrial disputes were outlined.[67] There was no provision for industrial departments or other semi-independent industrial unions within the OBU. The constitution also provided for "general units," in which workers would organize by geography when their numbers were too small to allow them to organize by industry. The document was remarkable for its lack of clarity and posed more questions than it answered. How would existing craft union locals affiliate? What would be the industrial divisions? How important was the concept of geographic representation to be? Were existing unions to continue to manage their own affairs while owing allegiance to the new union? The constitution was mute. Was the OBU to support electoral activity? Did it stand for revolution through the general strike? Would it seek or honour contracts with employers? Midgley and company were silent. The true believers of the SPC, who had seized control of the developing workers' revolt as early as November, 1918, had led it to Calgary in June, but the mountain disintegrated into a molehill.

Confusion and division were inevitable. Berg was very disappointed. He had fought successfully to keep the name One Big Union, and to build a referendum into the constitution, but had been thwarted in his attempts to borrow from the IWW and to establish a seven person, rather than a five person, executive board. He had wanted to use the constitution of the IWW as a foundation, but was stymied. He was bitter that Midgley and the rest of the central committee had installed themselves as the first executive board and was convinced the union would not work. In his mind the only way to attack the capitalist system was "to form the new society within the shell of the old."[68] This, however, would have meant the adoption of classical syndicalism and was clearly not acceptable to the SPC men in the saddle. The structure and policies of the OBU were almost solely determined by the sterile and somewhat fuzzy ideas of those SPC members who had been so important to its founding. It was designed by the maneuverings and machinations of a small handful of millenarians while the tens of thousands of western workers ready to revolt against capitalism and craft unionism had no chance to determine what the vehicle of their discontent would be like.

Chapter 6

Labour's Civil War

The Winnipeg general strike began May 15. It lasted six weeks and grew out of twenty years of increasing division between workers and their employers throughout the city. Labour's desire to win a real share of control over their daily lives, and the determination of the civic elite to fight them, created the basic polarization. The strains of war compounded these problems and created an atmosphere in which two ordinary disputes, in the metal trades over wages and union recognition and in the building trades over wages, exploded into the longest and most complete general strike in Canadian history.[1]

129

Fools and Wise Men

The Winnipeg labour movement was never as united as it was during those six weeks. The strike was supported by moderates and radicals alike because the underlying sense of grievance was felt by almost all. The wisdom of a general strike may have been questioned by some workers but they had faced common problems for many years and they all fought together. Moderates such as James Winning, J. L. McBride and Ernie Robinson were united with radicals such as Bob Russell, W. H. C. Logan and William Ivens, and throughout the strike, no public division emerged. Even after the Winnipeg labour movement was split into international and OBU factions, the general strike was never a serious point of debate. Robinson and others defended their role in the strike within the Trades and Labour Congress because the general strike was one thing most Winnipeg labour leaders could always agree on.

Such was not the case in other cities where sympathetic strikes were called to demonstrate solidarity with the Winnipeg strikers. In Vancouver, the trades council voted on May 22 to call its members out if there was any military interference in Winnipeg. A week later, the Council issued to the federal and provincial governments a series of demands to be met as a condition for calling off the sympathetic strike. Included were the right of collective bargaining, the six hour day, reinstatement of Winnipeg postal workers, better pensions and allowances for veterans and nationalization of abbatoirs, cold storage plants and grain elevators. A strike vote was conducted and a walkout called for June 3.[2]

But Vancouver workers were not solidly behind the strike, whatever appearances trades council leaders put forward. The results of the strike vote were not publicly announced until four weeks later because only 5 804 workers out of approximately 16 000 union members in the city had bothered to cast ballots, and, of this number, the majority in favour of a strike was a mere

806. The walkout dragged on for a month and started to fall apart when the street railway workers decided to return to their jobs on June 30 and the metal trades council began to poll its members to see if they too wished to go back. Towards the end of the strike many workers wanted nothing more than reinstatement, and there was bitter public debate in labour ranks about tactics. Jack Kavanagh, secretary of the strike committee, attacked the metal trades council for stabbing the strike in the back because they had not been invited to help run it. Welsh, of the metal trades council, claimed the strike had been "foredoomed to failure" and criticized the strike committee for even calling it. One trades council member called the walkout "folly" because of the small number who had voted in favour of it. Trades council secretary Smith, a committed OBU man, admitted that "if the strike vote had been published, those in opposition to us would have known the weak spots first hand."[3] In fact, some key unions, such as the civic employees and street railway workers, only voted to strike after the walkout began. The Vancouver sympathetic strike was certainly no example of spontaneous solidarity and not an instance when the overwhelming wishes of the rank and file caused the leadership to act.

The same can be said of Edmonton. On the evening of May 21, a meeting of union leaders resolved to take a strike vote of their members for purposes of calling a sympathetic strike. Within four days the returns indicated 1 676 in favour, 506 opposed, with 38 out of 49 locals voting. The strike began the next day. At first support was strong. The Railway Carmen were behind it as were two out of three machinists' lodges, most of the building trades and the street railway workers. The postal workers refused to join the strike, but the electrical workers did and the policemen would have but were instructed to stay at work by the strike committee.[4] Before long, however, many workers began to drift back to their jobs. Civic services were resumed by the end of May, sheet metal workers were back on June 11 and almost all strikers were working after Sunday, June 22. According to one student of the strike, no great disruption was experienced in the city after the first week due to the conservative leadership dominating the trades council.[5] That there was tension between the strike leaders and the Trades Council cannot be doubted. Carl Berg, a key figure on the Strike Committee, complained that the city could have been "closed down for some time" if some of the "so-called leaders had not got cold feet." Still, Berg considered the strike a success and was pleased that it had lasted as long as it did. Joe Knight disagreed and called Edmonton an "exaggerated farm village," and the strike "a tragic farce." The walkout had been "called and murdered by a clique of reactionaries, whom the press [were] eulogizing as safe and sane labor leaders." Even Berg came under fire: "with jesuitical cunning [he] is working against the O.B.U., but his having lined up with the reactionary element on the strike committee will eventually nullify his efforts."[7]

The strike in Calgary was the least serious of those in the major western cities. The sympathetic strike was endorsed by the executives of the city's unions at a May 21 meeting where a strike committee, headed by OBU advocate J. Hooley, was appointed to oversee strike balloting. Many unions did not cooperate with the committee. Less than 1500 out of approximately 6000 members voted. The crucial street railway workers refused to participate. On Monday morning, May 26, only 1500 workers left their jobs while teamsters, civic office workers, outside city workers, bakers, railway clerks, barbers, and most building trades workers stayed on the job. One strike committee official admitted that the workers had no grievances but were "duty bound to stand by Winnipeg."[8] When the electrical workers voted to stay on the job, the prospects for the strike becoming truly general were dashed. Only two groups actively supported the walkout, the postal workers and the Ogden shopmen, but this was not nearly enough. By the end of the second week in June, the strike had petered out completely.[9]

The collapse of this strike signaled the end of the influence of the railway shop radicals in the leadership of the Calgary trades council. A. G. Broatch was ridiculed by a group of shopmen when he tried to persuade them to stay on strike and Hooley, a boilermaker, resigned from the trades council presidency. A few days prior to the trades council elections on July 12, Alfred Farmilo arrived in the city from Edmonton and met with several locals in the city to gauge OBU strength. Farmilo persuaded the unions to purge the council of OBU supporters and all OBU proponents were dismissed from the council at its July 12 meeting.[10]

The sympathetic strikes directly affected One Big Union fortunes in Vancouver, Calgary and Edmonton. They added to the growing split between secessionists and those loyal to the international unions. Strikers in these cities were not acting for clearly defined local objectives; the list of demands issued by the Vancouver trades council was clearly a device to attract support from as many quarters as possible. The strikes were, therefore, deliberate acts of policy, without clear objectives. Whatever the general grievances of the workers in these cities, the sense of dissatisfaction was not enough to make these strikes a success. When they proved half-hearted, bitter public recrimination followed and those who led the strikes were usually the target.

Winnipeg was a different case. Here intense bitterness was generated amongst the strikers and their enemies over the operation of essential services. Government and Citizens Committee attacks brought the workers together. Here there were union martyrs respected by pro- and anti-OBU factions alike in the per-

133

sons of the arrested strike leaders. Here also there was unity between 'red' and moderate who organized, supported and led the strike from start to finish. The divisions which began to emerge within the Winnipeg labour movement prior to the strike were temporarily laid aside and the strike had no apparent effect either way. In the other cities, however, the splits hindered the conduct of the strikes and were aggravated by the obvious failures. This hurt the OBU—a sympathetic strike-oriented organization—and helped the internationals who counseled "moderation" and employed "tried and true" tactics.

Outside the cities, the sympathetic strikes had little impact in the short run and were only a brief interlude in the OBU's steady march forward because little organization or propaganda could be done until the last of the strikers returned to work. Midgley even ran into trouble with his colleagues for continuing his OBU duties instead of pitching in to run the Vancouver sympathetic strike,[11] while Pritchard's arrest in Winnipeg drained some OBU funds used to bail him out and retain a lawyer. But the dam broke when the strikes ended and quick progress was made in sweeping up the loggers, coal miners and hardrock miners of Alberta and British Columbia.

In the spring of 1919 working and living conditions in the logging camps were essentially unchanged from those prevailing a decade before. Many loggers still slept in double bunks on hay-filled sacks, went without toilets, baths or running water, and shared their surroundings with pigs.[12] But some relief was on its way from a new union formed in the early months of 1919 which gained a foothold in the scattered camps and battled for clean bunks with sheets, better food, open camps, higher wages and standardized hours. Unions had tried this before but none had succeeded. The AFL Shingle Weavers and the Industrial Workers of the

World alike had been crushed by the operators. The British Columbia Loggers Union, formed in January, 1919, was more successful. Helena Gutteridge, Birt Showler and Ernest Winch organized and directed this union which soon became one of the fastest growing labour organizations in British Columbia.[13]

The loggers faced tremendous obstacles. In one camp the timekeeper listened to the complaints of the men while the foreman wrote out their severance cheques. When the loggers were finished, they were handed their pay and fired.[14] The general unrest prevailing in the interior made organization hazardous. When Alex Mackenzie tried to sign up loggers in Cranbrook, his meeting was cut short by Great War Veterans Association members while the police stood by. After he returned to his room, the vigilantes hustled him out of the hotel, seized his receipt book and the initiation fees he had collected, and gave him two minutes to get out of town or "God help him."[15]

The loggers were swept up in the OBU enthusiasm from the very beginning. They were themselves organized as an industrial union: "For us it looks that if there is not to be 'One Big Union,' then the conditions of capitalist production will decree that there shall be 'no union at all.' "[16] Towards the end of April ballots were sent to over 4000 union members from headquarters in Vancouver asking for their votes on the six hour day and the formation of the OBU. About half responded by mid-May with 2032 in favor and 28 against. In early July delegates met in Vancouver and decided to affiliate with the OBU and change the name of the organization to Lumber Workers Industrial Union of the One Big Union.[17] The loggers did not join as individuals but affiliated through their industrial union which maintained its own newspaper, executive board and offices.

The Lumber Workers Industrial Union quickly extended its activities to Saskatchewan, Manitoba and Ontario, and continued to grow rapidly. By October, 1919, the membership mark topped ten thousand, and seven thousand more were signed up by the end of the year. Most of the coastal camps were completely organized and a rash of bush strikes brought immediate improvements in living conditions.[18] The union faced no opposition from any international union, and soon became unopposed master of the lumber camps.

In the coal fields of Alberta and British Columbia, the secessionist movement found solid support with individuals and locals quick to donate funds to the OBU. The District 18 board and policy committee voted 9 to 4 to "fall in line with the OBU" at a special meeting on March 29. P. M. Christophers left the chair to support the OBU and Frank Wheatley was the only Board member to oppose it.[19] The vote created immediate problems because the miners were under a contract with the Western Coal Operators Association that provided a checkoff to the UMW, and District leaders feared the mine owners would end the checkoff if they found out that the miners were about to join the OBU. This would seriously disrupt the flow of dues money into union coffers. District secretary Ed Browne thought the OBU central committee should deal with this problem by bringing District 18 into the OBU without delay. Joe Knight, who attended the meeting, agreed. He urged Midgley to take "immediate steps" to support the miners and warned that it would be a great mistake to allow time to elapse between the break with the UMW and the district's affiliation with the One Big Union.[20] But Midgley was reluctant to commit the OBU to any definite action until the referendum had been completed and the founding meeting held.

The OBU question was soon complicated by a dispute that arose between the miners and W. H. Armstrong, director of coal operations, over wages and hours of work for surface mine employees paid on an hourly basis. The district executive had approached Armstrong in late February, 1919, with a request that the collective agreement between themselves and the Western Coal Operators Association be extended beyond its March 31, 1919 expiry date. They wanted wages and working conditions to stay the same (subject to cost-of-living adjustments provided for in the agreement) and wanted to begin negotiations with the owners within "thirty days after the declaration of peace."[21] They were following policies laid out by the international which were intended to produce new continent-wide negotiations in the coal industry after the war. Armstrong agreed and, on March 6, issued an order which extended the agreement.[22]

The new status quo was upset by the British Columbia legislature which passed an eight hour law for surface mine employees. This effectively raised their hourly wages because they would henceforth be paid nine hours' wages for eight hours' work. To stay within the spirit of his March 6 order, which froze wages, Armstrong issued a new order which reduced the hourly wages of these men to keep their pay at the same levels as before. Although the hourly wage was restored, take-home pay was lowered because the men were working one less hour. The district officers objected to this reduction in earning power and strongly opposed it.[23] The British Columbia coal operators, on the other hand, particularly the Crows Nest Pass Coal Company, saw themselves placed at a disadvantage to the Alberta collieries because their miners would work fewer hours each week.[24] Armstrong, therefore, issued a second order on April 16 which extended the eight hour day to Alberta and provided that all surface workers in the two provinces formerly employed nine hours a day or more should receive nine hours' pay for eight hours' work. But this still did not satisfy Christophers and Browne. They complained that men formerly employed for ten or eleven hours would suffer and appealed to Armstrong for further action. He decided to seek the advice of Gideon Robertson who suggested that he refuse any other consideration of the union's demands until a new agreement had been worked out in the United States, at which time the contract in District 18 would again be reviewed.[25] Armstrong complied and told Christophers and Browne that if they objected to the April 16 order, he was quite willing to rescind it and put matters back to where they had been before March 6.[26] The union then conducted a stroke vote which indicated overwhelming support for the walkout. In the Lethbridge district alone, over 4000 miners voted yes, only about 150 dissented. The strike was set for the afternoon of May 25 and fanmen, pumpmen, firemen and engineers were called out in addition to contract miners and daymen.[27] This was an unusual move. The union usually gave fanmen and pumpmen special permission to work during strikes because they were responsible for keeping the mines gas and water free. But this time district leaders knew there would be no help from the international because of the One Big Union referendum[28] and needed to bring as much pressure to bear as quickly as possible.

The strike did not begin with any wild enthusiasm. There was, rather, a "dogged, fatalistic attitude" that this, finally, was the showdown. Many were convinced the strike was the start of the great social upheaval they had expected.[29] At first the strike was almost completely free of disturbances and only in one Drumheller mine was there any attempt to keep production going. Mounted Police and Alberta Provincial Police kept a close watch but refused to intervene. At Lethbridge there were disturbances on May 28 and 29 when small crowds of strikers stoned CPR trains taking maintenance workers to a mine. There were several casualties, but city police and Alberta Provincial Police had little trouble restoring order. Throughout the coalfields, miners dug in for a long struggle and searched for work.

Christophers and Browne led their willing, but un-prepared, followers into a long strike that completely tied up coal production in District 18. They might have picked a better time. Coal consumption always fell in the spring, and this, coupled to the drop in demand for fuels which came with the end of war, meant surplus coal stocks and less pressure on the operators to settle. Christophers and Browne claimed the issue was nine hours' pay for eight hours' work for the handful of sur-face workers who had formerly toiled ten or eleven hours. But was it? When this issue first arose, Knight warned Midgley and Pritchard that if the miners were left to themselves they might go back to the UMW and this would provide a powerful weapon for others to use against the OBU. But Pritchard and Midgley were un-moved. They claimed they could not deal with questions of wages and hours. It would be folly at this stage for the OBU to assume responsibility for, or attempt to take charge of, a strike of any description.[30] But, at the same time, it was general knowledge amongst coal operators and international union officials in western Canada that the OBU was making rapid headway. Christophers had publicly committed himself to secession; the rank and file were being asked to support the OBU and contrib-ute to the central committee.

When Midgley and Pritchard made their position clear, Christophers and Browne knew the OBU could not help them if the split with the United Mine Workers came too quickly. They had jumped the gun in commit-ting themselves to the OBU, or had been pushed into doing so by Knight or Berg, at a time when they most needed the support of the international. Now, they were between the frying pan and the fire—no help from the UMW and none from the OBU. This strike was an opportunity to unite their members behind them and force the operators and Armstrong to deal directly with them and by-pass the international. To do this they had to maintain the fiction that they were still the bona fide representatives of the UMW in the coal fields—this, at the very time district locals were discussing, and voting on, the preamble and constitution of the One Big Union. They fooled no one. The strike was long and hopes for a quick victory were fading fast. Christophers and Browne were incapable of the deft necessary to their cause and their attempts to cover up were nothing but heavy-handed blunders. Browne did not even care whether the local referendum meetings were open or secret as long as the vote was "in favor of the O.B.U."[31] To the operators and Armstrong he and Christophers put on a UMW face; to their own men, an OBU one.

In late June, Christophers and Browne asked Armstrong and the coal operators to re-open negotiations. Armstrong contacted UMW vice-president John L. Lewis for advice and was told that District 18 had never officially notified the international of the strike or the reasons for it.[32] When the operators learned this they refused to have anything to do with District 18 officials and called their actions "base treachery." In the meantime, Dave Irvine, international organizer for the UMW, told Armstrong that his union would probably put a number of officials into the area to replace the present officers and reorganize the district. He proposed that the current contract remain in effect until April 1, 1920, by which time agreements would have been negotiated and signed in the United States.

Browne and Christophers were desperate. Stories were now circulating that many miners were sick of the long strike and wanted to get back to work. Some move was needed to keep them in control of events and, consequently, Browne tried again to get negotiations started. His excuse for asking Armstrong to arrange a

Miner's union hall, Sandon,B.C.,1900. *Provincial Archives,Victoria,B.C.*

Trail, B.C., 1900. The Cominco smelter is on the hill.
Provincial Archives, Victoria, B.C.

Sandon, B.C., hardrock mining town, 1897.
Provincial Archives, Victoria, B.C.

Miner's hotel in Rossland, B.C., 1897.
Provincial Archives, Victoria, B.C.

Robert Dunsmuir, founder of the Dunsmuir coal empire.
Provincial Archives, Victoria, B.C.

Hatley Park, Victoria, B.C. Dunsmuir family residence.
Provincial Archives, Victoria, B.C.

Hardrock miners, Centre Star Mine, Rossland, B.C. *Provincial Archives, Victoria, B.C.*

Coal sorting screen and picking table, c.1914. *Glenbow—Alberta Institute, Calgary, Alberta.*

Coal trucks and "day" men, Frank, Alberta, 1902.
Glenbow—Alberta Institute, Calgary, Alberta.

Arrested IWW striker, Kamloops, B.C., 1912.
Provincial Archives, Victoria, B.C.

Coal miners on a man car wait to enter
the mine, 1910.
*Provincial Archives of Alberta. Photograph
Collection.*

Logging camp Vancouver Island, 1907.
Provincial Archives, Victoria, B.C.

Coal mine rescue team, Coal Creek,
B.C., 1912.
*Glenbow—Alberta Institute, Calgary, Al-
berta.*

Immigrant children, Winnipeg, 1916.
Foote Collection. Manitoba Archives.

Sorting and binding catalogues, Winnipeg, 1915.
Manitoba Archives.

Immigrant hovels, Winnipeg's North End, 1904.   *Manitoba Archives.*

Rossland, B.C. rock drilling contest, 1897.
Provincial Archives, Victoria, B.C.

A well-stocked logging camp cookhouse, B.C. *Provincial Archives, Victoria, B.C.*

After work in a B.C. logging camp.
Provincial Archives, Victoria, B.C.

Millcrest football team, May, 1914. Seven of these men died in the Millcrest explosion one month later. *Glenbow—Alberta Institute, Calgary, Alberta.*

G. Blaylock, General Manager of Cominco.
Provincial Archives, Victoria, B.C.

Mine surface buildings at Millcrest, Alberta, wrecked in the big explosion.
Glenbow—Alberta Institute, Calgary, Alberta.

Dominion Coal Commissioner W. H. Armstrong.
Provincial Archives, Victoria, B.C.

Funeral after a mine explosion, Strathcona, Alberta, 1907.
Provincial Archives of Alberta. E. Brown Collection.

R. A. Rigg.   *Manitoba Archives.*

This type of anti-Red propaganda was common in Canada in 1919.
Glenbow—Alberta Institute, Calgary, Alberta.

Look Out For The Snake!

CANADIAN LABOR
WILL CRUSH BOLSHEVISM

Many of our millionaires were once workmen. In Russia there is no advance for labor. All men there must work and you cannot quit your job. The boss has authority to beat you and to even kill. You must obey your orders rigidly. You receive paper money called rubles which was made by a printing press, but you cannot buy much with it. People go from the cities to the country to get food and the poor peasants have very little, because their surplus is taken from them by force. The factories in the cities cannot run if people are hungry. If nothing is produced, there is nothing to distribute. The agitator sits close to the money and the men who are clinging to power. You will be butchered without trial if you protest.

Bolshevism and socialism are similar theories and are children of autocracy. They spring up in defeated countries where great hunger exists. They appeal best to those who have nothing to lose. In Canada we cannot understand the hatred for government that you see in immigrants from despotic countries.

Canadians Cannot Feel Bolshevism

Our workers are well paid and many of them own their own homes. The foreigner who becomes naturalized and learns English soon becomes efficient, and like the rest of us becomes adamant against breeders of discontent and unrest.

A portion of the population in our industrial centres cannot speak English and very little attention has been given to these workers. This has been a fertile field for anti-government agitators and I. W. W. to recruit a following. Effort should be made to Canadianize these aliens.

The spirit of Canadianism is the best antidote as we are all citizens of a great and free democratic nation and do not want class distinctions. Employers and employees are getting closer together and the workers are participating in industrial affairs more and more every day.

Keep industry humming so that wages will not be reduced. Our returning soldiers must be given jobs. They are fighting men and will lend new energy to any industry. Now is the time to put your shoulder to the wheel and help adjust things so that we can get back to a peace basis as quickly as possible.

One of a Series of Articles Published by The Canada Firm

Victoria Park meeting during the Winnipeg general strike, May-June, 1919.   *Foote Collection. Manitoba Archives.*

W. A. Pritchard, c.1930s.
Provincial Archives, Victoria, B.C.

Hon. Gideon Decker Robertson,
Senator, May 1922.
Public Archives, Canada, PA-33996.

Railway shopcraft workers, Winnipeg, 1920.
Foote Collection. Manitoba Archives.

Anti-general strike parade, Winnipeg, June 4, 1919.
Manitoba Archives.

Winnipeg general strike, riot of June 10, 1919.   *Manitoba Archives.*

meeting with the operators was that peace had been declared.[33] The operators were puzzled. They pointed out that district officials had, some time ago, explained "peace" as "when peace was ratified by the United States Senate" and this, clearly, had not happened. The district officials, they concluded, had simply changed their minds. Armstrong agreed and refused to authorize any negotiations until the district officials were vouched for by the international.[34]

While these discussions were taking place, the OBU began to come out into the open in towns and camps throughout the district. The Crows Nest Pass Coal Company received letters from the local union, which they refused to answer, with the letters "UMWA" crossed out and "OBU" substituted, while the sign in front of the union hall at Canmore, Alberta, was changed to read "OBU." But even though the vote on the OBU constitution was in full swing, Browne still tried to keep up the fiction that the United Mine Workers were in good standing in the area. He told F. E. Harrison, Armstrong's assistant, as late as July 7 that less than one-fourth of the locals had reported their results: "some have accepted and some have rejected and that leaves us still working as a district under a charter of the United Mine Workers of America and as such we would be prepared to enter into an agreement with the Western Coal Operators Association."[35]

That very day a notice was nailed to the bulletin board near the mine at Fernie, British Columbia, announcing that local union officials had received a petition signed by thirty-five miners asking for a mass meeting to discuss the strike. Those who attended this meeting demanded that Christophers come to Fernie to explain "just what was being done in connection with the . . . strike." Christophers came the next morning and tried to explain the actions of the district executive. It was in vain. The miners repudiated the One Big Union, announced their intention to return to the UMW and instructed their local policy committee to resume negotiations with the operators to work out a new agreement and get them back to work.[36] This setback came amidst growing division in the ranks of the district executive itself. Browne told a Mounted Police detective in Calgary that he did not want Christophers at the head of the district if he tried to dissociate himself from the OBU. The Police were convinced that "Browne and Christophers [were] not pulling well."[37]

Under these circumstances district officers' efforts to end the strike intensified. On July 14 district leaders told assistant coal commissioner Harrison that they were prepared to send their men back to work, and accept the April 16 order, provided there was no discrimination. Armstrong was unwilling to concede even this until the UMW vouched for the reliability of the district officials. He was determined not to have any dealings with the OBU and to bring the UMW directly into the picture. Browne declared the government had no right telling the men what organization they should belong to.[38] It was now fully apparent to him that the miners were fighting "the Operators, the Government and the International Union which appear to have combined their forces to beat us into submission."[39]

The truth of this was clear after the arrival in Alberta of a commission of three representatives sent by the UMW's international board. By July 25, international board members Samuel Ballantyne from Iowa and William Dalrymple from Oklahoma had entered the area and, together with Dave Irwin, held their first meeting with Armstrong. (The third member, not yet arrived, was Samuel Caddy from Washington.) Armstrong told them he thought a housecleaning was in order. The present officers of the District were OBU and he would have nothing to do with them. The union men sat quietly and said little, but the next morning contacted

Lewis and told him that Christophers, Browne and vice-president McFagan were all OBU and recommended that the district charter be suspended.[40] Lewis did this and wired Christophers that the district was no longer affiliated to the United Mine Workers. Christophers, Browne and McFagan then told all the district locals of the revocation and urged them to form themselves into OBU units as soon as possible.[41] The District 18 executive gathered on July 31 and formed themselves into District #1, Mining Department, One Big Union. By August 1, 1919, as the strike dragged through its tenth week, the United Mine Workers had been reduced to a shell in western Canada and the One Big Union, with over seven thousand coal miners, ruled the coal fields. Ed Browne wrote a friend: "All supporters in western Canada is [*sic*] watching the Coal Miners, upon their action depends the future of the O.B.U. in western Canada."[42]

OBU success in the coalfields was matched in the hardrock mining country of the British Columbia interior. The men in Kimberly, Silverton and Rossland (about 650 miners) endorsed the OBU by large majorities in the referendum. The Consolidated Mining and Smelting Company, which controlled the mines at Rossland, responded by locking out its employees May 20 and ordering its shift bosses to discharge all OBU members. The rise of the OBU was only the latest disaster for the International Union of Mine, Mill and Smelter Workers (the name was changed from Western Federation of Miners in 1917) which had been steadily losing members in British Columbia for some time.[43] The hardrock mining industry was in trouble throughout North America because of shrinking markets caused by the onset of peace. In the United States the union was on the verge of breaking apart after years of internal division. In British Columbia, it had lost a long and costly strike against Consolidated Mining and

Smelting at Trail in 1917. In the winter of 1918 and the spring of 1919, miners were forced to seek employment as general labourers around mines and smelters. Few were happy with their union, especially because their leaders in the U.S. seemed more intent on smashing the IWW than securing better terms of employment or reorganizing the union for greater internal strength.[44]

Union president Charles H. Moyers was, nevertheless, determined to fight the OBU. He claimed there was no need for two rival unions in each mining camp and warned that miners joining the OBU would not be able to find work in the United States. They were drawing a line and building a fence around western Canada. These were the same mistakes committed fourteen years before by the IWW, he maintained.[45] But there was little hesitation among the miners and smeltermen. In the first week of July they sent delegates to Nelson to form an OBU mining department. There, the One Big Union constitution was adopted and District #1 of the Metaliferous Miners of the OBU was established, with a district board of five members presided over by Tommy Roberts. Local unions were requested to form grievance committees to deal with management in disputes over wages and working conditions and it was decided to demand a minimum wage of $5.00 per day in mines and smelters. The long-hated bonus and contract systems were strongly condemned.[46]

Like the loggers and the coal miners, the hardrock miners maintained a semi-autonomous existence in the OBU and paid their per capita to a district board rather than directly to the OBU. By August, the large Kimberly and Silverton Miners' Unions had left the International and Moyers was forced to revoke their charters.[47] In the third week of September the first regular convention of the OBU hardrock miners was held at Nelson. By now the district covered the Kamloops, Kootenay and Similkameen territories and included every local union in the area except that at Sandon where most miners had voted to join the OBU, but the international held a mortgage on the union hall and hospital. Hardrock mining had become an OBU preserve.

Elsewhere victory was not so easily achieved. When William Varley arrived in Winnipeg shortly after the general strike, he joined R. A. Rigg, recently appointed special western representative of Trades Congress president Tom Moore. Moore could not have chosen a better man. Rigg had been active in the Winnipeg labour movement as a president and secretary of the trades council, a member of the Social Democratic Party, a labour alderman and a member of the Manitoba legislative assembly. His speaking and organizational abilities were legend. He had strongly opposed conscription but volunteered for service with the armed forces in early 1918. During the Winnipeg general strike he had worked to rally the veterans' support behind the strike committee though he had serious misgivings about the wisdom of the strike. But, like many other general strike supporters, he was a loyal international union man.

Rigg was financed in a most unusual manner. The Trades and Labour Congress had been run on a small budget from its founding in 1886. Its permanent staff consisted of executive secretary P. M. Draper and a stenographer, and its facilities were limited to one small office in downtown Ottawa. This was not enough to mount an effective counterattack against the One Big Union, even though the American Federation of Labor was financing Varley and Farmilo, and different international unions were sending their own organizers into the west. Salvation came from the United Brotherhood of Maintenance of Way Employees and its president, Allen E. Barker. Barker, without the consent of his union's executive board, sent a cheque for $50 000 to Draper. One year later Barker was brought to trial charged with the improper handling of $172 000 of

145

union funds. Draper told the press at that time that he was "not at liberty to speak about [the money] because it relate[d] to private affairs of the labour movement." He refused to disclose how the money had been used except to say that Barker had been given a full accounting of it. Draper claimed that he had "acted privately" and not "as secretary of the Trades and Labour Congress of Canada."[48]

The battle between Rigg and the One Big Union in Winnipeg began July 15. At a meeting of the trades council a resolution was introduced to hear the report of the delegates to the OBU founding meeting in Calgary and to adopt the OBU constitution. Referendum results indicated an 8 841 to 705 margin in the city in favour of secession. Rigg was allowed thirty minutes to present his case to the meeting.[49] Those delegates opposed to the One Big Union, including the entire executive, were convinced they had no chance to stop the secessionists. The OBU resolution passed by a wide margin and the council then voted to draw up a new constitution in line with OBU requirements.

Rigg believed control of the council was the key to victory, but tried to avoid the appearance of directly interfering in council affairs. He spoke to the executive after the meeting and told them that since they still had the Trades Congress charter, they only needed to forge ahead with their regular business at the next meeting. Any delegate suspected of pro-OBU sympathies would be kept out. Rigg wanted to keep the velvet gloves on as long as he thought he was in control of events, even though he did not trust council president James Winning's motives and believed that Ernie Robinson was sympathetic towards the OBU, though opposed to disruption.[50]

Rigg's plans were upset when OBU supporters brought in a petition for a special council meeting to settle the constitutional question. Winning had no choice but to call the special meeting for Tuesday, July 29. If Rigg had seized control of the charter and put himself in the chair, as he had the authority to do, he might have averted what followed: Winning was too much the hesitant compromiser to keep control of the meeting. His first mistake was to forget to follow the regular order of business. He moved immediately from the officers' roll call to the report of the credentials committee and failed to challenge the delegates from union locals which had already gone to the OBU. They could have been replaced with delegates loyal to the Trades Congress.[51] Winning then ruled that he would not accept the report of the council's bylaw committee because it was designed to change council into an OBU body. He was challenged and voted down. As far as Russell was concerned, the trades council was meeting legally under a TLC charter and, as such, had the right to wind up its own affairs, transfer its property to the One Big Union and return its charter.[52]

Rigg had miscalculated. He was silent as the meeting roared around him. One motion instructed secretary Robinson to return the charter and seal to Ottawa and "not hand it over to any so-called representative of the Congress who might be in the city."[53] Another directed the executive to turn all funds and property over to the OBU and send for an OBU charter. At the end of the meeting, W. A. Pritchard took the chair and the council, newly constituted as the Winnipeg central labour council of the One Big Union, proceeded to elect temporary officers.

Early the next morning Rigg went to the labour temple to take the charter and seal. He ordered Winning to disregard the motions passed the previous evening, and told him he expected full cooperation in purging the OBU from the council. He then called another special meeting for Friday, August 1. This time there were no mistakes. Rigg invited only those whose loyalty he was certain of, and even they were closely questioned by a specially-appointed committee.[54]

Rigg called the meeting to order with Winning in the chair, and told the delegates that the last meeting was illegal and that they were still in business. He then handed gavel, charter and seal to Winning. A special vote of confidence confirmed the executive in their positions. A press committee was appointed with responsibility for keeping control of the *Western Labor News*. Now there were two councils in Winnipeg, one affiliated to the AFL/TLC, the other to the One Big Union.

With the trades council on a firm footing, the battle for control of union property began. The trades council ordered the bank not to honour cheques signed by Ivens and Harry Veitch, chairman of the old press committee. Ivens was allowed to keep his job on condition that he agree to the trades council authority, but when the August 8 issue of the *News* was sent to the printers it was discovered that the subscription forms stated the paper was now OBU. Ivens was immediately fired and an injunction was secured which threw him out of the editorial office. Alderman W. B. Simpson, former circulation manager, replaced him.[55] For a brief time the One Big Union continued to claim ownership of the paper, but it soon urged all OBU units in the city to cancel their subscriptions and, on August 12, issued the first edition of the *One Big Union Bulletin*.

The Winnipeg central labour council of the OBU first met on August 5 in the same building, and at the same time, as the re-invigorated trades council. Elections established long-time socialists such as C. P. Cooper and W. H. C. Logan in executive positions, while R. B. Russell became secretary-treasurer. The council abolished initiation rites, which were considered "monkey shines" peculiar to the craft unions.[56] Delegates were chosen and business conducted in much the same fashion as the trades council, but with the crucial difference that this body was designed to control and coordinate the local units affiliated to it, not to be controlled by them as in the AFL system. The central labour council was a key element in the OBU structure because it welded "the workers of a district into a cohesive unit."[57] Under this principle the One Big Union was not based on federations of industrial unions, but upon a highly centralized local council organized across trade, craft, and industrial lines. This was much like the structure of the old Knights of Labor, and very different from the Industrial Workers of the World.

The central labour council was also very different in its emphasis upon educating OBU members in working class economics, science, philosophy and other subjects. Education was necessary because working class progress depended upon the workers knowing that they produced all the wealth but received only a small portion of it in return. Then, too, the progress of the One Big Union depended upon countering propaganda which accused it of being nothing more than a group of reds and Bolshevists.[58] Thus, classes were established all over the city and workers were urged to attend these or start their own. The economics were unabashedly Marxian, or what passed for it in the minds of those Socialist Party of Canada members who invariably taught the courses. By November, 1919, a literature committee was beginning to order, stock and sell pamphlets and booklets, and a small OBU library had been set up. Serious thought was given to establishing a labor college patterned after, but less ambitious than, similar institutions in Britain and the United States.[59]

Educational programs, however, won few battles in the fight to destroy the international unions. It was soon clear that an informal alliance was being forged between the AFL/TLC and city employers in a bid to freeze out the OBU. On construction sites, in factories, at the sprawling railway yards, OBU members were harassed, excluded, dismissed. Employers refused to listen to OBU grievance committees or bargain with OBU units. The railroads dealt only with Division 4 of the internationals,[60] even though the vast majority of shopcraft workers had followed Russell, Johns, and Logan into the OBU. Distribution of the *One Big Union Bulletin* was forbidden at shop and factory gates. Closed shop agreements were concluded between employers and international unions. At some establishments workers were forced to sign oaths that they would never join organizations which sanctioned "the principle of a sympathetic strike,"[61] a tactic aimed directly at the OBU. Railway shop managers had strict orders to bar OBU activity on company property, while international organizers were allowed into the shops and posted meeting notices on company billboards.[62] Workers could join the OBU if they wished, but they would only have grievances heard, wages raised, or working conditions improved, through the international unions.

One Big Union leaders always insisted that they wanted to strengthen workers in their daily battles while getting them ready for the inevitable revolution. The latter goal was to be achieved by building a class-based union and educating workers in Marxist fundamentals. This was often misunderstood because OBU leaders never had any intention of causing a revolution, though they certainly hoped to help it along. In the period from the outbreak of the Russian revolution to the collapse of the western Canadian general and sympathetic strikes in June, 1919, Midgley, Pritchard, Russell, Johns and others had every reason to hope that the revolution was about to begin. They waxed enthusiastic at conferences and conventions about what the future would bring and how the workers must ready themselves to enter the promised land. By late summer and early fall of 1919, however, it was becoming clearer that the 'inevitable' revolution was not around the corner.

In November, 1919, the *One Big Union Bulletin* published a lengthy analysis by Chicago economist Thorstein Veblen which asserted that conditions in America did not "offer such a combination of circumstances as would be required for any effectual overturn of the established order." Put simply, "Bolshevism [was] not a menace to the vested interests."[63] If revolution was not to come soon, it was the One Big Union's duty to its membership to concentrate on the daily struggle and leave the revolution to providence, or whatever passed for it. Workers in Winnipeg had endured a long general strike with little support from their unions. The radical rhetoric of late 1918 and early 1919 was increasingly drowned out by growling stomachs. It was clearly time for work and wages, time for the OBU to deliver on its more mundane promises. This was not lost on OBU leaders in the city. A *Bulletin* editorial of February, 1920, proclaimed: "This paper is published by the Winnipeg Central Labor Council of the OBU, a strictly labor organization. The business of a labor organization is simple. It is . . . to afford aid to its members in making collective bargains and to resist encroachments against the rights of the [workers]."[64]

The One Big Union's attempt to organize Winnipeg's garment industry reflected these sentiments. By November, 1919, the OBU had signed up most of the city's garment workers and began a campaign to urge its members to buy OBU label clothing. The employers had a closed shop agreement with the international union and refused to deal with the OBU. There was a short strike which ended when the employers promised to think about dealing with the OBU once the current agreement expired.[65] The One Big Union was hardly acting in a revolutionary way with its stress on the union label and its willingness to honour an enemy's contract. OBU carpenters displayed the same attitude when they were rebuffed by the Builders Exchange, an employers' organization. The carpenters wrote, "We are out solely for business and are not looking for any trouble in the building line. You desire your work to go on as speedily as possible, and we are willing to cooperate to that end."[66] When a dispute arose over pay scales for OBU painters employed by contractors who had signed agreements with the international union, the OBU took the case to the provincial Industrial Disputes Commission.[67] On another occasion, the *One Big Union Bulletin* replied to charges that the OBU was only concerned with general strikes with the statement that although the OBU did not reject such tactics, it would need "a most serious crisis in the relations of capital and labor" before resorting to them.[68]

The concentration on "bread and butter" struggles, waged in a conventional way, created serious internal contradictions. The OBU now appeared to want to play by the established rules of negotiation, recognition and contract. At the same time, however, its constitution provided for the use of sympathetic strikes, which, of necessity, would violate contracts. If the OBU was designed to appeal to radicals, it was limiting its effectiveness by emphasizing traditional union tactics. If it was intended to attract traditionalists, it should have given up sympathetic strikes and Marxist educational campaigns. Without a Marxist accent and the sympathetic strike principle, however, the OBU was little more than a conglomeration of craft union locals, with different journeymen carrying a common card, using the same tactics and for the same purposes, as the established unions.

Whatever the OBU was, it was unacceptable to employers and governments. The provincial administration of premier T. C. Norris appointed two trades council representatives to its Joint Council of Industry, shutting out the OBU, while the federal government continued to spy on the OBU and strengthen its militia forces in anticipation of OBU-created difficulties. According to some federal observers, strikes were most likely to come from the OBU and warnings about impending mass strikes (which never materialized) were repeated over and over.[69]

The fight between the OBU and the internationals centred around OBU efforts to capture international union locals intact and the attempts of international organizers to preserve these locals. There were many individual battles. When a local of the plumbers' union in Winnipeg threatened to secede, international organizer John Bruce called a special meeting to confront the OBU. He asked how many were prepared to stick by their charter because he had enough names to keep the local in business. It was a warm day. Bruce doffed his coat, put it on the back of the chair, and walked to the front of the platform: "Well, here is the charter. I want to remain and know who is going to follow this charter and those who are not going to follow it will kindly leave the room and there will be no ill feeling." Someone answered, "We'll hang the bloody thing around your neck." Bruce picked up the charter: "You and who else?" There was a chuckle in the room and five men got up and walked out. The plumbers stayed with the international.[70]

Despite the large sums poured into Winnipeg by the various international unions and by the American Federation of Labor and the Trades and Labour Congress, the OBU gained steadily. By October the One Big Union claimed 9 000 members in Winnipeg, a figure substantiated by the Mounted Police who reported, at the end of January, 1920 that the OBU had captured three-fourths of the trade union movement in the city.[71] The OBU was heavily represented at the major railway shops and had units of garment workers, painters and decorators, bakers, confectionery workers, tailors, teamsters, operating engineers and metal workers. Later in the year the street railway employees, about nine hundred strong, seceded from the International, stayed independent for seven months and then joined the OBU in August 1920. The victory marked the peak of OBU strength in Winnipeg. According to the Mounted Police, there was, at this point, a margin of about two thousand OBU over international union members in the city.

The Winnipeg trades and labour council was no slave of Moore, Morrison or Gompers even after the split. At the 1919 Trades Congress convention in Hamilton, Ontario, a strong Winnipeg delegation, which included Ernie Robinson, George Armstrong, F. G. Tipping and R. A. Rigg, proposed resolutions favouring the six hour day, greater autonomy for Canadian sections of international unions, and the right of the Trades Congress to determine its own membership without dictation by the AFL. Other resolutions attacked Tom Moore for sitting on the Royal Commission on Industrial Relations, Congress secretary P. M. Draper for "going to Britain as a self-constituted representative of Canadian labour," and Senator Gideon Robertson because he had "no seat in the House of the people's representatives." George Armstrong urged "the immediate withdrawal of troops from Russia" and proposed that the TLC "go on record endorsing the Soviets as administering affairs to the best interests of the working class."[72]

By the fall of 1919, Rigg, Varley and other international organizers had put the AFL/TLC unions back on a firm footing in Winnipeg. The One Big Union was still powerful in the city and had a strong emotional appeal to workers due to its native western Canadian birth,[73] and because many workers still believed it offered the industrial unionism they wanted. The international unions were still on the defensive, but Rigg and Varley, along with other international union organizers, managed to keep an active AFL/TLC presence in the city. At the moment it was all they could hope for; in the long run it was all they needed.

The battle against the One Big Union in Vancouver was fought along the same lines. When the Vancouver trades council endorsed the OBU shortly after the sympathetic strike ended on July 4, Frank Morrison ordered Alfred Farmilo to Vancouver. He arrived in the last week of July and on July 31, took possession of the trades council's charter and seal. A week later he called the first meeting of the newly-organized trades council to order. He told delegates representing sixteen local unions that he had been instructed to protect the charters of the AFL and the TLC in the city and to make arrangements for those unions who wished to retain their affiliation with the two congresses. Farmilo knew it was important to create the impression that the new council meeting under the old charter was the only legitimate successor to the original trades council chartered by the Trades and Labour Congress in 1888. This was crucial not only for the morale of the craft unions but to keep control of council property—a $45 000 investment in the Vancouver Labor Temple and 5 000 shares of the *B.C. Federationist*.

Now there were two councils functioning in Vancouver, both using the same name, and considerable confusion followed. Some local unions tried to stay neutral, but Farmilo forced them to make a choice: "Every union in the city must declare itself," he stated, "no union can have representation in both councils."[74] Soon many locals began to declare themselves by affiliating to the international council. By the end of the summer, the international council was functioning smoothly and Farmilo told AFL headquarters that it had a majority of the trade union members in the city. Even if this were untrue, it had been very easy for him to accomplish his mission in a city where the labour movement had been more radical, and for a longer time, than any other in Canada.

In September, 1919, the Trades and Labour Congress met in convention at Hamilton, Ontario. The meeting was quite different from that which had taken place at Quebec City the previous year. The convention was orchestrated towards condemnation of the disruption that had taken place within international union ranks since the fall of 1918. The Congress executive attacked the One Big Union and warned its members against "too frequent or too wide use of the strike weapon." The constitution was amended to give the executive broad powers to suspend or revoke the charter of any federation, trades council or directly chartered local where the officers encouraged or advocated secession. Further, the executive was empowered to replace wayward officers with a three-man commission in charge of the affairs, funds and property of the body concerned.[75] These provisions allowed the Congress to punish affiliates who were not also chartered by the AFL and was aimed directly at the British Columbia Federation of Labor, whose executive were solidly OBU and which still controlled the important *Federationist.* Federation officers were not about to wait for suspension. At the end of September they returned their charter and condemned the constitutional changes as "autocracy of the worst kind."[76] It was clear that a battle for control of the *Federationist* and other property was just beginning and that a major court fight loomed. To avoid that prospect, Federation officers decided to dissolve their organization. When the annual convention met March 21 and 22, 1920, delegates were told: "If the workers are all in one union the need for a Federation of units ceases." The executive expressed the hope that the Federation would be "superseded by a more powerful and intelligent form of organization."[77] But, notwithstanding these claims, dissolution was the best way to avoid a court battle and keep control of the *Federationist* because the majority shares of the paper had been purchased from the Federation by the OBU.

The international unions had plenty of help in the fight against the OBU in Vancouver just as they did in Winnipeg and elsewhere. The local Employers Association declared publicly, as early as June 23, 1919, that it was "desirable to support those men who have retained their affiliations with Unions in good standing with the Internationals" and "that under no circumstances do we recognize affiliations with the so-called O.B.U."[78] At least one company entered into a closed shop agreement to keep out the OBU while the international-affiliated trades council refused to recognize "unfair" declarations directed against employers by the OBU. Employers in the lower mainland, particularly in the lumber and shipbuilding industry, continually urged the federal government to provide jobs to undercut radical influence. Even the Mounted Police believed that a public works program was necessary "to provide a means of livelihood for those who are unemployed."

Farmilo, Varley and Rigg concentrated their efforts on the key centres of Vancouver and Winnipeg, but the rapidly widening civil war was being fought in every town and city that had a union local. Generally Varley and Rigg covered the territory from the Lakehead to the Saskatchewan/Alberta border while Farmilo covered Alberta and British Columbia. The three confined their efforts to urban centres and left the work of fighting the OBU in the mining regions to the representatives of those unions directly concerned. All three received the complete support of the international organizers crowding into the west on the orders of their particular unions and at the urging of the AFL itself. Some of the most active of these representatives were John Bruce of the Plumbers, James Sommerville of the

Machinists, whose home was in Saskatchewan, H. Kempster, also a Machinist, William McCutcheon for the Boilermakers, and Robert Hewitt of the Railway Carmen.

By the beginning of August the battle was joined across the west. Rigg set out for Regina on August 11 and was joined by Varley a few days later. They found the labour movement divided with trades council president Hazeltine and secretary Sambrook openly espousing secession, while the street railway men had withdrawn from the council because of its OBU tendencies. The council was in a sorry state. Attendance at meetings was poor and the executive was incapable of giving leadership.[79] Rigg and Varley had little trouble. Hazeltine and Sambrook recognized that the OBU had lost its popularity after the sympathetic strike epidemic had died out and were unwilling to fight a hopeless battle. On August 25 the trades council reaffirmed its affiliation with the international union movement and accepted the resignation of five executive members, including Sambrook and Hazeltine.[80] The OBU was beaten in Regina though it did not immediately disappear. Hazeltine and Sambrook continued to carry on propaganda work for another year and succeeded in organizing an OBU miscellaneous unit.

Rigg and Varley found little OBU support in the rest of the province. The officers of the Moose Jaw trades council supported the internationals. In Saskatoon serious internal division over an attempted sympathetic strike in May undermined OBU popularity. Rigg, however, was not complacent and warned Tom Moore that there was in Saskatchewan, as in the rest of western Canada, "a strong sense that the majority of the international union officials do not pay sufficient attention to this section and that the movement in general is seriously neglected."[81]

In Calgary and Edmonton, the situation was much

the same as in Saskatchewan. OBU councils functioned in both cities; that in Edmonton headed by Carl Berg; the one in Calgary by J. Hooley. The internationals had no trouble keeping their property or the allegiance of a majority of union members in both cities. In Calgary some contact between the two factions was maintained under the umbrella of the Dominion Labor Party, much to Farmilo's chagrin, but in Edmonton even this was not tolerated: a labour candidate for city council was forced to withdraw his name when AFL/TLC supporters pointed out that he was not a member of the international union.[82]

By January, 1920, the One Big Union no longer posed a real threat to the internationals in any western city except Winnipeg. There were tens of thousands of OBU members scattered across the country and in concentrations of OBU strength in places like Vancouver. One Big Union organizers such as P. M. Christophers, who resigned the leadership of the OBU Coal Miners District Board to become a paid organizer, continued to travel across the west speaking to local unions and trades councils, and continued to sign up One Big Union members. But the One Big Union had not chased the internationals from the west. In every important city the internationals defended themselves and survived. Even if the OBU was to win a definite majority of union members in western Canada, what would it accomplish? There was still the east and the United States. OBU victory depended on quick capture, intact, of the councils, federations and locals which already existed and the property that went with them. This had been the stated plan as far back as April, 1919. It had not succeeded.

The One Big Union's growing isolation was increased by its failure in central Canada. Joe Knight, OBU organizer in Ontario and Quebec, was convinced that "if the OBU [was] to conquer it must be prepared to throw its resources into the Eastern fight." Knight's first stop was Toronto. A struggle for control of the Toronto trades council between two factions held up his efforts. He was advised to "lie low" until the progressive faction, led by socialist James Simpson, won the election. But after Simpson won, he launched a vigorous attack on the OBU in the columns of the *Industrial Banner,* which he edited. Several trades council officials who had confided their sympathies for the OBU swung behind Simpson. Knight was disgusted. He thought about returning to the west but stayed in Toronto and organized a miscellaneous unit, two units of carpenters and a central council. The council was small but "composed of good fighters."

Knight had few good opportunities to spread the OBU message. Most doors were slammed in his face and the daily press was still engaged in the crusade against Bolshevism. He made a deal with the editor of the Hamilton-based *New Democracy,* who agreed to use his paper as the official eastern organ of the OBU in return for a guaranteed weekly sale of five thousand copies. But Knight had little money and, after six weeks, the paper closed.

From Toronto, Knight went to Montreal and found that an OBU council, which had been formed earlier, had collapsed. He spoke to several unions, distributed a great deal of literature and set up a new council. His work was handicapped by his lack of French and the timid attitude of the needle trades workers, "mostly Jews of many nationalities," who told him that if they joined the OBU, "the cry of alien organization [would] be raised immediately." Knight tried unsuccessfully to attract members from the British-based Amalgamated Society of Engineers, whose union was winding up its affairs in North America.[83]

The Montreal OBU was small but very radical. The intelligence department of Military District 4, responsible for Quebec, kept them under close surveillance. Regular meetings attracted several hundred English, French, Russian, Polish and Jewish workers who listened to speeches extolling the OBU and announcing the impending revolution.[84] Knight addressed them whenever in town, as did other visiting radicals from Canada and the United States, but for the most part local socialists such as Rebecca Buhay, described by one undercover agent as "an English Jewess, rather attractive in appearance and quite young, possibly 24 years of age," carried the ball. The local OBU members tried to organize workers in the railway shops and at the Vickers yards, but made little headway.

The Montreal OBU remained active, and was rewarded with the attention of at least four secret agents, but the Toronto OBU was, in one member's opinion, "a dead letter" by July, 1920. The OBU's general executive board continued to devote some attention to the east, and Knight and other organizers and speakers continued to travel there during 1920, but no progress was made. In Montreal the organization was, in reality, a cover for immigrant radicals, mostly Russians and Jews, who had little knowledge of the OBU. In Toronto the movement was soon dominated by "budding commisars," as Knight called them, who knew "more about the political and economic conditions of Russia than Lenin and less about the situation in Toronto than a Zulu." Knight was disappointed with the results of his trip, but urged his OBU colleagues not to abandon the east because that was where their "strength or weakeness" lay.

On the morning of January 26, 1920, the first regular convention of the One Big Union got underway in Winnipeg. The meeting had been postponed from October because of the trials of the Winnipeg general strike leaders. Twenty-four delegates, representing over 40 000 dues-paying members, gathered to consider the progress of the last six months and lay plans for the future. Midgley had issued over 47 000 membership cards and would have sent more out had the printers been able to keep up with the demand. The general executive board reported they had purchased 5 005 shares in the *Federationist* to ensure that the paper "conform with the policy of the O.B.U." Christophers, Kavanagh and Knight had carried out most of the organizing duties, but were hampered by a shortage of funds because many members were not paying dues.

No obvious difficulties emerged at the convention, aside from the dues problem, but the course of debate underlined the confusions that had emerged in the OBU at the local level. The Calgary central labour council introduced a resolution advocating reorganization "industrially," with six major departments such as mining, manufacturing and building, which was not unlike the structure of the IWW. It was tabled. Later, however, the meeting decided to put one member from each of the lumber workers, railway workers, coal miners and hardrock miners on the general executive board. Thus the delegates continued to waver between organizing the OBU into semi-autonomous industrial divisions and wiping out all internal distinctions by forcing members to pay their dues and owe their allegiance directly to the general executive board. The larger industrial divisions (referred to as district boards) were accorded unofficial, semi-autonomous, status with their representation on the general executive board, but nothing more. In elections Ernest Winch, Phillip Christophers, Tommy Roberts, Dick Johns, Joseph Naylor, W. H. C. Logan, W. H. Cottrell and Joe Knight were chosen for the board. Victor Midgley continued as secretary while W. A. Pritchard stayed as chairman.[85]

This convention, like almost every other union meeting in the west, international or OBU, passed a resolution condemning the trial and conviction of the Winnipeg general strike leaders. These trials, and the efforts of almost all unions to defend the men and provide for their families and legal expenses, were the last bond holding western labour together in common cause. It was a tie that the internationals had to break because, without exception, every one of the accused was a member of, or sympathizer with, the OBU.

The Winnipeg Defence Committee was created, soon after the general strike ended, to raise money for the arrested leaders. The committee was headed by an executive with both international and OBU men. It issued the *Workers' Defence Bulletin,* sent speakers from Winnipeg to every part of the country, and organized demonstrations and parades such as that held in Winnipeg on Labour Day in September, 1919, with over seven thousand marchers.[86] Contributions were regularly made to the committee from locals and councils antagonistic to the OBU such as those in Edmonton and Calgary. One anti-One Big Union machinist summed up the prevalent attitude: "The fact of being in different organizations [does not] in any way relieve us of our obligations to the brothers now in the clutches of the law. . . . we are united and undividable in demanding justice for Labor and fair and impartial treatment for our leaders."[87]

The strike leaders' trials dragged on until December, 1919, when all, with the exception of Heaps, were convicted. (Dixon, tried separately on charges laid by the provincial government, was found innocent in February, 1920.) As long as the trials were in progress, all those working on behalf of the strike leaders operated through the defence committee. When the trials ended, the internationals wanted to change tactics and put direct pressure on the federal government for the men's release. This could only be done by the Trades Congress.[88] Charges were soon made by P. M. Draper in Ottawa, Ernie Robinson in Winnipeg, and Alex Ross and W. Smitten in Calgary, that the defence committee was controlled by the OBU, spreading OBU propaganda and secretly channeling money into OBU coffers. Though the defence committee denied these charges, the Winnipeg trades council severed all connections with it in early April, 1920. They claimed that OBU representation on the committee meant that "antagonisms of the shop and factory have continually shewed [*sic*] themselves" and asserted that a combined movement of the Trades Congress and the international trade unions would secure better results.[89] Without the balance provided by the international union representatives, the defence committee was doomed. A Defence committee convention held a few days after the withdrawal passed resolutions threatening a two-day strike in Winnipeg every week until the men were released—an empty, quixotic threat at best.

Elsewhere, labour's civil war continued. The OBU was powerful in Winnipeg and, by the Trades Congress's own admission, still had considerable members amongst the railway shopmen at Port Mann, B.C., Saskatoon, Saskatchewan, and Fort Rouge and Transcona, Manitoba. The OBU also dominated the Port Arthur trades council and was strong amongst the Finnish and other foreign workers in the lakehead elevators. In Sault Ste Marie, Ontario, the steelworkers were strongly sympathetic to the OBU, and this was also true among smeltermen at Sudbury. Joe and Sarah Knight made Ontario their special domain, aided by Tom Cassidy who worked out of Windsor. OBU members persuaded the Carleton Place, Ontario, trades council to secede from the international union movement and attracted a Federal Labor Union in Pembroke, Ontario, into the OBU. In Montreal the OBU remained small but started up *The Worker/Le Travailleur,* published in French and English. Midgley reported to the federal department of labour that the OBU had, in 1920, 41 150 members in 101 branches mostly in the west. But, by the spring of

1920, the OBU had clearly ceased to be a force of any consequence in Calgary and Edmonton and was rapidly losing members in Vancouver.[90]

On May 10, 1920, a special conference of representatives of different Trades Congress affiliates met at Ottawa to consider some of the problems facing their unions. After a thorough examination of the labour picture in Canada, they concluded that the OBU had reached its zenith.[91] They had good reason. After one year, the days of sweeping OBU victories were over. The international unions were beginning to make progress in their drive to win back members, and the OBU's ability to withstand the counterattack was increasingly undermined by internal dissensions. The divisions among the OBU leaders which started to emerge in early 1920 may have resulted from a lack of strong hands at the helm—Russell, Johns and Pritchard were all languishing in prison. But the difficulties were mostly due to the leadership's continuing failure to define the basis upon which the OBU was to be organized and what role the major industrial units, such as the coal miners and loggers, were to play.

The dispute which eventually tore the OBU apart was triggered by the success of the Lumber Workers. The unit had grown to over 12 000 members by January, 1920, and had won many improvements in camp conditions. The rapid expansion brought many members of the Industrial Workers of the World into the union, and conflict grew between them and the Lumber Workers' leadership headed by Ernest Winch. Winch managed to beat back an IWW challenge at the union's January, 1920, convention but the threat was only temporarily averted and bitter internal conflict continued. The infighting grew so serious that a special committee was appointed to bring some of the plots and attempted character assassinations into the open.[92] But even though Winch had no intention of knuckling under to the

IWW, he must have realized that they had considerable claim on the emotional allegiance of many loggers with their long history of struggle in Canada and the United States, their legacy of martyrs such as Frank Little, Wesley Everest, and Joe Hill, their pantheon of colorful characters such as "T. Bone Slim" and Sam Scarlett, and their morale-boosting ditties printed in the famous "Little Red Song Book." There was considerable pressure, therefore, for him to tacitly adopt IWW positions.[93]

The union's expansion also caused it to move outside the logging camps and into the lumber mills and harvest fields. This was a natural evolution for any organization of this type because the logging labour force was always on the move from harvest field to forest to mill. In July, 1920, the union changed its name to Lumber, Camp and Agricultural Workers Department of the One Big Union.[94] This worried Midgley. He thought the Loggers were beginning to organize workers which were properly in the fold of the OBU itself and fretted about an attempt to capture the entire OBU.[95] These worries were not reasonable but were fueled by a growing personality conflict between himself and Winch and by different views on what the OBU should be like. Midgley believed that true OBU principles could only be followed if every worker was first and foremost a member of the OBU and the organization itself was only informally divided into geographic districts for convenience sake. Winch believed the OBU should have a structure not unlike the IWW with every worker belonging to the industrial department best suited to his work and, through that department, the One Big Union itself.[96]

The second convention of the One Big Union was due in October, 1920, at Port Arthur. Winch was not happy about the location, because he wanted to send as many delegates as possible, and tried unsuccessfully to have the meeting moved to a more westerly point. There were rumours that Joe Knight was going to try to shift the OBU's headquarters from Vancouver to Winnipeg to be more in touch with the east. Winch opposed this too. Midgley and Winch each thought the other was trying to oust him from the OBU's leadership. Midgley turned out to be the better plotter. His weapon was money.

The One Big Union was in financial difficulties. Though more than seventy thousand membership cards had been issued, less than half the members were keeping up with their dues.[97] One of the most delinquent organizations was the Lumber Workers who had stretched their financial resources beyond the breaking point. They were maintaining executive offices in Vancouver with branch offices in Fort William, Le Pas, Sudbury and Montreal. They were contributing substantial amounts to the *Federationist,* the *Searchlight* (a Calgary paper), the *One Big Union Bulletin,* and *The Worker/Le Travailleur* in Montreal. They had also spent far too much on recent conventions. Midgley took advantage of this and issued a circular establishing the basis on which delegates to the Port Arthur convention would be seated—actual per capita paid.[98] The lumber workers were at this time $2 100 in arrears. When the convention opened on September 20, 1920, seven delegates from the Coast District of the Lumber Workers were seated but Winch, along with two other delegates, was refused accreditation. After discussions, which lasted until the next day, failed to resolve the dispute, the loggers pulled out of the convention and resolved not to be bound by any of its decisions. Winch had been dethroned. When elections were held for the general executive board, his name was absent.

The OBU convention proceeded as if nothing unusual had happened. Midgley reported on the financial problem. He claimed that members were paying their dues directly to central councils and district boards which were using the money for their own purposes and not passing it on to headquarters. He urged that dues be paid directly to the general executive board in future. This would also reduce the power of the district boards and central councils, and increase the power of the executive, though he did not say so. Midgley also recommended moving the headquarters to Winnipeg, as was rumoured because, he claimed, it was more central.

This convention marked a clear victory for those opposed to industrial unionism. A resolution passed unanimously which called for the creation of one central office through which all OBU members would conduct their business. Another resolution, repeating the proposal made by the Calgary membership the previous January to organize the OBU into definite industrial departments, was defeated. The preamble to the constitution was changed and all reference to organizing workers according to industry was deleted.[99] In this way "industrial unionism," which to most workers meant "organization by industry" whether in a highly centralized union such as the IWW or in an independent organization such as the United Mine Workers, was disposed of. The whole history of the OBU demonstrated that in the minds of the Socialist Party ideologues, this had never been a serious concern. The drive for industrial unionism had been a major component of the workers' revolt to begin with, but that revolt had been channeled by Midgley, Pritchard, Russell and their allies into the creation of the One Big Union. The struggle had come full circle.

The split between the One Big Union and the loggers grew wider in the weeks following the convention. Reams of paper were devoted to the battle as the principals aired their views in public and spread the blood of the OBU into the open for all to see. OBU men were whistling in the graveyard with their assertions that the split was not serious and that most loggers agreed with the convention's decisions. One result was the loss of

Carl Berg. He supported Winch against Midgley and Knight, whom he had little love for. He repudiated the executive of the OBU in December, 1920, and the small One Big Union organization in Edmonton was split in two. Berg had great influence amongst the foreign workers in the northern part of the province,[100] and his loss was bound to hurt the organization.

On January 17, 1921, the loggers opened their own convention at Vancouver. The executive reported to the delegates what had transpired at Port Arthur and, after much discussion about the future of the organization, the convention passed a resolution to withdraw from the OBU and form "a Lumber Workers Industrial Union of Canada until such time as the One Big Union conforms to the principles of democratic industrial unionism." A referendum, designed to back up the executive's actions, already in progress but in which only 1600 loggers had voted, was ordered continued.[101] The split was complete and, at one blow, the OBU lost approximately one-quarter of its members. Midgley had few regrets. He claimed the loggers had been only loosely attached to the OBU for some time and attributed their action to "a mass of undigested syndicalist propaganda." He predicted the Lumber Workers' experiment would fail because "an effective working class organization cannot recognise divisions of either craft or industry."[102]

The Lumber Workers did decline. In January, 1924, the union, a shadow of its former self, applied for membership in the Trades and Labor Congress and was turned down.[103] Internal division between pro-and anti-IWW factions, the state of the lumber economy and the continuing drive of the operators against trade unionism took their toll. Not until the rise of the International Woodworkers of America in B.C. in the 1940s would the loggers find the organization they had sought for so long. But the OBU also declined. The loss of the

Fools and Wise Men

Lumber Workers, their "chief strength" in the opinion of Tom Moore, was a serious blow from which there could be no recovery. In pursuit of the dream that had inspired the Socialist Party members from the very beginning, Midgley and his allies gave up any realistic possibility that the OBU would continue to be a force of real consequence in Canadian trade unionism. The workers' revolt was betrayed, not deliberately, but by an unreasonable fixation with an impractical and unrealizable form of organization.

Chapter 7

Invading the United States

The One Big Union was never meant to be a national organization. No one advocating the OBU ever objected to the idea that a union should reach across international boundaries and OBU leaders were determined to do just that. Midgley was confident the movement would "ultimately cover the entire North American continent,"[1] while Pritchard believed success in the United States was vitally necessary to the cause. As Alex Ross had scornfully pointed out in the Calgary trades council in April, 1919, an OBU restricted to western Canada would not be a One Big Union at all but a "dinky little union" with a handful of members. There was, therefore, never any question that the OBU would, at the right moment, become an "international" union itself.

That moment came in April, 1919. Workers in the United States' Pacific northwest, and particularly Seattle, Washington, had been increasingly restless for some time. There was strong IWW influence in the area because of the proximity of the extensive logging industry around Puget Sound, while the young and bustling city of Seattle attracted thousands of workers prepared to make their fortune on the northwest frontier in much the same fashion as those settling in the cities of western Canada. The labour movement, though nominally loyal to Samuel Gompers and the American Federation of Labor, displayed disquieting signs of independence. The most dramatic of these was the general strike of February 6 to 10, 1919, called by the Seattle central labor council in support of shipyard workers locked in a dispute with the government-owned Emergency Fleet Corporation. This walkout was strongly condemned by the AFL, which also took partial credit for ending it to the disgust of many in the Seattle labour movement.[2] But the general strike was only one sign of Seattle's refusal to play by AFL rules. Another was "Duncanism," named for central labour council secretary James A. Duncan, which stood for strong control of local unions by the council, close cooperation amongst kindred trades and efforts to get agreements in a single industry to expire at the same time.[3] In a campaign launched by the central labour council in early March, 1919, this informal system was standardized into the Duncan Plan to reform the American Federation of Labor from within. The proposition called upon AFL members to vote on the reorganization of the Federation into twelve industrial units to provide the unions with a more effective strike weapon. Thus, there was significant dissatisfaction with the AFL in Seattle just when western Canadian

workers were rising in revolt against the Gompers system. It was natural for some Seattle workers to look with
more than passing interest at the One Big Union.

When OBU leaders received inquiries about their
campaign from Seattle they decided to go there to tell
their story. Pritchard and Midgley appeared before the
central labour council in April to speak about the OBU
and received great applause when they declared that "a
class conscious labor movement must at once take the
place of the old craft form of organization in which one
set of workers are pitted against . . . another."[4] The
council did not debate the merits of the OBU at that
time, but Midgley left with the belief that Seattle would
eventually break from the AFL. On the same trip Pritchard spoke to a large group of longshoremen and
plans were laid for a later expedition to Tacoma.

Though Midgley and Pritchard did not realize it, they
were getting themselves into the midst of a local argument over the Duncan Plan. Harry Ault, editor of the
daily *Seattle Union Record*, backed the Plan and tried to
make it appear that Pritchard and Midgley did also.
After the B.C. duo departed Seattle, Ault published an
article which gave the impression that Pritchard approved of the scheme. "If the Duncan plan succeeds,"
he was purported to have said, "we will be back in the
reorganized A.F. of L. almost automatically."[5] This
story upset OBU supporters in Seattle who quickly
wrote Pritchard to let him know what was happening.
They insisted he send a letter of denial as soon as possible and that he send it not to Ault whom they referred
to as a "God Damn Labor Faker" but directly to them
for insertion in the paper. This Pritchard did, declaring: "Since . . . time is denied us, and the problem demands, and will continue to demand, immediate action,
it seems . . . the height of folly to expect any sudden
move [to reform] on the part of the A.F. of L."[6]

When Canadians appeared before Washington labour bodies to talk about the One Big Union, they were essentially outsiders, at the mercy of rules and gavel. But when they participated in meetings as delegates their influence was bound to be greater. It was, in fact, as representatives to the convention of the Pacific Coast District of the International Longshoreman's Association in May, 1919, that they were able to firmly plant the OBU seed in Seattle soil. Joseph Taylor of Victoria was district president, while other Canadians, including Jack Kavanagh, were in attendance. Kavanagh was determined to "use his influence on behalf of the OBU" following Pritchard and Midgley's foray in April and, given the honour of delivering one of the convention's opening addresses, told the gathering about the OBU and outlined the plan upon which it proposed to operate.[7] He also took advantage of his presence in the city to address the Seattle central labour council. After explaining why western Canadian workers were resorting to secession, he claimed that the "one big union idea [was] growing by leaps and bounds, and had applications for membership from local unions from the Atlantic to the Pacific Coast." Even though he attacked the council's pet Duncan Plan, he was "listened to with great interest" and received "much applause."[8]

Kavanagh and the other Canadian delegates were successful. The ILA convention went on record "in favour of forming an industrial union patterned after the British Columbia One Big Union" and declared its intention of submitting an OBU proposal to all ILA, dock work, and marine transport unions on the coast. Taylor issued a circular to all members explaining the action and outlining the structural layout of the proposed American OBU. He claimed this had nothing to do with the IWW and noted that the Canadians who had met at Calgary the previous March as well as the delegates to the Coast ILA convention were "men who had been in the Trade Union Movement for many years."[9]

Having been converted, the Longshoremen now set out to spread the word. In late May they asked the Seattle central labour council to consider Canada's "secession movement," but the council was not yet ready to entertain such notions and, instead, resolved to ignore "all communications and persons advocating secession from the A.F. of L."[10] But this was only a temporary setback for the OBU. The big prize was the State Federation of Labor itself, and OBU supporters made considerable effort to send a large delegation to the Federation's annual convention scheduled to open in Bellingham, Washington, on June 16, 1919. William Short, president of the Federation, warned Frank Morrison that One Big Union advocates planned to control the Federation and capture the executive. As the convention drew near, policy and ideological issues were increasingly boiled down to a fight over the executive election in which Short and Charles Perry Taylor, Federation secretary, represented "the more conservative element" while Thomas Russell of Tacoma and L. W. Buck of Seattle were the 'progressive' candidates.[11]

Monday, June 16, 1919, the Washington State Federation of Labor met in its eighteenth annual convention. Delegates were in a boisterous mood and feeling somewhat defiant of AFL authority. On the first morning they voted to support Seattle Local 40 of the Operating Engineers against its international officers who had suspended the local's business agent for boosting the Duncan Plan and advocating general strikes. It was clear from the discussion that many delegates were really using the opportunity to show their support for the February general strike.

Canada received considerable attention at this meeting. Jack Kavanagh was back, this time in his capacity as president of the British Columbia Federation of Labor, to tell the convention about the Canadian strike situation. He claimed that the Canadian government did not dare put troops into Winnipeg and Vancouver because it could not trust its own soldiers. He declared that the sympathetic strikes were directed "against the government of Canada" because it had interfered on the side of the employers. The convention answered his appeals for help with a "heavy collection" and a pledge of "full moral and financial support to the general strikers of Winnipeg, Vancouver and all Canadian cities."[12]

In the executive elections William Short was returned but Charles Perry Taylor was defeated by L. W. Buck. This was not, however, a clear victory for the 'progressive' bloc because Taylor, a paid AFL organizer, had made many personal enemies over the years and Buck, a socialist, was not of the "ultra-radical type" as Short put it. On the last day of the convention, however, when many Short-supporters had departed,[13] the 'progressives' scored their major victory. A resolution proposed by Harry Wright, Tacoma longshoreman and secretary of the Pacific Coast District of the ILA, which called for a referendum on the holding of a One Big Union conference, was adopted by a wide margin despite the opposition of the resolutions committee.[14] Short's fears had been realized; the One Big Union campaign was launched.

Though Wright and other OBU supporters borrowed much of their ideas and terminology from Canada, there was no actual connection between the Canadian and Washington OBU. Canadian speakers supported it, gave their ideas to it and, in part, provided the example but they could not give real leadership nor lend financial aid. It was vital to their interests to see the One Big Union succeed in Washington, but they were too fully preoccupied with their own battle north of the border to do anything but cheer from the sidelines.

By mid-July, after one false start, the State Federation's executive council settled the referendum details and printing and distribution of ballots began. The One

Big Union issue was, as Harry Ault observed, the most important question that had faced Washington labour in a long time and the debate heated up as the voting began. There was bitter division. In a stormy two-hour session of the Tacoma central labour council a motion was introduced to spend council funds to spread the referendum message. Conservatives demanded a roll call vote while OBU supporters, led by Harry Wright, threatened to use the council newspaper against them. Many OBU opponents stormed out of the meeting and warned they would withdraw their unions if any money was spent on OBU propaganda. The council president struck a compromise by ordering AFL organizer Louis Beard to speak at local meetings about the importance of the referendum. This fight over funds was echoed several days later in a Seattle Machinist Lodge where it was charged that money raised to support Canadian strikers was being channeled into the OBU.

To facilitate an exchange of views, Ault opened the columns of the *Seattle Union Record* to different expressions of opinion. Harry Wright used the opportunity to explain that the movement in Washington was "entirely different in its inception and fundamentally different in nearly every way from that of Canada." The proposition was not intended to lead to secession. He claimed the labour movement could, and should, be reformed from within, but thousands of workers were calling for change of some kind and it was better to thrash the issues out at a conference than to allow real splits to take place. Wright denied that the OBU was connected in any way with the IWW, but even if it was, he reasoned, this would not be cause to oppose it any more than an American flag should be thrown away because it was made of Japanese silk. His OBU would organize the unorganized, reconstruct the labour movement along industrial lines, assure that agreements in kindred trades expired at the same time, eliminate jurisdictional squabbles and establish a universal transfer card.[15] Above all it would never secede.

Wright's was the very voice of moderation and reason, but Short was not convinced. He pointed out that if the resolution passed, a convention would be called to form "One Big Union along industrial lines." This meant secession which, he warned, meant failure and defeat. The resolution voted upon at Bellingham, he charged, was an "exact copy of the one introduced in the Calgary conference which brought about the Western Canadian OBU."[16] Charles Perry Taylor supported Short: "We don't want any OBU. What we want is closer affiliation. The colored gentlemen in the woodpile [is] the IWW . . . The OBU is on a par with the general sympathetic strike in Seattle, which, as the Union Record said, is going 'no one knows where.' "[17]

Wright disavowed secession and claimed that he had never seen the Calgary OBU resolution but the charge was the most effective weapon OBU opponents could use. Robert Harlin, president of District 10 of the United Mine Workers, speculated that Wright was acting for other individuals who hoped "by trickery" to secure a favourable vote. If there were moves afoot to stampede the membership, he threatened, a day of reckoning would come.[18]

While the battle over the referendum was raging in Washington, hardrock miners in Butte, Montana, climbed on the One Big Union bandwagon and in late June, began to lay plans for an OBU convention. Labour councils in the northwest were invited to send delegates to discuss the feasibility of forming a state OBU in Montana preliminary to the establishment of a national One Big Union. Frank Morrison reacted quickly. He warned the Silver Bow trades and labour council in Butte not to send delegates to the meeting and to withdraw credentials already issued, and he sent as many international organizers as possible into the area.

Gompers threw his weight into the battle with messages to the presidents of the Machinists, Boilermakers and Electrical Workers seeking their aid in maintaining the integrity of their unions. But even with these efforts the convention went ahead. *The Butte Miner* welcomed "Bolsheviki" delegates from Canada and the Pacific Coast, and Joe Knight delivered the keynote address. There was no IWW representation at the meeting, even though theirs was the largest miners' union in the area, but one local IWW leader who was invited told the meeting that his union would not cooperate with the OBU. Despite the threat, a metal miners' unit was formed and there was discussion of linking the OBU of Washington and Montana.[19]

With the OBU challenge now moving south of the Canadian border, the AFL intervened. After obtaining an assessment of the situation in the State of Washington from Short, Morrison canvassed AFL executive council members to seek their advice. James Duncan (no relation to the Seattle central labour council secretary) suggested that the State Federation be ordered to cease the referendum immediately or have its charter revoked and placed in the hands of a special delegate. W. D. Mahon believed any organization holding an AFL charter had no right to submit such a referendum to its membership and should be expelled from the AFL for doing so. He urged Morrison to take a firm stand and bring the "one big union nightmare to a close as soon as possible." Matthew Woll echoed his fears: "We must prevent the poison now injected in the movement of the northwest from spreading to other parts and we must put out the smouldering fires now raging in that part of the country which may at some future time blaze up into a great conflagration in many of our industrial centers."[20]

On August 2, 1919, Morrison sent a toughly-worded letter to the State Federation. He reminded them of their statutory obligations according to the AFL constitution and told them that the Washington State Federation of Labor had "ignored its pledge to recognize and support the principle of the autonomy of the National and International unions." The State Federation had no authority to assume powers that belonged solely to the individual unions that comprised the AFL, Morrison wrote. If the referendum now underway was not immediately halted, the AFL executive council would revoke the State Federation's charter, establish "a bona fide state organization" in its place and seek to have the national and international unions affiliate with the new State Federation.[21]

The order, coming as an edict from Olympus, created almost as much dissension in Washington State as the referendum. Short, who had opposed the OBU movement all along, was upset by the abruptness of the ultimatum. He had assured Morrison earlier that things would not get out of hand and had asked that the state labour movement be allowed to handle the matter in its own way because he was confident that the "level headed unionists would steer . . . . through the dangerous channel without disruption.[22] Harry Ault sympathized with this view and believed the AFL executive council had been misled by the resolution's wording into believing it was a move toward secession. In a front page editorial he appealed for calm assessment of the new realities facing labour in Washington and suggested another referendum calling for a conference to discuss closer affiliation, the high cost of living and other matters.

The Seattle central labour council was not about to give in to AFL dictation. At its August 13 meeting it considered a resolution submitted by the Longshoremen condemning the AFL action and demanding a continuation of the referendum. There was an attempt, supported by L. W. Buck, to sidestep a vote on the motion

by passing it directly to the executive of the State Federation, but this was easily defeated and the resolution
passed. Some council delegates maintained that federation officers could not ignore council demands even
though compliance with the motion could well mean secession. The State Federation was now caught between
the Seattle labour movement and the American Federation.[23]

The following day the State Federation executive met
to decide its future course. Faced with the power of the
AFL, uncertain of the extent of grass roots support for
the OBU and with serious internal opposition to the entire referendum, they gave way. Letters, telegrams and
resolutions from locals and councils condemning the
AFL were to no avail and a motion was unanimously
adopted to obey Morrison's instructions. But they did
not submit meekly. They told Morrison they would go
along because, as officers of the AFL, they had no
choice, but they objected to the way the matter had been
handled. They asserted they should have been con-
sulted about the order and expected such consideration
in future. The OBU referendum issue was being handled satisfactorily prior to the AFL's interference, they
claimed, and would have been resolved without disruption. Now, they charged, there would be serious difficulties: "Your action . . . has precipitated a situation that
will require the most careful handling to avoid serious
injury to both state and national bodies. We regret your
action exceedingly, and sincerely trust that in future . . .
you will at least ask for advice from . . . those of us who
are on the grounds here."[24]

With the State Federation's surrender, opposition to
the AFL faded rapidly. The last battle was fought in the
Seattle central labour council the evening of August 20,
1919. OBU supporters condemned the State Federation
executive's action and demanded that the council stop
its per capita payments. A letter from Harry Wright

urged that the Seattle and Tacoma central labour councils continue the vote and proceed to organize the OBU themselves if the majority of the rank and file so decided.[25] But Wright and his supporters could defeat Short and his, including L. W. Buck and James Duncan. The final vote on the resolution to sustain the State Executive's action passed by a wide margin, even though the One Big Union advocates had, in Morrison's words, "considerable following."[26] The OBU in Washington had been dealt a fatal blow.

Given the vicious battle raging north of the border, the One Big Union had been dispatched with little fuss. In part this was due to the strong oposition of William Short and his executive to the OBU—even L. W. Buck never defended the referendum. Their indignation over Morrison's order to halt the voting may have been genuine but it also helped keep rank and file support behind them. And they, after all, were committed to the AFL and to carrying out its orders. But failure also resulted from the timid tactics of the OBU supporters. Harry Wright claimed from the start that he was not a secessionist and that the Washington OBU could be built inside the larger American Federation of Labor. Thus the One Big Union was presented as an alternative to the Duncan Plan. Perhaps this was because he and his allies believed that the workers of Washington wanted reform but would never agree to secession; certainly almost all the actions, pronouncements and editorials of the state craft union movement pointed to a desire for change short of revolt. But in trying to sell the OBU as nothing more than a reorganization of the State Federation within the AFL, Wright probably alienated the IWW-oriented radicals who demanded more while scaring the 'moderates' who wanted less. Under the circumstances it was impossible for the OBU advocates to build a strong enough base of support to oust the state federation leadership and defy the authority of the AFL executive council.

Despite the setback, the One Big Union continued its efforts elsewhere in the United States. Isolated OBU supporters spread literature here and plastered stickers there. Jack Kavanagh was sent to California but was hindered by the almost universal confusion of the OBU with the IWW. In September, 1919, Bob Russell went to Chicago to help a small group of dissident shopmen set up a local OBU unit. The men were angry at their leaders for ordering an end to a strike the previous month and decided to begin a secret OBU organizing drive in the city's railway shops and roundhouses. But despite these efforts, and despite the brave hopes of some that an American stampede to the OBU was imminent, only five units were operating in the entire country by the end of October,[27] and only one—the Butte metal miners unit—sent a delegate to the January, 1920 convention in Winnipeg.[28]

The big push began in the spring of 1920. Tom Cassidy was ordered into Chicago to organize amongst the city's railway shopcraft workers. He arrived on Friday, April 23 and immediately began to make contact with friends and supporters throughout the city. The next few days were filled with speeches—to representatives of OBU railway workers, to shopmen at the Northwestern Roundhouse, to secessionist machinists who called themselves the Amalgamated Metal Workers. At one point he secured a set of false credentials and snuck "incognito" into a gathering of Illinois Central sheet metal workers, but when he tried again at a meeting of Chicago, Eastern and Illinois Railroad carmen, he was thrown out. After one week's efforts, Cassidy left Chicago on May 1.[29] Midgley was elated with his accomplishments and the general executive board wired him to go back to Chicago as soon as possible to continue his work in the railway shops.

OBU organizing also continued on the Pacific Coast with most attention focused on the San Francisco Bay Area. Two editions of the *O.B.U. Bulletin of Oakland,* affiliated with the "One Big Union Movement of America," were issued during a shipyard strike. The first issue proclaimed, "this organization does not advocate any acts of sabotage, violence or terrorism,"[30] in an obvious effort to allay fears that the One Big Union was really the IWW in disguise. The tactic did not work. In Oakland a party of unknown men raided OBU headquarters and damaged typewriters and office furniture, while in San Francisco five OBU members were jailed on charges of vagrancy after police raided their office. In Los Angeles, the state attorney set out to prove that the IWW and the OBU were the same organization.[31]

The IWW had used the name "One Big Union" unofficially for years. Throughout this period it continued to maintain that it was the true OBU and that workers should join its ranks to build the One Big Union. The confusion, in the public mind, of the two organizations was a continuing problem for the One Big Union in the United States. In fact, the IWW was enthusiastic about the appearance of the OBU in the spring of 1919 and thought the new union's program was enough like its own to allow both to forget the differences. They urged that the report of the Western Labor Conference be put in pamphlet form and distributed throughout the United States.[32] But this attitude quickly changed as the IWW realized that the OBU was not a close, or even a distant, cousin and was determined to keep itself free of IWW influences. In July, 1920, "Wandering Wobbly" charged that the OBU was "safely in the hands of a very few doctrinaire Canadian and English 'commodity struggle' socialists who seemed to want the workers to think the [OBU was] the same as the IWW and the authorities to think that it was not."[33] In the fight between the loggers and the OBU executive, the IWW quite naturally sided with the former. They derided the concept of geographically-based organization and called OBU leaders "politico-geographical opportunists."[34]

Despite opposition from the IWW on the left, the AFL on the right and local government officials and employers on every hand, the general executive board in Canada felt confident enough about OBU progress in the United States to urge American members, particularly the Chicago railwaymen, to hold their own founding convention and set up their own financial/administrative structure to take control of OBU units in that country.[35] The meeting was held at Chicago June 29 and 30, 1920, when forty-three delegates, claimed by the One Big Union to represent 40 000 workers in California, Montana, the midwest and the east, gathered at the Briggs House to launch the American OBU. A nine-member general executive board was elected with members from Buffalo, New York; Sioux City, Iowa; Altoona, Pennsylvania; Moline, Illinois; Madison, Wisconsin; Milwaukee, Wisconsin; Great Falls, Montana, and Chicago. Convention chairman R. M. Kephart, a machinist, claimed in his keynote address that railway units, one of which contained five hundred members, had been organized on five railroads in the Chicago area, and that the OBU could count over three thousand adherents in the city. The press was excluded from the meeting "to express [the delegates'] supreme contempt for these inmates of the journalistic houses of prostitution." Little time was spent agonizing over a constitution since the Canadian version was adopted word for word.[36] The convention did not exactly throw the AFL leadership into a panic. Morrison was sceptical that it had even taken place, even though he received the proceedings from an AFL organizer in Pittsburgh, and distributed copies to the AFL executive council and Tom Moore.[37]

Whatever the real state of the OBU in the United States midwest in the summer of 1920, a full-time organizer was needed on the spot if any progress was to be made at all. Accordingly, Tom Cassidy arrived back in

185

Chicago in the third week of June and resumed his speaking and organizing efforts amongst the railway workers. After the founding convention he went to Gary, Indiana, to launch an OBU campaign among the city's steelworkers, but his efforts were cut short by growing OBU financial difficulties. Midgley was having great trouble collecting dues and in mid-August called Cassidy back to Canada "owing to lack of funds."[38] He was later to return to Chicago for a brief period but was never again able to resume full-time organizing in the United States. After Cassidy's departure, the OBU in Chicago began to deteriorate rapidly. The so-called general executive board of the United States OBU, based at Chicago, simply disappeared while the secretary of one of the railroad units helped himself to the unit's treasury.[39]

Through all this adversity, the OBU in Canada clung to the dream of a flourishing movement challenging the AFL on its home ground. In the midst of a depression that gripped Canada and the United States from October, 1920 to the winter of 1921, the *One Big Union Bulletin* claimed American workers were "coming over to the OBU."[40] while the *Federationist* predicted "a landslide to the OBU as soon as the unemployment situation improve[d]."[41] This dream prompted continued efforts in San Francisco where a group of secessionist workers labelling themselves the Rank and File Movement were won over to the OBU in January, 1924. But the most peculiar story of continued OBU involvement in the United States focuses on the mill town of Lawrence, Massachusetts.

Lawrence had become a by-word among American workers during an IWW-led strike of textile workers in 1911. It was a long and bitter campaign sustained by sacrifice and sheer guts which saw strikers send their children to live with sympathizers in other cities and IWW leaders jailed. The IWW won the strike, in part because of a rare display of public sympathy, and Lawrence earned a permanent place for itself in the annals of the American labour movement. In late 1920 a group of workers, aided by volunteer organizer Ben Legere, formed an OBU unit which became one of the most active of the small American OBU.

Legere was a Hollywood actor and a former Wobbly. He and his wife, Barbara Parrington, also an actor, earned a living from plays and movies and both devoted two months every summer to work—free—for the OBU. Legere had been touring western Canada with a road company when the OBU was being launched in the spring of 1919 and quickly became a supporter. A good speaker, he used his acting talents to "put it on dramatically," in Russell's words.

In April, 1922 thousands of unorganized workers in Lawrence struck to protest a wage reduction. The OBU in Canada launched an appeal for funds and the Winnipeg central labour council sent an initial donation of $100.[42] From this point on the Canadian OBU became increasingly responsible for the financial support of the Lawrence unit as well as another textile workers unit established in nearby Dover, New Hampshire. When Legere was busy with acting or organizing for the OBU in places as far removed as California and Cape Breton, Bert Elmsley directed affairs in New England. The Lawrence unit managed to launch a newspaper, *Lawrence Labor,* but could only sustain it with financial backing from Winnipeg.[43]

In the spring of 1924 the IWW reappeared in New England. OBU members in Lawrence remembered the past associations of their town with the Wobblies and decided to cooperate. In the words of Bert Elmsley, "our differences . . . are on matters of structure, secondary matters, not in revolutionary purpose and working class solidarity."[44] On April 4, the unit resolved to "extend a cordial invitation to the IWW to come to Lawrence and

hold a meeting with the co-operation of the OBU."
Elmsley told the IWW that "the OBU was ready to meet
[them] in a spirit of solidarity."[45] This alliance was the
beginning of an IWW effort to swallow up the OBU in
New England.[46] There was not much left to digest. The
American OBU had been, for some time, little more
than a mirage in the minds of leaders sitting at Executive Board meetings in Winnipeg, half a continent
away.

Chapter 8

Battle for the Mining Frontier

The Hardrock Miners

The One Big Union had many enemies in the hardrock mining country of British Columbia, but few were as tough and determined as Selwyn Gwillyn Blaylock, general manager of the Consolidated Mining and Smelting Company. Cominco, with headquarters at Trail, was the largest corporation in the region and had been founded by Canadian Pacific to develop mining and smelting properties acquired in 1897 when plans for the Crows Nest Pass line were being laid. It had access to

189

cheap and dependable transportation and valuable ore discoveries, and after a long-term agreement was concluded with the Crows Nest Pass Coal Company to supply fuel for its smelters, rapidly became lord of the B.C. interior.

Blaylock's star rose with the company. He was born in Quebec, and educated at McGill University. He came west in 1899 to work as an assayer in the Trail smelter. He was soon promoted to chief chemist, and supervised several Cominco-owned mines and smelters. He became assistant general manager in 1911 and general manager in early 1919. He was a rugged man who enjoyed hunting and fishing amongst the peaks in which his mines and smelters nestled, and was not unlike many other professional managers in his intense dislike of unions. In 1917 he inflicted a humiliating defeat on the International Union of Mine, Mill and Smelter Workers during a strike at Trail.

Blaylock hated the One Big Union. He ordered miners carrying OBU cards locked out of Consolidated mines at Rossland in May, 1919, before the mass secession to the OBU had started. When the OBU, led by T. B. "Tommy" Roberts, approached the company for a dollar-a-day wage increase in early September, 1919, Blaylock refused to talk to them and within a few days the Sullivan, Tunnel and North Star mines at Kimberly—all Consolidated properties—were struck.[1] But the men were in trouble from the start. An influenza epidemic of the previous fall and winter had drained the treasuries of the local unions and miners were short of strike funds. After two weeks the district Dominion Fair Wage Officer tried to arrange a settlement, but Blaylock refused to have anything to do with the One Big Union and insisted that his men sign a written repudiation of the OBU before he would allow them back to work. He announced that he would run his own business and would not be dictated to "by any organization of muck pile orators."[2] The men refused to give him the assurances he demanded and the strike continued.

On October 9, Blaylock ordered the miners in Kimberly off company property. There were about fifty families and the men decided to stand fast rather than undergo the hardship of dispossession. That same day a group of strikers, reinforced by a contingent of OBU loggers, met a train from the east carrying a small group of strikebreakers. Fifty had started out from Winnipeg, but the prospect of trouble discouraged most as they headed west and less than twenty arrived at Kimberly. After leaving the train, they nervously passed a few "pleasantries" with the strikers, claimed their baggage and hurried aboard the same train just before it pulled out of the station.[3]

But this was a small victory in a large campaign. The Sullivan and North Star mines had large ore reserves from before the shutdown, and continued to ship to the Trail smelter during October while the trickle of strikebreakers recruited by Consolidated grew with each passing day. By November, 1919, production was almost back to pre-strike levels. Mining continued at Nelson, the smelters and concentrators were operating at Trail and about two hundred non-union miners were working at Rossland. The zinc plant at Kimberly curtailed some of its operations, but the company imported ore and concentrates from elsewhere to keep it going.[4] As fall became winter and the snow and cold isolated the small towns and camps, production slowed to a crawl. Hundreds of miners and smeltermen tramped up and down the valleys looking for work, and they, together with the strikebreakers, provided all the manpower Blaylock needed to replace the hated OBU strikers.

There was little hope for the OBU through the dead of winter. The Sullivan mine continued to ship ore to the smelter at Trail, while the Rossland mines were shut down by the depressed market. By February all hope for victory was gone and the strike was ended March 1, 1920. The OBU was forced to admit its failure.[5] A former executive officer of the international commented sarcastically: "[Their] general strike weapon had inadvertently been left in a damp place and got rusty and when [they] finally got it cleaned and oiled it was too late, and so another golden opportunity slipped by."[6]

Despite the defeat, Roberts and the OBU prepared to do battle again. This time the enemy was twenty-five mines situated in the Slocan district between Nakusp and Castlegar, British Columbia. The companies refused to meet a demand for a dollar-a-day increase and 400 miners struck on May 1, 1920. Three operators, including the large Silversmith mine, signed agreements with the OBU to raise wages fifty cents a day, supply blankets to the men, and comply with the Health Regulation Act in every detail. All the others stood firm[7] and nine of them opened negotiations with Anthony Shilland, representative of the Mine, Mill and Smelter Workers in New Denver, B.C. The miners themselves played no part in the discussions. An agreement was quickly reached granting a seventy-five-cents-a-day increase (with twenty-five cents of this returning to the companies for board), and stipulating that the operators would, "insofar as practical," hire their men through the nearest Mine, Mill local. OBU members would have to renounce their affiliation before working. This agreement was not presented to the miners for ratification but was, instead, accepted by Mine, Mill president Charles Moyers who wired his approval from Los Angeles.[8] Since the nine operators also agreed to comply with the Health Regulation Act, the major difference between this and the OBU settlement, aside from the closed shop clause, was the supply of blankets. The Mine, Mill declared the strike ended on May 18, 1920, while the OBU threw pickets around mines at Silverton and Sandon. Roberts claimed only twelve men in the district had returned to work, and vowed to fight "to a finish."

The operators were armed with a contract which gave official Mine, Mill sanction to the importation and use of strikebreakers—every scab working in a Slocan mine was to be blessed with Mine, Mill membership. OBU supporters throughout the region were forced to keep a sharp eye out for strikebreakers. Fortunately for them, there were only a few routes to cover. Rail connections were poor and the best way to move men into the strike district was to use the boats plying the waters of Lake Kootenay. Men could be brought up from Nelson, landed at Kaslo and trucked over mountain roads to Arrow Lake which ran through the centre of the Slocan. With OBU men hiring on to provincial road crews to watch for strikebreakers, and picketers covering the boat landings, it was almost impossible for the operators or the international union to slip men in unnoticed.[9] Four representatives of Mine, Mill combed the region for strikebreakers throughout June and July, 1920, but in vain. R. H. Grimes, manager of the Slocan Silver Mining Company, tried to bring twenty-one men in from Medicine Hat, Alberta. He met their train at Nakusp and boarded with a case of pick handles which he began to distribute as the train rolled on to Rosebery. One man, a returned soldier, asked what to do with the weapons and was told there might be a fight and he should not be afraid to use them. Some of the men pitched the clubs out of the train and, when the group arrived at the vicinity of the mine, thirteen decided not to continue while the rest were escorted to the workings by a gun-toting mine employee.[10]

At the end of July, the Third International Mining Convention, an organization of operators representing southern British Columbia and Washington state mining concerns, was held at Nelson. The meeting was dominated by discussion of the deteriorating labour situation and the One Big Union came in for repeated condemnation. The delegates charged that the OBU was a seditious and disloyal organization fomenting "unnecessary labour troubles" which made it impossible to attract outside investment. They called on the federal government to launch an immediate investigation of OBU activities in the mining regions, warned employers not to conclude agreements with the OBU "in furtherance of selfish interests," and demanded the enactment of laws to "ensure eradication of open defiance of orderly government."[11] Fred Starkey, secretary-manager of the Convention, wrote Senator Gideon Robertson that although the mine owners had "made arrangements" with the international union, OBU "agitators" were carrying out a policy of intimidation. He threatened that if the authorities failed to stop OBU men from waylaying strikebreakers, "the people in their might" would be "forced to take the law into their own hands and deal summarily with those who curtail their production and deliver unprovoked attacks upon their vital interests."[12]

The operators were hurting because the strike, now three months old, was holding. *The Northwest Mining Truth,* a pro-Mine, Mill newspaper, noted at the beginning of August, 1920, that "practically every mine of prominence [in the Slocan district]" was "closed down" and a large proportion of the unmarried men in the region had left. One mine at Sandon, employing about sixty men, had capitulated to the OBU but the other operators were determined to hold out. The paper predicted that the trouble would "never be settled rightly or permanently until every blatant spokesman of anarchy [was] swept from the district."[13] By the middle of the month enough strikebreakers had been brought in for a limited resumption of production at a few mines. The *Truth* believed the worst was over, but conditions in the region made the optimism ring hollow. In most towns of the district stagnation had set in, businesses were closed and streets deserted. Sandon and Silverton, OBU strongholds, were particularly hard hit. Rumours of vigilante action against OBU leaders circulated, but the strike remained peaceful and pickets confined themselves to "verbal persuasion" in their efforts to turn back strikebreakers.[14] As long as construction and maintenance work was available, the OBU appeared to be able to carry on indefinitely because striking miners could sustain themselves while keeping watch for strikebreakers. One Mounted Police survey in the Penticton region revealed that almost half the men working on a government irrigation project were OBU members, eighty percent of whom were from the Slocan.[15]

The price of metals on the international market, the crucial factor which determined the opening, expansion, or closing of mines and smelters throughout the world, dropped sharply at the end of the war, rose rapidly from the early spring to the late summer of 1919, and dropped again until the end of the year. From then until the end of August, 1920, they remained fairly constant. Then, just as the trickle of strikebreakers into the Slocan brought in enough men to begin new operations, and OBU members started to drift back to work, they dropped again and kept dropping until the summer of 1921. Lead, silver, copper and zinc fell to their lowest prices in six years.[16] The impact on mining in the British Columbia interior was immediate and disastrous. Mines and smelters began to close, unemployed miners, smeltermen and millworkers were thrown out of work.[17]

But the strike was still on, at least in Roberts' mind. Midgley was leery of maintaining the strike in the face of a falling market, and asked Roberts if it was good tactics "keeping the men out on a long strike."[18] What he apparently did not realize was that the men were not being kept out by the OBU but by the depression. The strike was never officially called off; Roberts simply proclaimed victory: "The OBU miners in the Slocan District have a clear field now after their long strike," he declared. "All the mines that tried to operate under unfair conditions have closed down."[19]

If there had been any victory in forcing a closure of the mines, it was a hollow one because the depression and its unemployment, coming after a strike lasting more than six months, wore away the One Big Union. By April, 1921, conditions rendered it impossible to do any organizing in the region.[20] When Slocan operators persuaded Mine, Mill members to accept a general wage reduction in May, 1921, Roberts was powerless to do anything other than write a letter to the editor of the *Nelson Daily News* claiming that Mine, Mill represented only 5% of the miners. The OBU still had a working agreement with the Silversmith mine, but it was employing only a very few men. Two years after the OBU entered the valleys of the west Kootenays, Tommy Roberts and a small handful of die-hards were all that remained to keep the faith.

The Coal Miners

The battle for control of the coal fields began with the May, 1919 coal strike and continued with the miners' switch to the One Big Union in late July, 1919. To combat the OBU, an alliance of business, government and international unions took shape rapidly under the guiding hand of William Henry Armstrong, director of coal operations in District 18. Armstrong was a portly businessman from Vancouver who made his fortune in public works contracting after coming west from Ontario to work for the CPR in 1883. When chosen by the Borden government to control the western coal industry during the 1917 strike crisis, he was head of his own contracting firm and land company. Aside from a passion for motoring (he owned the first automobile to appear in Vancouver in 1899), he had few interests other than making money.

The relationship between Armstrong's office and the United Mine Workers was formalized July 29, 1919. That day, after several meetings with the UMW commission and W. F. McNeil, secretary of the Western Coal Operators Association, Armstrong prepared and signed an order which was left undated in the hands of his assistant. It was nothing less than an instruction to operators to accept miners back to work vouched for by the United Mine Workers and to meet and bargain with the UMW to work out a new agreement. The order was to be issued when UMW officials were satisfied that they had completed enough of a reorganization of the district to be able to take advantage of it.[21] The deal was made with the full knowledge and agreement of the operators, one of whom told the press that he would "have no dealings with the One Big Union nor officers of any organization representing that sentiment."[22]

Since it was apparent that Armstrong would not talk to the One Big Union, P. M. Christophers and Ed Browne were forced to make a direct appeal to the operators. On August 2, 1919, OBU headquarters in Calgary sent letters to mine owners in the Drumheller Valley seeking meetings "to make the necessary arrangements for a resumption of work." But Jesse Gough, owner of one of the larger mines in the region, told a Mounted Police officer there was "no chance" any of the operators would agree. He had been personally asked by Ed Browne if he would sign with the OBU and had flatly refused. There was, thus, little surprise when a general meeting of the Western Coal Operators Association passed a resolution on August 6 promising to "give the International Commission [the Association's] moral and solid support in their efforts to organize District 18 for the International, and have operations resumed."[23]

Aside from minor disturbances at Lethbridge at the end of May, the strike was free of disorder during the first nine weeks. This was primarily due to the lack of any real effort to keep the mines open or to import strikebreakers. But at Drumheller, topography made it necessary to pump water from the mines to keep them from flooding. There was danger that violence might erupt as OBU strikers tried to stop fan and pump men from working. Arthur Meighen took an interest in this situation, and persuaded Newton W. Rowell, president of the privy council and minister in charge of the Mounted Police, to order Commissioner Perry to protect the mines.[24] With the fans and pumps going and the Mounted Police and Alberta Provincial Police ensuring order, small numbers of veterans began to work in the mines. Drumheller Valley operators were determined to get production back to normal and laid plans with the Great War Veterans Association to sign GWVA members into the UMW and start work as soon as possible.[25]

The OBU, locally led by John Sullivan and John Roberts, and heavily supported by the large Italian and Slavic community, was determined to keep the mines in the Valley shut and mounted a massive picketing operation on the road from Drumheller to the Midland Mine. Early on the morning of August 7, RNWMP Corporal Charles M. Paris rode out to the mine to investigate reports that men going to work were being harassed. He found twenty pickets blocking the road and escorted a group of strikebreakers through. There were a few jeers. Sullivan told him that the Mounted Police had once been "the finest organization in the world, but the Winnipeg strike dragged your name in the dust."[26]

On Saturday morning, August 9, violence erupted.[27] Sullivan was rousted out of bed by five men determined to march him out of town, but he was saved by his own quick thinking and a neighbour who covered his escape with a rifle. All that day groups of strikers milled around in Drumheller while the veterans hurried to and fro in cars, unmolested by the four Mounties and the six Alberta Provincial Police stationed in the town. There were few physical encounters, but taunts and insults kept tension high and the town police busy. The next day Sullivan came out of hiding and, with Browne, Christophers and other OBU leaders, addressed a strikers' meeting. The veterans made no attempt to stop them, and the day passed peacefully.

Early Monday morning a cavalcade of cars swept along the dusty valley bottom roads to the miners' shacks strung out along the south side of the Red Deer River. The cars stopped quickly, veterans jumped from seats and runningboards, and ran towards the cabins. Miners, awakened by the whoops and yells, ran for the thick brush that grew to the rear of the staggered shacks. As the attackers drew near the huts, miners threw rocks, firewood—anything handy—and stopped the charge. Both sides stood their ground as missiles and shouts filled the air. Then slowly the pursuers began to retreat to their cars. The miners followed and chased the veterans back toward the cars until gunfire began to echo through the valley. More cars were coming to reinforce the attackers. The miners quickly turned in panic and ran to the hills.

In the earlier charge on the shacks, Mrs. Nicholas Babyn fired two shots at the veterans from a small bore hunting rifle. When they grabbed the weapon from her hands, she dashed back into her shack and brought out a revolver which was also wrestled away. She was not arrested, but when her husband arrived home later he was seized by police and charged with being an alien illegally in possession of arms and ammunition.

Through the day, strikers and their leaders hid in the

hills and were hunted by the veterans. Some were caught and roughed up, but Christophers, Browne and Sullivan managed to stay free. The mine owners and veteran leaders in town issued an ultimatum to the strikers to return to work or be driven out of the valley and, in the evening, Dave Rees held a UMW organizing rally attended by 250 men and encountered no opposition. The strikers were defeated and began to drift in from the hills and return to work. Most of the mines reopened on Tuesday morning, August 12, but the reign of terror was still not over for the aliens who were afraid to return to their homes and wandered the outlying areas in large numbers. The mine owners swore-in returned men to act as "special constables" who continued to terrorize OBU supporters. Christophers and two other OBU leaders were seized by several carloads of these "specials" from a meeting at Wayne, Alberta, brought to a kangaroo court-martial at Drumheller and thrown out of town. Sullivan was also caught and driven out of the district.

The OBU in Drumheller was now in complete disarray. Few of its supporters were ready to give up their allegiance but, for the time being, they swallowed their pride and threw their lot in with the UMW. The vigilantes had done the trick while the Mounties, Alberta Provincial Police and Drumheller town police stood by. There was coal to be dug and the local economy was sagging. Legal procedure had been trampled. The *Calgary Daily Herald* admitted that the veterans had acted in "an unorthodox way" but considered their actions "excusable" under the circumstances.[28]

The Drumheller affair was the climax of the District 18 strike. In the days following there was a slow but steady drift back to work throughout the district. There was considerable pressure to resume coal production for the coming winter and Senator Robertson, speaking at a Calgary meeting, made it clear the government was backing the international unions and was satisfied "with the way in which they conduct their business."[29]

On Saturday, August 16, 1919, the One Big Union Policy Committee met at Lethbridge with Christophers, Browne, Sullivan and other district leaders attending. Within a few hours a decision was reached to send the miners back and a telegram was flashed to all OBU locals advising them to "return to work under the U.M.W. of A."[30] Later, Christophers told a group of miners that he would never join the UMW but urged them to "study their wives and children" and ask themselves if they could stand another month without pay. "Remember the O.B.U. principle," he shouted, "By God there is another day coming." The men then decided, almost unanimously, to return to work under the international union. Charles Peacock, a leading OBU supporter, remarked that "he never felt so humiliated in his life."[31]

In the next few days miners throughout the district met, discussed the situation, voted and returned to work. In Fernie on the 16, Taber, Michel and Natal on the 17, Brulé, Hillcrest, Bellevue and Canmore on the 18, miners abandoned the strike. The letters "OBU" painted so proudly on the Canmore miners' hall a month before, were rubbed off. Christophers pledged that "the OBU would come to life later on in the coming winter" but for the moment, the Union was in disarray.

Despite the return to work, operators refused to re-employ former OBU leaders or supporters. At Coleman and Canmore, firebosses and aliens were particularly singled out.[32] This caused bitter feeling and brought threats of further strikes or slowdowns. The men resented the discrimination and UMW officials thought the policy would create OBU martyrs who would continue to rally anti-UMW sentiment.[33] Some action was necessary to soothe the miners, allow the UMW to appear to be in control of the rank and file and still give

operators the chance to make a "reasonably careful se-
lection" of the men working for them.[34]

The solution was arrived at during a meeting in Edmonton between UMW officials, Senator Robertson,
W. H. Armstrong and his assistants, and several operators. The union men stated that former district officers,
executive board members and policy committee representatives would not be given UMW cards until their
cases were heard, and a decision as to their fate reached,
by the international executive board. The question of
"objectionable" miners was then raised and Robertson
suggested that if an operator had men in his camp
which he objected to, he should submit their names to
the UMW commission which would examine their cases
before issuing cards.[35] With this policy the UMW commission, with the full cooperation of the owners and the
government, became a tribunal acting completely outside the law with the power to deprive men of their livelihood and blacklist them from employment in the coal
fields. This was surely one of the gravest excesses ever
committed by Robertson in his crusade against the One
Big Union.

Commission hearings were quasi-judicial in character.
They were held in company offices throughout the coal
fields with the "accused" present to defend himself but
without legal counsel. In a typical hearing at Fernie on
September 6, 1919, Samuel Whitehouse, former president of Gladstone Local Union, was accused of stopping
production at the Crows Nest Pass Coal Company mines
in violation of the contract, and causing serious losses to
the company. His "tribunal," which browbeat him mer-
cilessly, consisted of F. E. Harrison, W. F. McNeil of the
Western Coal Operators, W. R. Wilson of the company,
and three members of the UMW headed by Morgan
Lewis. Company and union officials tried to discover his
relationship to the OBU:

Mr. Houston (UMWA):
> Now Mr. Whitehouse we have had at least thirty men put through the same process of examination that you are now undergoing. They had knowledge of the O.B.U. and they were prepared to give an honest answer. These evasive answers are not conducive to your best interests, if you want re-employment from this Company. Do you or do you not believe in the O.B.U.? You were president of this Local Union. You claim that you have been more or less out of the community, but it is not reasonable to claim that you had not some knowledge of the strike situation as it existed in this camp.

Mr. Whitehouse: There were three weeks that I never . . .

Mr. Houston: Possibly so, Mr. Whitehouse, but you were president and you . . .

Mr. Whitehouse: Well, if you want me to say Yes or No to the O.B.U., I will say No.[36]

Following hearings such as this, the UMW commission provided special cards for those men "cleared" to enable them to work in the mines. Throughout September and October, 1919, the commission travelled throughout District 18 and heard cases involving close to one hundred miners.

But the United Mine Workers could not hope to win the allegiance of the men in this way. Many had gone back to work under UMW auspices only because they had been urged to do so by the OBU leaders. If the United Mine Workers was to have any real hope of rebuilding its shattered organization in western Canada, positive action was necessary. Throughout November, 1919, little was possible because a coal strike in the central Pennsylvania fields demanded close attention by international headquarters while Canadian UMW officials were unwilling to begin negotiations with the operators until a settlement was reached south of the border. In early December, following a forced end to that strike, and a fourteen percent increase imposed by the U.S. federal government, international officers Ballantyne and Dalrymple returned to Alberta from Indianapolis to resume their commission duties and Armstrong arranged for joint bargaining to begin.

The OBU was also anxious to begin talks with the operators. At a convention held the first two days of December, it was decided to try to start negotiations aimed at the same fourteen percent increase won by miners in the United States. If this failed, a strike at individual mines would be considered. Significantly, Christophers, who urged an immediate strike, was beaten out for the presidency by Henry Beard, a Michel miner. The general sentiment of the meeting was to delay a walkout decision until the trials of the Winnipeg strike leaders were over.[37] After the convention, Ed Browne sent the coal operators and Armstrong a note asking them to meet the OBU "for the purpose of making a new contract."[38] The approach was supported by the Hillcrest, Blairmore, Bellevue, Fernie, Michel, Carbondale, Nordegg, Coleman and Brulé locals of the UMW, which passed a resolution condemning the UMW-operators alliance, pledging to stick by the One Big Union, and calling on their executive to convene a district board meeting to consider further action if Armstrong refused to meet the OBU leaders before January 1, 1920.[39] This was a hollow threat because the OBU was broke, and without funds, a new strike would have been more disastrous than the first.

Negotiations between the Western Coal Operators

and the United Mine Workers, held under the auspices of Armstrong and Robertson, began December 16. A fourteen percent increase, retroactive to December 1, 1919, was agreed on as a temporary measure until conditions had settled in the United States, and a fuller, more permanent agreement could be negotiated in Canada. The increase was to be granted to UMW members only and the operators agreed to collect UMW dues through a compulsory checkoff. If men wanted work in the mines they would have to become UMW members. The agreement was finalized December 19 and, a few hours later, promulgated by Armstrong as Order 141.[40] The coal operators, who had denounced the UMW as alien extremists in 1917, now held the very same union in loving embrace.

The One Big Union was furious. *The Searchlight*, a pro-OBU paper published in Calgary, denounced the checkoff to an "American organization" as "an extraordinary thing for a minister of the Canadian government to insist upon." In Calgary Alderman Broatch told a meeting of Alberta mayors that the coal fields would be shut down if the Robertson arrangements were enforced. But even *The Searchlight* admitted there was "no sentiment in favor of a strike."[41] Several miners locals threatened to fight any attempt to force their members to join the United Mine Workers but also admitted that it was "essential that there should be no disruption in the Coal Industry."[42]

Despite such sentiment, there were a few brief anti-UMW strikes during December, 1919, and January, 1920, when the whole district was in a state of flux. To the public there appeared to be two unions struggling against each other but, in reality, many UMW locals were strongly sympathetic to the One Big Union. When pro-OBU resolutions were passed and forwarded to Armstrong, they were often typed on UMW stationery. McNeil summed matters up at the end of December when he told W. R. Wilson, president of the Coal Operators, that the UMW did not appear to be making "any great amount of progress."[43] One secret Mounted Police report placed UMW strength at the beginning of 1920 at 4027 members out of 9155 miners in the district,[44] but even this figure did not reflect those who were OBU members carrying UMW cards for convenience. Hard core UMW members were still a small minority.

On January 3, 1920, the OBU miners' executive met at Calgary. Order 141 was discussed and OBU members were urged to accept the increase it contained, but were told to refuse to accept the checkoff. Should any of the men be locked out for refusing to agree to the checkoff, the Board pledged that the whole district would rise to their defence.[45] This was a needless worry, however, because in the following weeks most operators paid the fourteen percent increase while bundles of checkoff slips lay unused in managers' offices. The checkoff was only enforced in the small number of camps where the UMW was strong. After the long 1919 strike, operators were not interested in forcing the issue at the local level, especially since they knew their men were still backing the OBU.[46] Nevertheless, one thing remained constant throughout this period—Armstrong would not talk to the One Big Union. An approach made at the end of February, 1920 was brushed off, and Armstrong told Beard that he had "no faith in any promise you or your organization may make, because of your past actions and utterances."[47]

Order 141 remained the ideal instrument for the destruction of the OBU because, if put into effect throughout western Canada, it would cut off all dues monies to the OBU and place all the miners under UMW discipline. In March, 1920, Armstrong decided to enforce it and put an end to the uncertainty that had dogged the district since the end of the 1919 coal strike. Orders went to coal operators to enforce the closed shop against the One Big Union. The miners resisted. On March 9, three hundred and forty were locked out at Bellevue and the next day three hundred more at Blairmore.[48] Between March 22 and 29, collieries at Coleman, Hillcrest and Canmore were forced to close. By the end of March, approximately 1800 miners were on strike or being locked out over the checkoff. One prominent Coleman citizen told a Calgary newspaper: "I don't see how the government can enforce that order. If the miners don't want to belong to the American organization, I don't see how they can be compelled to. The operators should be left to make their own agreements with their men."[49] The Calgary *Albertan* called Robertson's tactics "sledge hammer methods" and pointed out that most operators had been reluctant to enforce the order because they did not want strikes. Some operators still refused to go along with the government, and men continued to work at Fernie, Michel, Coalhurst, Commerce, Nordegg and Monarch.

The Industrial Disputes Investigation Act, on the statute books since 1907 and applicable to all industrial disputes falling under federal jurisdiction, including those in coal mines, stipulated that a board of conciliation had to investigate any disagreement within the Act's jurisdiction before there could be a strike or lockout. Since this had not been done, the OBU laid a complaint against the manager of Canmore mines for violating the Act.[50] But the law offered no hope. The manager asserted that Armstrong's order took precedence over the Act and that no one had actually been locked out for not signing the checkoff. The case was dismissed.[51] The OBU appealed to the Appellate court but was defeated again. As a direct result, the miners yielded to the checkoff order and returned to work by the end of April, 1920. The

Fools and Wise Men

strike/lockout had extended over several weeks, observed the *Federationist*, and the miners were "interested in the persistent question: when do we eat?"[52]

The UMW moved quickly to capitalize on the OBU defeat. On May 5, 1920, Morgan Lewis approached the operators to begin discussions aimed towards a new contract, and by June 10 a collective agreement was signed. It was intended to run to March 31, 1922 and to be retroactive to April 1, 1920. The closed shop/checkoff was included as was a statement that the contract was "for the sole use of the members of the United Mine Workers of America and the members of The Western Canada Coal Operators Association." A 27% wage increase was granted, and the 1917-1919 contract was agreed to be the basis for working conditions.[53] Since District 18 was still under "trusteeship," there was no elected scale committee and the agreement was worked out directly between the international commission and the operators. Many miners refused to vote on it. At Michel, Coalhurst and Monarch, not a single miner cast a ballot. In the Drumheller Valley less than 20% voted. In Fernie, forty men voted out of six hundred. Though the contract was approved by a three-to-one margin, only about 3700 voted in the entire district—less than half.[54] W. R. Wilson of the Crows Nest Pass Coal Company was unimpressed. "Show us that you can control the men," he told the UMW, "and we will make the checkoff compulsory."[55]

During the March dispute, or the uneasy truce which followed, there had been little real violence. But violence had dogged the One Big Union from its very beginnings. P. M. Christophers found out in July, 1920 that the legacy was hard to shake.[56] He had been a paid OBU organizer since his ouster from the presidency in December. His travels took him to every part of the coal fields, and on June 30 he arrived at the little southern Saskatchewan town of Bienfait, not far from the American border, to begin organizing work among the area's soft coal miners.

On Saturday night, July 3, Christophers retired to his bedroom in the King Edward Hotel at about 10:30, read the newspaper for an hour and then tried to sleep. Shortly after closing the light there was a loud banging on his door. Christophers opened it, and seven or eight men crowded into the room and began to demand his nationality and his business in Bienfait. Christophers told them he was an OBU organizer and was neither an American nor a member of the IWW, but the vigilantees ordered him to get dressed and told him they were going to take him out of town. Christophers was scared and appealed to them not to use force or "rough play." They assured him that if he submitted quietly, there would be no trouble. He dressed and was marched downstairs. In the lobby, Christophers tried to pay his bill but could not find enough money. His captors shuffled impatiently as he tried to cash a money order. After a few strained moments, one man told the clerk he would "fix the account up" and Christophers was pushed through the door and shoved into the back seat of a waiting car. Five men climbed in and the car drove off into the night.

After heading east for about twenty minutes, the car drove through the deserted streets of the nearby town of Estevan and drew to a halt. Christophers stayed in the back seat as the men piled out, moved away from the car and argued about what to do next. One man stuck his head in the window and threatened that if Christophers came back to Canada he would be tarred and feathered. Christophers now realized that he was not going to be lynched but kidnapped to the United States. Five men then clambered into the car and the party drove south to the boundary. They sped through the dark for several hours and arrived at Noonan, North Dakota at 2:30 in the morning. Later, after lunch,

Christophers was freed. He shook hands with one of his kidnappers and thanked them for not roughing him up. "We had to do it to get you away from the crowd," the other replied. Christophers walked to Portal, North Dakota, and crossed back into Canada.

Seven Estevan men were later charged with transporting Christophers out of Canada against his will. One of them, George Hunter, was a corporal in the Saskatchewan Provincial Police, but assistant police commissioner Tracey swore, at the preliminary hearing, that no orders and no instructions had ever been issued to remove Christophers from the country.[57] OBU allegations of official involvement were never proved, and the entire episode was a disaster for the OBU. After the kidnapping, miners in the area refused to touch the One Big Union, and all efforts to organize these fields ended abruptly.[58] Once again, vigilantes left their mark on events.

Despite the kidnapping, coal miners in Alberta and British Columbia clung tenaciously to the One Big Union. In July and August, 1920, strikes directed against the checkoff stopped production twice at Fernie, B.C. and at Coalhurst, Drumheller, Commerce and Wayne, Alberta. Over three thousand miners were involved and more than ten thousand man days of work were lost. But these strikes were little more than short guerilla actions in the OBU campaign. The real push would not come in the summer months when demand for coal was low; it would come in the fall.

OBU leaders had said for months, publicly and privately, that late August or September would be the ideal time to launch a campaign for recognition backed by a "general tie-up in the mines." They urged their members to return to work under the UMW label during the March, 1920 fight at Bellevue and Blairmore because they believed the time was not right for an all-out campaign.[59] As a result, Armstrong's drive to enforce the checkoff had the ironic effect of pushing unrepentent OBU men into UMW lodges, and helping the OBU maintain control of many of them. The leaders of the Fernie lodge were all OBU sympathizers while eighty percent of the men at Hillcrest, Bellevue and Coleman continued to pay OBU dues.[60]

On Saturday, September 13, 1920, representatives of the OBU miners met at Calgary to plan the campaign against the checkoff. Delegates wore badges proclaiming "the checkoff must go," and made it clear to the press that this fight was not about wages or working conditions, but a battle against the United Mine Workers. This may not have been the best time for a strike, but in the opinion of most delegates, it was the only time, and unless action was taken soon, nothing further could be done for at least another year. Their deadline was October 1; unless the checkoff was abolished and negotiations entered into between the OBU and the operators by that date, the mines would be struck.[61] This challenge was sent to the membership by Arthur Evans, newly elected to succeed Ed Browne as secretary. At least one newspaper pointed out that this was "the first time that the O.B.U. officials have called a strike openly and for their own principles."[62]

There was little widespread enthusiasm for the battle.[63] The men had been striking on and off since May, 1919, and many thousands had lost months of pay in the fight to expel the UMW from the coal fields. Some were paying dues to two organizations at once. Others had struggled to regain old positions against the anti-OBU discrimination practised by the operators. It had been a long and costly fight. Now, at least, there was steady work, and as much as a man needed. Coal production had increased steadily since the early part of the year.[64] Digging was good and the pay envelopes were fat, particularly with the increases paid out by the operators to bribe the men back into the UMW. The men strongly supported the OBU but were hesitant about a strike.[65]

The time was ripe for the United Mine Workers to try to drive another wedge between the miners and the One Big Union. UMW leaders approached the operators with a demand that their contract be re-opened for negotiations because recent settlements in the United States put the average pay of non-contract miners there higher than in Canada. The operators objected strongly, but ran into the intervention of Gideon Robertson who arrived in Calgary September 28. Robertson had been touring the west with a federal tariff commission and rushed ahead to Calgary to keep a close watch on events. He met the operators to try to convince them to agree to the UMW's demands, and told them that they must re-enter negotiations with the UMW to avoid losing men to the One Big Union.[66] Before this was done, the OBU strike began, when two collieries at Drumheller and one at Wayne were closed September 30. The next day twelve more were struck at Wayne, Drumheller and Midlandvale. At first the walkout was almost completely confined to the Drumheller valley and only affected a large number of small domestic coal operations.[67] In the Crows Nest Pass frantic OBU efforts to get the men at Fernie and Michel to join were rewarded on October 5 and 6. In the north, five hundred miners at the Brazeau collieries quit work on the seventh. The strike was far from total—not a miner in Lethbridge joined[68]—but despite widespread reluctance, 3492 men were still willing to show their support for the OBU and put their faith in its leaders.

This time that faith was misplaced. Confusion reigned at OBU headquarters and a general feeling of pessimism weighed the strike effort down. Evans told miners in each section that those in the other sections were prepared to strike to back them up.[69] False stories were spread about the extent of the walkout and claims were made about numbers of men striking that were patently untrue. Christophers tried to convince Lethbridge miners to join the walkout, and suggested a rotating strike to make their funds last, but they refused and stayed at work.[70] Executive members travelled up and down the province with little coordination and less planning, sometimes for the sole purpose of raising money for their own salaries. Internal divisions appeared between old and new executive members, while the strains of an empty treasury showed everywhere.[71] To add to OBU problems, mine operators told UMW officials that they would discuss re-opening the contract and awarding a wage increase to the daymen if they would return to work.[72] Robertson played his usual role of threatening to use federal might to "protect" working miners while labelling the strikers foreign agitators who were members of "secret soviet societies."[73] The whole affair, in the words of one RCMP report, had "an air of lightheadedness."[74]

On Saturday, October 10, 1920, an injunction was issued against the OBU for failure to abide by the requirements of the Industrial Disputes Investigation Act and attempting to convince UMW miners to break their contract with the operators.[75] Beard, Christophers and the others were defiant, but it was the beginning of the end. Throughout the district the drift back to work began. Slowly at first, and then in greater numbers, miners met, discussed the situation, and decided that further struggle was useless. The hardier OBU supporters could not hold them. On October 15 the OBU leaders, recognizing their failure, issued a call to return to work,[76] and the next day miners in seven collieries responded. All over the coal fields the trickle became a flood stopped here or there only momentarily by a reinstatement problem or some other local grievance. The strike had never amounted to the general stoppage that would have been necessary for victory. The funds to sustain a long campaign were not available and with more than half the mine workforce continuing on the job, production was never crippled enough to make the strike hurt. Despite empty threats of future action, the OBU was finished as a force of any consequence in the coal fields. Frank Woodward, secretary of the Winnipeg central labor council of the OBU, attributed this to lack of effective support: "although the men are all back now they are wiser and realize that thorough reorganization must be carried out to prepare for future eventualities."[77] But Woodward was fooling no one. In the western coal fields, the OBU's future was past.

On June 14, 1921, delegates representing coal miners throughout Alberta and the Crows Nest Pass gathered at Calgary for a special convention called by the committee overseeing UMW affairs in western Canada. The international was now confident enough of their control to begin the re-establishment of full autonomy to District 18. There were, undoubtedly, still OBU members and supporters in the area, but none dared challenge the international. The special convention was a carefully orchestrated celebration of UMW benefits and condemnation of the wayward former district officers.[78] A new constitution, milder than the old in its basic acceptance of the principles of business unionism, was adopted and full autonomy was restored August 1, 1921, almost two years to the day after it had been suspended. The return of District 18 to full-fledged membership in the United Mine Workers marked the end of the battle for the mining frontier. The OBU revolt in the coal fields was over.

Chapter 9

Hard Times

On Saturday, December 13, 1920, Bob Russell was paroled from Stony Mountain penitentiary. He was the first of the 1919 general strike leaders convicted and the first freed. On February 28, 1921, Ivens, Johns, Queen, Armstrong and Pritchard joined him. His imprisonment, together with Pritchard and Johns, deprived the One Big Union of three of its most forceful leaders during a crucial period in its development. The OBU they left had been a growing power in western Canada; the OBU they returned to had fallen on hard times.

By the winter of 1920-21, the One Big Union had lost

the west coast loggers, British Columbia hardrock miners and coal miners of District 18. In Vancouver, once a major OBU centre, few members remained. Not one delegate from there attended the October, 1920 convention at Port Arthur. Only a handful of supporters could be counted in Edmonton, Calgary, Regina or Saskatoon. In Winnipeg, 4438 members were organized into sixteen units.[1] They worked mainly in the railway repair shops and marshalling yards, while others were in the building and garment trades.

Since its birth,the One Big Union had fought governments, employers and craft unions during a post-war boom. In May, 1920, a sharp drop in the price of raw silk on Japanese markets set off a chain reaction soon felt throughout the industrialized world.[2] Prices fell, unemployment rose and wages were cut as a new depression tightened its grip on Canada. In the fall of 1920 the unemployment rate for trade union members began to rise sharply until it stood at 13.07% by January, 1921. Spring conditions helped ease the tight job market in some seasonal industries such as water transportation, but generally the situation continued to deteriorate and the unemployment rate for trade union members in May, 1921 stood at 16.48%.[3] The rise in unemployment matched a fall in wages. In all parts of Canada, and in every industry, pay packets shrank. Average wages dropped fifteen percent. Many workers could not afford to pay union dues and government statistics reflected "very heavy losses" in the number of union members and locals in the country.[4]

The depression killed any real hope OBU leaders may have had to hold the line. Headquarters were moved from Vancouver to Winnipeg in March, 1921, and the Pender Street OBU hall in Vancouver stood empty and virtually unused. It was almost impossible to secure British Columbia delegates for the fall, 1921, OBU convention in Winnipeg. The OBU's decline on the coast prompted AFL headquarters to release Alf Farmilo from active service[5] while an effort, launched by the Vancouver trades council, to recover property lost to the OBU in the summer of 1919, was hampered because the records were missing and no OBU officers could be found in the city.[6]

Membership losses made the OBU's financial situation worse. When the general executive board sent a representative to the west coast in February, 1921, a bitter argument broke out in the Winnipeg Central Labor council because some delegates were convinced there was no money for organizing. Tom Mace, who took over as general secretary when Vic Midgley resigned and returned to the coast, begged Tommy Roberts in Sandon, B.C., to pay some of the dues owing to headquarters. "The G.E.B. is just about broke," he pleaded, "and has a bunch of bills yet to pay."[7] The all-important *OBU Bulletin* was an intolerable drain on funds.

The paper, and the OBU treasury, was saved by one of mankind's oldest urges—gambling. An idea, proposed in November, 1921 by a member of the Winnipeg central labour council, to publish English football scores soon developed into a proposal to run a weekly football lottery. The aim was to increase *Bulletin* circulation by printing a coupon in each issue which, when submitted with twenty-five cents for a three week subscription, allowed each entrant one chance at a modest cash prize. The workers "would gamble anyway," exclaimed one central labour council delegate, lest anyone complain that the OBU was corrupting its followers. Anything which helped the *Bulletin* survive ought to be considered, implored editor Frank Woodward. If circulation increased several thousand the whole thing would be justified. Besides, someone else reasoned, "even when the coupon was clipped from the paper, the paper would be left lying around the house and the other occupants would read it." Since OBU lawyer W. H. Trueman approved the idea as "legal in every way," the council decided to go ahead.[8] On December 8, 1921, the first coupon-bearing *Bulletin* was published.

Public reaction to the contest was overwhelming. The pool of prize money rapidly swelled to the point, in July, 1922, when more than eighty-eight thousand dollars was paid out to contest winners in one month.[9] The *Bulletin* handled more than one-quarter of a million dollars from February to September, 1922, and kept the lucrative contest going when the soccer season ended by switching to major league baseball. By mid-April, 1922, more than 150 000 entries a week, each clipped from a copy of the *Bulletin*, poured into the OBU-owned Plebs Hall in Winnipeg.[10] An entire staff of contest room girls and newsboys was hired to work on the lottery, forcing OBU leaders into the queer position of having to negotiate wages and working conditions with their own workers.

In June, 1922, the Manitoba Court of Appeal ruled the contest illegal. A change of tactics was called for and the Winnipeg central labour council decided to allow readers to enter the contest free provided they did so on a *Bulletin*-printed coupon. The money continued to roll in, but now as outright purchases of the paper instead of subscriptions. Huge bundles of the paper were sold by the hour. It was rumoured that more than a few found their way into city law offices and the Grain Exchange, and that A. J. Andrews himself, one-time leader of the Citizens Committee of 1000 and chief crown prosecutor in the strike trials, took fifty copies a week.[11] But this scheme was no more acceptable to the Crown than the first and the OBU was forced to find another solution. This time it was a weather guessing contest. The lottery rolled on and the money flowed in. Such maneuverings and subterfuges between Crown and OBU leaders continued until 1927, by which time a host of imitators, including the *Western Labor News*, had been spawned and interest in the lottery had cooled. Nevertheless, at its highpoint, half a million copies of the *Bulletin* were printed every week[12] and the earnings were staggering.

The windfall kept the OBU going. Though the government kept a close watch on contest funds to assure that earnings, less expenses, were paid out as winnings, the union executive managed to use lottery funds to purchase supplies and materials, pay at least one full-time organizer (Tom Cassidy) and purchase shares of the Plebs Hall Company which owned the building where the OBU hall and offices were located.[13] Eventually the *Bulletin* assumed the entire Plebs Hall mortgage. In 1926 the OBU seriously considered purchasing the Charles Kerr Company of Chicago, a world-renowned publisher of labour and socialist literature, and negotiations continued for several months before being broken off. Though this method of spreading the OBU gospel did not work out, another, less lofty, was tried. A car was purchased and plastered with OBU slogans and advertising so that the OBU message was spread on the streets of Winnipeg every time Russell or the others went on official business. Some of Winnipeg's working class children benefited directly from the lottery when the OBU summer camp was opened at Gimli, Manitoba in 1926. Throughout the summer, 250 children a week were brought to the camp free. There were classes in Marxism and socialism, sing-songs and the usual entertainment and recreation. There were also four meals a day and all the milk they could drink. The union spent about $40 000 for bungalows, dining room and other facilities.[14]

The lottery money made survival possible, but an active, thriving union needs members and towards the end of 1921 a new challenge threatened the OBU's hold on its faithful few. In March of 1919 the Soviet regime held the founding meeting, in Moscow, of the Communist International (Comintern), designed to impose unity, discipline and Soviet leadership on the growing world Communist movement. At the second Comintern congress in March, 1921, twenty-one conditions were adopted which established the organizational structure, procedures, tactics and lines of authority binding on all member individuals and parties. Radicals around the world were invited to affiliate to the Comintern, provided they agreed to abide by the twenty-one conditions. In Canada, where the question of affiliation had been an important topic for socialists since the Comintern's founding, the twenty-one conditions complicated matters because they clearly aimed to establish Moscow's primacy and some Canadian radicals refused to accept this. Debate inside the Socialist Party of Canada grew so bitter by December, 1920, that the party was ripped apart and suffered wholesale defections.[15]

Some of the SPC members who favoured the Comintern were OBU supporters. On the coast, Jack Kavanagh and *Federationist* editor A. S. Wells, and in Edmonton Joe and Sarah Knight, threw their lot in with the communists. In February, 1921, Knight published an article in the *Alberta Labor News* advocating the formation of a Communist party in Canada based on the revolutionary movement that already existed in the west. Though no such party had yet been founded, and no Canadians had been delegates at either the first or second world Comintern meetings, individuals were joining communist parties based in the United States and were receiving help and direction from North American Comintern representatives.[16] In the spring of 1921, Ella Reeve Bloor, working as a member of the Communist Party of the United States and an important American link to the Comintern, went to Winnipeg to urge Russell to go to Moscow for the third world Comintern congress and be the Canadian representative at the founding meeting of the International Congress of Revolutionary Trade and Industrial Unions (Profintern) scheduled for July. Russell refused and Joe Knight, then working for the OBU in Ontario, went in his place as an officially accredited OBU delegate.[17]

Knight travelled to Moscow with the American delegation. He attended some of the Comintern sessions and helped work out a program of action for the American section of the Profintern. In this role he gave his enthusiastic approval to the "united front" policy which called on revolutionaries throughout the world to get into the established trade unions and "bore from within" to convert them into revolutionary instruments. In the words of the official Profintern proceedings: "The revolutionary struggle should be waged and built up around *winning the unions*, i.e., the millioned masses united in the old unions, and *not by destroying them*."[18] The long-run implications for unions like the OBU in Canada or the IWW in the United States were clear: faithful communists in North America were ordered back to the American Federation of Labor. Until these decisions were translated, published, distributed and adopted by the various Comintern and Profintern affiliates, however, Canadian Communists tried to hide the harsh truth from friends in the OBU through a deliberate policy of hedging and confusion.

The secret founding meeting of the Communist Party of Canada was held at Guelph, Ontario in late May, 1921, while Knight was in Moscow. The Party endorsed and adopted the Comintern's twenty-one conditions and declared itself to be "an underground, illegal, organization." The Party's primary role was to spread the idea that violent revolution was inevitable and necessary for the establishment of a proletarian dictatorship "based upon Soviet power." The delegates took the view that the AFL leadership had forced radical western workers to withdraw from the craft unions but that secession had left those unions in the control of reactionary officials.[19] This was a straight adoption of the "boring from within" policy advocated by the Profintern.

At the OBU's third annual convention, held at Winnipeg September 26 to 29, 1921, Joe Knight described the events he had witnessed in Moscow, and urged the OBU to affiliate itself to the Profintern as quickly as possible. At least three other resolutions echoed Knight's appeal, and R. B. Russell favoured it, but the resolutions committee claimed that OBU members were not clear about the exact nature of the Comintern or the Profintern and declared that "an educational campaign" should be carried out first. Knight promised to provide information about the Profintern and the committee's resolution was adopted with only two dissenting voices.[20] This compromise may have been designed to steer a middle course to avoid the bitter internal debate that had torn apart the Socialist Party of Canada and the Lumber Workers Industrial Union. The pro-Communist sympathies of Knight, Wells and other members were well-known and a considerable faction had developed inside the OBU which supported affiliation. On the other hand, there was little solid information about the Profintern, and affiliation under those circumstances could have proven disastrous.

If further clarification was the aim, Knight and the Communists refused to cooperate. Knight's written report of the Profintern meeting was confusing and misleading. In it, he admitted that the Profintern had no use for secessionist organizations and that Canadian revolutionaries must use the "boring from within" tactics that had been used in Europe. Any group that wanted to affiliate to the Profintern had to adopt this policy without exception. These were strong words for the OBU because, if accepted, they were an admission that the secessionist struggle had been in vain. But Knight also claimed that the Profintern had adopted a resolution urging the OBU to align itself with a communist party to form committees to work inside the craft unions to unify "the entire organized labor movement of the country through one national executive."[21] (He did not reveal that a communist party already existed.) If true, the OBU could indeed play a useful role in the revolutionary struggle as a distinct organization, but it was impossible to verify. When copies of the Profintern proceedings were finally secured from other sources, no such resolution appeared, and when Russell wrote Comintern representative Carl Jansen in Toronto to seek clarification, Jansen was evasive because he was unsure and was forced to rely on American party sources for his news.[22] This confusion, in itself, created resentment towards the communists, as did the thought that outsiders, from another country, were telling western workers how to conduct their struggles. One member could not see "how Moscow could tell an organization like the O.B.U. to go out of existence; the thing was silly!" he proclaimed. Another warned that the communists were out to "smash all existing revolutionary organizations" so that they could have a clear field for themselves.[23]

While OBU members were debating affiliation, the communists were preparing to establish an open, legal party capable of launching a broad appeal to Canadian workers. The foundations of the new organization, to be known as the Workers Party of Canada, were laid by Communist Party leaders in December, 1921. Their plan was to continue the Communist Party as an underground institution controlling the open Workers Party. In a speech to a Vancouver meeting in January, 1922, Jack Kavanagh claimed that a militant party of the working class was necessary, but that a Communist Party could not be formed because "we don't know yet whether it is legal or not. We are obliged to keep within the law. We recognize power when we see it."[24]

The founding convention of the Workers Party was

called to order in Toronto on February 17, 1922. Representatives from all over Canada attended, including Bob Russell, who had been invited as a fraternal delegate and could not ignore the invitation whatever his personal reservations may have been. In Toronto, Russell finally learned what the communists had in store for the One Big Union. The resolution embodying Workers Party trade union policy called upon revolutionaries to work within the major existing unions to bring about their amalgamation. When there was one union for each industry they were to be revolutionized and affiliated to the Profintern. Russell strenuously objected and claimed the OBU had the only practical form of organization. Street railway employees in one city did not need the support of street railway employees in other cities, he declared, but of the other workers in their own city. He was immediately attacked by twelve other delegates including the Knights and Jack Kavanagh. Joe Knight claimed that the OBU still had strength in Winnipeg only because the workers there refused to swallow their pride. To Sarah Knight the AFL or the OBU was not the issue; the main question was "the best method of getting behind the working class." Kavanagh declared that if the OBU refused to return to the craft unions, the opportunity to create a revolutionary trade union movement would pass. Others, such as Michael Buhay of Montreal, a member of the underground Communist Party, were not so kind: "Delegate Russell has delivered the same kind of speech as the A. F. of L. bureaucrats . . . We want a policy to unite the working class. What is Russell's policy? Join the O.B.U.? We have been talking about unifying the labor movement. Western Canada was yours, but not to-day"; or Maurice Spector of Toronto, another member of the underground party: "Russell's speech [is] the last dying kick of the syndicalists in Canada"; or Robertson of Winnipeg: "The O.B.U. had its origin in idealism. Those who were then recognized as leaders have to-day forsaken it." Hardly a voice was raised, from Winnipeg or elsewhere, to defend the man who had gone to jail for them all. Maurice Spector summed up the Workers Party's position in his closing address to the convention: "It has been demonstrated once and for all that the cant of 'East is East and West is West, and never the twain shall meet' has no place in the revolutionary movement."[25]

The Winnipeg delegates knew the OBU was still popular in their city and the job of selling the new communist policy would not be easy. Some of them, led by H. M. Bartholomew, implied, after their return, that although workers were being urged to go back to the AFL elsewhere, it was not expected of those in Winnipeg because the OBU was the major union there.[26] This did not suggest suicide, merely truncation—perhaps easier to swallow since the bulk of OBU strength clearly lay in Winnipeg anyway. When Russell reported otherwise to the central labour council, of the OBU, the communists called him a liar. When the council voted to hear the official minutes of the Toronto meeting (no verbatim account was yet available) to determine the truth, they protested vigorously and left the hall.[27] Two weeks later *The Worker*, official organ of the Workers Party, edited by Jack Kavanagh, published an account of the founding meeting of the Workers Party which left little doubt of its anti-OBU tone. The Winnipeg communists were unrepentant and refused to apologize to Russell. During the following weeks, the issue of OBU affiliation to the Profintern became confused with the narrower question of the Workers Party's attitude to the One Big Union. The *Bulletin* continued to advertise Workers Party meetings and Workers Party members continued to sit in OBU governing councils. But the Party's attitude could not fail to change this. *Bulletin* editor Woodward declared: "we would have been far better pleased had a different attitude been taken."[28]

The future of the OBU-Workers Party relationship was decided at three successive open membership meetings on April 28, May 5 and May 12, 1922. They were called to discuss the resolution on trade unions passed at the Workers Party convention in February and to decide whether or not the One Big Union should join the Profintern. Workers Party members naturally urged affiliation. Jacob Penner claimed that "secessionist movements in the past [had] not brought . . . any success." Another Workers Party member warned that "by holding aloof from the Red International we become a sect like the Holy Rollers. By lining up with the Red International we will become a part of the general labor movement of the world."

Russell struck back: "Comrade Penner . . . stated clearly, after rambling around, that the A.F. of L. was the most reactionary organization in the world. They all say this, and then [tell us] 'go back into the A.F. of L.' Hammond and Robertson said that [my] report was a fabrication. They say this is not the policy as far as Winnipeg is concerned. . . . I know that the [Workers Party] is out to destroy the OBU, because I was at Toronto. But the members of the [Workers Party] deny this." He challenged any Party member in the hall to admit the truth. None did. One claimed he did "not wish to break the OBU, nor does the [Workers Party]," while another asserted that the communists meant to "go within the A.F. of L. and work there for the OBU."[29]

This pattern changed little during the next two meetings. OBU supporters, led by Russell, attacked the contradictions in the communist position and pointed out that one Party member said 'abolish the OBU' while another said 'but not in Winnipeg.' At the final meeting on May 12, a resolution was proposed calling the communist position "retrogressive and decidedly against the best interests of the working class." The debate at this meeting was particularly bitter. One anti-Profintern member asked why the Workers Party urged others to join the Profintern, but were not themselves connected with it. (They were not but the illegal Communist Party was.) Bartholomew, for the Workers Party, accused OBU leaders of sabotage and not carrying out the instructions of their September, 1921 convention. At the end of the meeting, the resolution passed—the Workers Party, and affiliation with the Profintern, was rejected.[30]

The feud now developed into open warfare. Editorials in the *Bulletin* and *The Worker* grew more bitter. Jack Macdonald of the Workers Party was particularly sarcastic: "The problem . . . is simple to our fervid OBU-ists. Once the worker is initiated into their organization he ceases to think [in craft terms] but thinks and acts from then onwards as a member of the working class . . . why? one may ask. Because the OBU is a class organization. If you doubt it, read its preamble."[31] But the war was not confined to words. All across the west Workers Party members campaigned within individual units to undermine the influence of the OBU leadership. Complaints were received in Winnipeg from Vancouver, Edmonton, Lethbridge and Sudbury. Workers Party members concentrated on Winnipeg railroad workers and were particularly active within the OBU units at the Transcona and Fort Rouge shops. Some OBU members complained that the only union getting "bored from within" was the OBU. Finally, in November, the Winnipeg central labour council, led by Russell, Mace and Woodward, and after much agonized debate, threw Workers Party members out of all executive positions in the union.[32]

The One Big Union lost some of its most able leaders in this fight and needed all its resources to save what little remained of its strength. Organization—bringing the OBU message to shop and factory—was now more necessary than it had been since 1920. In the early spring of 1923 Bob Russell went to Ontario in pursuit of new members. In the west, Tom Cassidy, salary and expenses paid by the *Bulletin,* continued to drive the rutted roads in his battered old car to visit small towns like Melville, Watrous and Humboldt in Saskatchewan, to repeat his oft-told message that craft unions were obsolete and the OBU the only hope. But there was not enough money to sustain these efforts. The *Bulletin* was closely watched by government officials to ensure it did not pay OBU bills or sustain OBU campaigns out of lottery funds. Cassidy's expenses were as far as the rules could be stretched. Further belt tightening was necessary and at the end of March, 1923, the position of general secretary was dissolved. Tom Mace was out of work, but without his salary to pay, Russell could be sustained.

The organizing drive continued in April. Russell touched most of the small railroad towns between Winnipeg and Sudbury, and concentrated his efforts in the Fort William/Port Arthur area where he stayed for a week. Cassidy drove into Alberta to attack the Workers Party in Edmonton, one of its chief strongholds in the west. He hammered out the principle that the OBU was controlled by its members, unlike the craft unions: "when I belonged to the church I had no say in hiring or firing the Pope or running the Vatican, and these members [in the craft unions] have no say in what their leaders will do except collect the money."[33] These meetings had to be self-sustaining if the OBU treasury was not to be emptied. The usual practice was to pass the hat after Russell or Cassidy had finished their presentations and answered questions. The collection was then used to pay the cost of the hall and the printing and advertising. If anything was left—and this was not too usual—it was pocketed as expense money.

The campaign brought no spectacular results. In mid-April Russell returned to Winnipeg to battle the international unions in the CPR roundhouse but he was soon on the road again, headed west, to take over from

Cassidy who went home to care for his seriously-ill wife. Russell concentrated on railroad workers as he headed towards the mountains, stopping at Dauphin, Humboldt and Prince Albert. Progress was slow and hindered by the small amounts collected at meetings along the way. In the third week of May he arrived in Edmonton and spent several days working around the railroad shops of the Canadian National and Edmonton, Dunvegan and British Columbia Railways. Then it was on to Calgary, tired, and short of money. The weather was cold and rainy, attendance at meetings sparse. Russell managed to dig up enough cash to print five hundred meeting notices but when he went to the refineries in the pouring rain to hand them out, he discovered that the men were not working because of the weather. Through the rest of the day he walked in the downpour trying to nail the posters to telephone poles. He was usually an incurable optimist as far as his beloved OBU was concerned, but he had few illusions about Alberta: "I don't think . . . that you will get any big landslide just at present," he wrote of Edmonton.[34] Calgary did "not look very promising . . . I will just have to take things as they come."[35]

By the end of May, Russell was back in Winnipeg. The OBU now had so few paid-up members that it was necessary to ignore the constitutional provision of one delegate for every five thousand dues payers when plans were laid for the August, 1923 annual convention. Winnipeg's position as the main base of OBU strength was acknowledged with five delegates out of the expected twenty. When the convention was opened on August 3, fewer than 3100 members were represented and the entire first day was taken up with individual delegate reports on the state of the OBU in each district. General secretary Catherine Rose, who was the Winnipeg central labour council's stenographer, provided small consolation with her assertion that "it is the proof of the strong desire of the workers for such an organization as the One Big Union that in a period of industrial depression and intense opposition from all sides, we have been able to hold our organization together." The dominant concern, expressed by most delegates, was that systematic organizing outside Winnipeg had stopped after Russell's return from Alberta at the end of May. "We must not use all our energies in one place," warned Calgary's A. G. Broatch. "We must find some method different to what we have adopted in the past for organising at outside points."[36]

In mid-September, Ben Legere travelled from Winnipeg to the west coast, at his own expense, to rough out a strategy for future organizing. Only in Sandon, British Columbia did he find a healthy and functioning OBU unit under Tommy Roberts' leadership. Wherever he went, meetings were sparsely attended and collections small. He blamed the inabilities or laziness of local OBU representatives. In Nanaimo, for example, "Comrade Barnard," whose wages from the OBU had been cut when the membership of the local miners unit had almost disappeared, "started a stationery store and is now one of the little business men of the town, with anything but the right O.B.U. psychology." Legere minced no words. The whole existing machinery was useless and there was no use sending out organizers to wander aimlessly trying to pay their way as they went. It would be necessary for permanent, full-time organizers to settle at key points for periods up to a year. After a month or two, Legere believed, there should be enough local members to share expenses for the organizer and his needs. Legere suggested Calgary for the first office and pointed to Tom Cassidy as the ideal man.[37]

Cassidy had been a pillar of OBU organizing effort for years. He had travelled from Toronto to Chicago to Vancouver for the One Big Union, and he knew every Dauphin, Humboldt and Medicine Hat in between. But his usefulness to the OBU was at an end, regardless of what Legere had in mind. He was a sick man—tubercular—and he was controversial. He considered himself an apostle of the "new revolutionary morality" and occasionally lectured on birth control and abortion. In the summer of 1923 he scandalized audiences at the Brandon and Winnipeg labour churches with his views on sexual freedom. In September, rumours circulated that he had three wives in western Canada and had engaged in sexual adventures with OBU secretary Catherine Rose in a Brandon hotel.[38]

The OBU had never faced a problem like this before. The executive's first solution was to separate Rose and Cassidy as quietly as possible. A request for organizing help from Port Arthur provided the excuse to relieve Cassidy from his position as Winnipeg organizer and send him east. At the same time, discreet approaches were made to Rose, through her father, to secure her resignation in return for a favourable employment recommendation. She refused to quit; Cassidy refused to go to Port Arthur. He insisted that the executive was hiding the real reason they wanted him to go east which was "his moral character." He was, accordingly, suspended and called in to face them.[39]

The meeting was held September 26, 1923. At first several executive members fenced with Cassidy about his refusal to follow orders, but Cassidy grew impatient and told them to "act like men and get at the real reason." Woodward spoke up: "Would not, say the episode at Brandon, in view of the fact that you were general organizer and Miss Rose was secretary of the [general executive board] and of the [central labour council], would the Executive not be justified in taking the action they did?" Cassidy proclaimed his innocence: "Prove the Brandon episode . . . when the charge is made I will then present my defense. Rumor has it also that I was drunk in Swift Current. I was too, and I admit it . . . but

Fools and Wise Men

I am not going to be a victim of a frame up . . . I have a reputation to look after . . . and I don't propose to leave here or sneak out quietly with a cloud hanging over me."

"You admit the truth of the rumor of being drunk. Why won't you either affirm or deny the affair at Brandon?"

"Just let a charge be laid . . . I will admit that I was registered at a Brandon hotel as T. Cassidy & wife. I will also admit that Miss Rose was seen in my company at that time, but even admitting all this I can knock any charge that is made into a cocked hat." Woodward sarcastically pointed out that Cassidy, who had "gloried in having the only real revolutionary morality" was now "seeking to hide it."[40] When Rose refused to resign quietly, she was dismissed. The executive charged the couple with being "egotistical enough to consider the vindication of their moral standards of greater importance than the development of the movement" and threatened the central labour council that they would all resign if their actions were not upheld.[41] Rose and Cassidy tried to defend themselves before the council— Rose charged that she was the victim of discrimination, "a fine thing for a rank and file movement"—but they had no chance. Tom Mace reminded the delegates that the Socialist Party of America had been smeared with a "free love" label by the press not too long before, a lesson not lost on other members. The executive was upheld after an emotional and angry debate.[42]

Cassidy refused to let the issue die. He was getting sicker by the week but he continued to haunt OBU headquarters and attend council meetings though he was not a delegate. The OBU leaders wanted to dispose of the affair as quietly as possible but Cassidy wrote letters to units outside of Winnipeg complaining of the treatment he had received. Each time one of these units wrote the council for more information, there was a sharp debate and Cassidy was accused of having nothing better to do than disrupt the organization. Russell complained that he was "dissipating the energies" of the council and implored the membership to forget the matter and get down to business.[43] But his advice was ignored and a special committee was elected to look into the entire affair after Cassidy accused Woodward of having him investigated by a private detective. Cassidy also threatened to write a book exposing the executive but he was sicker than most realized. On February 13, 1924 he died. He was thirty-six. Short weeks before, Woodward and the executive had attacked Cassidy's refusal to surrender quietly and had accused him of endangering the One Big Union. Once he was safely in the ground, Woodward blamed "the system" for his death and lamented a "distinct loss to the working class movement."[44]

Cassidy's demise meant the loss of yet another of the radical vanguard which had led the One Big Union to the peak of its success in 1919. By February, 1924, Cassidy and Houston were dead. Joe and Sarah Knight, Jack Kavanagh, Becky Buhay and A. S. Wells had deserted to the Communist Party. Dick Johns quietly faded out of the scene after his release from prison and turned his mind to education and vocational instruction. Bill Pritchard made a rousing return to the coast in the spring of 1921, but soon drifted back to the longshoremen's union. In the great Vancouver dock strike of 1923, in which the union's hold on the docks was smashed by the Shipping Federation in a two-month struggle, Pritchard edited the strikers' newspaper and was helped by Vic Midgley. Midgley drifted back to Vancouver, after the transfer of the OBU head office to Winnipeg, and rejoined the lathers union. In February, 1923, he was elected that union's delegate to the Vancouver trades council, but some delegates refused to forget or forgive Midgley's OBU sins and engineered his expulsion from the council two weeks later. When he tried again in May, 1924, he was successful. He continued to write to Russell but took no active part in OBU affairs. P. M. Christophers, who also kept in touch, had been elected to the Alberta legislature for the Rocky Mountain House constituency in 1921. Of the old guard, only Tommy Roberts in Sandon, A. G. Broatch in Calgary and Bob Russell, now secretary of the Winnipeg central labour council, were left.

The Rose/Cassidy matter left a bitter aftertaste. Members in Winnipeg and elsewhere continued to talk about it even after Cassidy's death. But concern for the struggles of the living soon pushed the unpleasant memory into the background. Towards the end of 1923 there were signs that the One Big Union might have a future after all. The struggles of Nova Scotia coal miners and steel workers against the giant British Empire Steel and Coal Corporation (BESCO), lord of almost the entire steel and coal industry in the province, were complicated by a battle between left and right inside the union, and the desire of the United Mine Workers' leadership in the United States to purge the local radicals. The confusion gave the One Big Union its first real chance to break new ground since 1920. The Cape Breton coal fields and the Sydney steel mill were the scene of mounting worker discontent and frustration since early 1922. In that year a BESCO drive to cut coal miners' wages touched off a series of slowdowns in the collieries that lasted from mid-March, 1922 until early summer. United Mine Workers' headquarters created considerable resentment in Nova Scotia with their advice to accept wage cuts in the face of rising unemployment and a depressed coal market. In June, 1922, a left-wing slate led by J. B. "Jimmy" McLachlan and "Red" Dan Livingstone captured the executive of District 26, which was composed of Nova Scotia and New Brunswick miners, with a pledge to resist wage cuts with a 100% strike (including fan and pump men) if necessary. This strike began August 15 and lasted to the end of the month. Twelve thousand miners were off the job and troops were used to guard company property and protect BESCO strikebreakers. The strike ended when BESCO agreed to restore 12% of a 30% wage cut imposed previously.[45]

The miners' strike set the scene for a strike of steelworkers the following June in Sydney. These men were members of the Amalgamated Association of Iron, Steel and Tin Workers and were also defending themselves against a wage cut. For a brief time the strikers seized part of the steel plant, and pitched battles with company and provincial police followed. On July 1, 1923, provincial police attacked the Whitney Pier section of town where many strikers lived, and beat and arrested many of them and members of their families. When news of the raid reached the mining towns, the District 26 executive presented Liberal premier E. H. Armstrong with an ultimatum—pull the police out or face a general strike of the mines. On midnight, July 3, the strike began, and by July 12, all the men were off the job. Six days later, UMW president Lewis revoked the district charter because the strike was in violation of an existing contract. McLachlan and Livingston were removed and replaced by a provisional executive, faithful to Lewis, headed by international organizer Silby Barrett. By the end of July, the strike was over. The miners and the steelworkers had been defeated.[46]

The relationship between the Nova Scotia miners and their union was strained to the breaking point by these events. As far as the miners were concerned, the union had not supported their fight against the 1922 wage cut and had betrayed their campaign to help their fellow BESCO employees in the steel mills in 1923. As far as Lewis was concerned, the Nova Scotia miners were being misled by Communists such as McLachlan, who had tried, in the summer of 1922, to withdraw from the UMW and join the Profintern and who had telegraphed Lenin to seek his support in the strike. The situation was ripe for the One Big Union. Initially, it was the Sydney steelworkers, led by Forman Waye, a machinist elected to the Nova Scotia legislature under the Farmer-Labour banner in July, 1920, who showed the greatest interest in the OBU.[47] There was no hesitation in Winnipeg and by the end of 1923 OBU literature was pouring into the region.[48]

On January 15, 1924, the District 26 miners struck once again against a BESCO wage cut. Barrett and other district officials went to Montreal to bargain with the company and publicly pledged to restore wages to pre-1922 levels. Within days they announced a settlement and ordered the men back to work, but when the terms of the arrangement were revealed, it was apparent the miners were only slightly better off than before. The men felt betrayed and locals at Stellerton and Thorburn in Pictou County came close to open revolt. In early March, district officials held a referendum on the agreement, the miners rejected it by a 3-to-1 margin and the vote was completely ignored. On March 24, UMW headquarters replaced Barrett with William Houston, and one month later UMW headquarters and BESCO arranged a special wage deduction to recover UMW funds expended in the January, 1924 strike. The money was to go directly from the miners' pay to BESCO and then to Houston. This was the last straw and in mid-May an unauthorized meeting of representatives of all locals in District 26 met at New Glasgow, Nova Scotia to discuss the situation. A committee was appointed to prepare the ground for a full restoration of autonomy and district-wide elections.[49]

The Nova Scotia miners were on the verge of a full-scale revolt against the UMW but for the moment Russell could do little more than write letters. Nova Scotia was full of potential, and Russell was confident of a major breakthrough;[50] but Winnipeg, and particularly the railway shops, were where a large number of the remaining OBU members were concentrated. In the early spring of 1924, the OBU's hold on these workers was directly challenged by the fixation of craft unions and management alike, with a new worker-management cooperation scheme known as the Baltimore and Ohio Plan.

The B & O Plan was first worked out by the International Association of Machinists and the Baltimore and Ohio Railroad in early 1923 after a nation-wide shop-craft strike in the United States in July, 1922. The agreement was first instituted at the B & O shops at Glenwood, Pennsylvania to provide increased union-management cooperation and greater worker reward through increased productivity and output. The president of the IAM, William Johnston, saw it as a way of introducing industrial democracy to the work place: "If . . . we want to lay claim to the arguments, as the theory of industrial democracy stipulates, that industry can afford better wages and working conditions when its workers share in the management of it, then we must be prepared to assume definite responsibility for better industrial performance."[51]

In early 1924, Division 4, representing Canadian shopcraft workers, and the management of the Canadian National Railways began to examine the B & O Plan. The One Big Union reacted angrily, attacked the "slave scheme" and called on the rank and file to "stop its inauguration."[52] This was due not only to a basic mistrust of, and disagreement with, "industrial democracy," which smacked of employer-dominated works councils and company unionism, but also to the threat posed to the OBU. Management-craft union cooperation in the past had destroyed the OBU in the coalfields and the hardrock mining country and severely dam-

aged it elsewhere. The craft unions had already succeeded in keeping the OBU powerless in the Winnipeg
railway shops by freezing it out in signed contracts between Division 4 and the railroads. The B & O Plan
could be the final blow.

The annual meetings of Division 4 in Montreal in
mid-April endorsed the plan but the OBU continued to
battle against it. Meetings were held, literature distributed and editorials published to rally the workers. In
mid-June, two OBU members, Jack Clancy and Bill Foster, were fired from the Canadian National's Transcona
shops because of their anti-Plan activities. The OBU
tried to force their reinstatement with one hour strikes
but were unsuccessful.[53] The craft unions wanted it, Sir
Henry Thornton, president of Canadian National,
wanted it and the OBU was incapable of mounting the
pressure necessary to stop it. In early 1925, Canadian
National began instituting the plan on a trial basis.

While the OBU was fighting a losing battle in the CN
shops in Winnipeg, prospects for success in Nova Scotia
never looked brighter. In June, 1924, the general executive board decided to send Ben Legere into District 26
with instructions to work with local OBU sympathizers
to swing "the miners and steel workers into the O.B.U.
at the earliest possible moment."[54] With expenses covered by *Bulletin* lottery money, Legere travelled the
byways of Cape Breton spreading the OBU message
while he attacked BESCO, the Communists and the
leadership of the United Mine Workers. His first minor
success came in mid-August when a handful of Sydney
steel workers formed a small OBU unit.[55]

At the end of August, 1924, while Houston was in the
United States attending to personal business, UMW
headquarters suspended the charter of the Westville
local. Westville had been one of the Pictou County locals
leading the revolt against the provisional leadership of
District 26 since the imposed settlement of February

and March, 1924. The Nova Scotia miners were in no mood to bow to Lewis' threats. They launched a court action against Houston, who returned to Nova Scotia in early September, for failing to fulfill his responsibilities as president of District 26. Lewis backed off almost immediately and instructed Houston to call a convention at Truro, Nova Scotia on September 29. But the Pictou dissidents had no intention of waiting for the outcome of the Truro meeting. In the third week of September the executives of the three locals—Thorburn, Stellarton and Westville—set September 29 and 30 as the dates for a membership referendum to decide the future affiliation of their locals. They urged their members to vote for the OBU.[56]

Ever since June, Legere had been like a whirlwind for the One Big Union in Nova Scotia. He had capitalized on the tensions within UMW ranks and had managed to head off the influential Workers Party in the Pictou area. He was a thorn in the side of too many important people. On September 18, he was arrested by immigration authorities, charged with violations of the Immigration Act and ordered deported pending a hearing.[57] In Winnipeg, there was no question of leaving Legere to fend for himself and Russell rushed east while funds were raised to provide for Legere's defence. *Bulletin* editor Frank Woodward was furious. He blamed the arrest on the Communists and warned: "we can assure any pervert who has sought to drive the O.B.U. out of Nova Scotia by any such methods that the O.B.U. is in Nova Scotia to stay."[58]

The referendum in Pictou County appeared to confirm Woodward's claim. The vote produced a solid majority for secession and the *Halifax Herald* observed: "the One Big Union is the dominating branch of the labour movement in Pictou county as a result of the ballot . . . It was an overwhelming win for the One Big Union which got a combined majority in the towns of Thorburn and Stellarton."[59] On October 3, the Stellarton local withdrew from the UMW and joined the OBU, and was followed by the Thorburn and Westville locals before the month was out. The three then formed the Pictou County central labour council. To add to the good fortune, the charges against Legere, freed on bail shortly after his arrest, were dropped after the government decided it had no reason to deport him.[60]

With Legere free, he and Russell began to operate as a team. On one occasion they were addressing a packed meeting from a boxing ring in a small auditorium. Legere launched a vigorous attack on the Communists whom he accused of fabricating the stories that went into *The Worker*. Malcolm Blue, a diminutive boxer of local note, who had been a member of the Socialist Party in Regina, jumped on the apron of the ring and demanded that Legere "take it back." Legere landed one solid punch and knocked Blue off the ring. Russell, fearing a riot, took off his jacket, rolled up his sleeves and appealed for calm. He was still something of a martyr because of his trial and imprisonment—"a little Jesus" in his own words—and succeeded in restoring order. Then he threw out a challenge: "is it a fight you want, it's a fight you'll get, but we fellows from the west we fight a different way from what you fight here. . . . If you want us to bring down our boxers . . . we'll give you a show but out in the west we fight with our tongues and our heads." He then challenged Blue to a debate but Blue refused to return to the ring. Russell and Legere kept their skins and captured the audience.[61]

Despite the gains in Pictou, the OBU was unable to make any dent elsewhere. Russell and Legere were barred from the Truro convention even though they had been invited to address the delegates by Forman Waye. (Malcolm Bruce of the Workers Party was also denied entry.)

The convention was anything but a gathering of the

meek to pay homage to Lewis. A temporary executive, chosen to administer the district until a full pithead election was held in November, were all left-wingers and were headed by John W. Macleod, a friend and ally of Jimmy McLachlan. McLachlan himself was barred from running for district office by a Lewis edict, but was given a standing ovation when he spoke to the delegates.[62] The leadership emerging to take control of the district after more than a year of direct UMW administration was as militant as before. If the OBU counted on Lewis imposing a submissive executive on the district that would further alienate the rank and file, their hopes were in vain. Besides, OBU strength was not even certain in Pictou county. The Communists charged that hundreds of miners had not taken part in the referendum and OBU vote totals appeared to prove those claims.[63] In Stellarton and Thorburn, UMW locals continued to function.

For most coal miners, this was not a time for secession and division. Late in November, 1924, BESCO proposed a 20% wage cut as the basis for a new agreement to commence January 1, 1925. Macleod and the District executive put up a militant front and refused to consider it. They had fought BESCO tenaciously in each year of the previous three and were prepared to resist any further erosion of their living standards. BESCO wavered somewhat in the face of this steadfast opposition and eventually reduced its demand to a 10% reduction. But there it stood. Preparations for a strike went ahead as clerical staff were recruited to run pumps and fans. On March 3 and 4, credit was cut off at company stores in Glace Bay, Reserve, New Waterford and Sydney Mines and the collieries were closed. On March 6, miners in the rest of the district walked out and the fourth 100% strike in four years began.[64]

The Glace Bay miners' strike of 1925 was one of the longest and most violent in Canadian history.[65] It was a labour war and before it was over in early August, the miners and their families had been reduced to starvation, company and provincial police had run wild in police riots, pitched battles for plants, power stations and water sources had been fought and miners and their families had been beaten, shot, run out of their homes and killed. Once again militia patrolled the area and machine gun nests, electrified barbed wire and unsheathed bayonets became common sights in the coal towns. In June, before the arrival of the militia, frustrated miners and their families burned company stores and mine surface structures throughout the district. Stories of the privation and hardship suffered by the miners spread throughout Canada and relief poured in from every conceivable source, including the OBU which contributed indirectly through the Glace Bay Co-operative Store. The United Mine Workers, supporting a strike of 200 000 miners and facing lawsuits in the United States, was hard pressed to support its membership in Canada.

Any OBU activity aimed at undermining the UMW during the strike, or the months of tension leading up to it, would have been foolish and perhaps fatal. Thus, attacks on the leadership of District 26 were notable by their absence as the OBU concentrated instead on the Communists, who were accused of betraying the miners, and Lewis, who was berated for the UMW's weak financial support.[66] The Communists charged that the OBU was secretly trying to negotiate a deal with BESCO,[67] but this was unlikely, given the temper of the rank and file miners. Russell summed up the OBU attitude at a mass meeting of Glace Bay miners in July when he urged them to "Win your fight first, change cards after."[68]

The strike finally ended on August 10. The newly-elected Conservative government of E. N. Rhodes worked out a settlement which included a partial wage cut and guarantees against discrimination. A provincially-appointed royal commission was promised to investigate the affairs of BESCO and to determine the company's ability to pay. It was a bad deal for the miners, especially since BESCO ignored its promise not to establish a blacklist, but they had little choice. They had lost over 7 million dollars in wages and could fight no more.

With the strike over, OBU organizing efforts were stepped up and plans laid for a permanent resident organizer and an OBU office on the Nova Scotia mainland at New Glasgow. But even though the UMW had been defeated in the strike, it was still the major union force in the coal fields as far as most miners were concerned. The OBU made no progress against the UMW in the face of the tremendous apathy and weariness that settled over the miners in the remaining months of 1925 and the first months of 1926. In Pictou county the OBU's grip remained weak with hundreds "sitting on the fence" and many others still faithful to the UMW.[69] These men were a thorn in the OBU's side and showed up to disrupt a mass meeting on at least one occasion. UMW plans, in early 1926, to enforce a checkoff for all BESCO employees were more dangerous but OBU indignation meetings failed to rouse any support. Few miners bothered to attend OBU rallies or protest demonstrations and OBU organizers were embarrassed time and again by empty halls and unfilled seats. In early July, 1926, they reluctantly decided to discontinue public meetings and recommend to Winnipeg that they be withdrawn and that further organizing be done by local part-time men only.[70]

In late July, miners at three collieries in Glace Bay, New Waterford and Sydney Mines struck when three of their number, OBU members, refused to sign the UMW checkoff. They scored a complete victory at New Waterford but were blocked in Sydney Mines and Glace Bay when Macleod and several other UMW officials were charged in court with threatening to throw OBU men down a mine shaft.[71] The brief respite gave OBU leaders in Pictou County a chance to prepare for the next assault which came on August 24. The first blow was struck at Stellarton against two collieries operated by the Acadia Coal Company, a BESCO subsidiary. At first the company remained neutral, but on August 31, the company issued a statement that told its employees to join the UMW if they wanted to work and barred 200 miners from going underground until they signed the checkoff. Four who refused were fired.[72] The OBU charged that "District 26 officials [were] going to pimp for BESCO" and appealed to the provincial government, but aroused little sympathy in the area.[73] Within weeks, the remnants of OBU strength in Pictou melted away, though a handful of miners in Thorburn struggled to keep their unit alive.

The losing struggle over the checkoff and the pessimistic outlook of the permanent organizers almost inclined the general executive board to cut its losses and pull out. But under Russell's constant prodding, it roused itself to further efforts.[74] Russell either had little grasp of the realities or felt, like Tommy Roberts in Sandon, that a withdrawal from Nova Scotia after all the time and money that had gone into it, would have "a detrimental effect on the organization."[75] Thus, in the face of all reason, the office in New Glasgow was maintained and a new organizer sent in.

In the rest of 1926 and most of 1927, the OBU continued its hopeless fight for survival in Nova Scotia. An Inverness unit continued to exist as a functioning body and a few scattered members kept the faith in towns such as Sydney Mines. More money was poured into the New Glasgow office and the one full-time organizer busied himself in the fruitless search for members until February, 1927. Several part-time organizers, paid on the basis of members recruited, were also used, but were notoriously unreliable. One list of names submitted to Winnipeg came straight from a Cape Breton cemetery.[76] In Winnipeg, countless lengthy and sometimes bitter debates over future tactics in Nova Scotia occupied the general executive board, as if the fate of thousands of workers hung in the balance rather than a mere handful. None of the OBU leaders dared admit that their dream of a phoenix-like rise to power in the east lay shattered.

By the spring of 1926 it was obvious to all, even Russell, that the OBU was in deep trouble. In May, the general executive board tried to end the OBU's almost complete isolation. For several years the IWW had sought merger or working agreements with the OBU but had always been rebuffed. This time the IWW suggested a unity conference with the OBU and the newly-formed Mine Workers Union of Canada, composed of western miners who had seceded from the UMW.[77] The OBU was not interested in the IWW proposal, but did send feelers to other independent unions, particularly the Canadian Brotherhood of Railway Employees headed by Aaron R. Mosher. The CBRE had been expelled from the Trades Congress in 1920 because it was dual to the AFL-affiliated Brotherhood of Railway and Steamship Clerks. Mosher was interested, but worried that some unions would not respond because the call had come from the OBU.[78] Nonetheless, plans for a unity conference took shape. Mosher spearheaded the campaign along with the small Canadian Federation of Labour, a remnant of those unions expelled by the Trades Congress for dualism at the Berlin, (now Kitchener) Ontario, convention of 1902. A preliminary meeting at Toronto in late November, 1926 decided to hold the unity conference in Montreal in March, 1927.[79] Invitations were issued in early February, 1927, and four OBU representatives were chosen to attend, including

Russell. Not once, in all of the discussion inside the Winnipeg central labour council, the General Executive Board, or the *Bulletin*, was there any mention of the implausibility of a union which held the principles the OBU still claimed to be faithful to, joining a congress of other unions.

"Bands of Solidarity Welded at Conference," proclaimed the *Bulletin* as the founding meeting of the All Canadian Congress of Labour got underway in Montreal on March 16.[80] The convention was attended by 107 delegates representing eight unions, the largest of which was the Canadian Brotherhood of Railway Employees. The Congress claimed to represent 46 269 workers, but if this was based on the 19 245 members publicly claimed by the OBU, there were probably closer to 25 000. The OBU actually paid dues on only 1600 members to the new Congress for 1927.[81] Congress membership was restricted to Canadian unions of either the craft or industrial variety and Mosher was elected first president. The preamble to the constitution of the ACCL proclaimed that it was founded to: free Canadian workers from the "reactionary influence" of United States unions; promote the general welfare of Canadian workers; procure higher real wages and better working conditions, while recognizing that workers could not "under the present system . . . obtain the full value of their labour"; and promote, amongst the workers, a thorough understanding of working class economics.[82] The four OBU delegates were assigned positions on various Congress committees and one was given a place on the executive board. When the One Big Union's fifth general convention met at Winnipeg in early May, 1927, the first held in almost four years, the merger with the ACCL was endorsed without objection.[83] This would have been unheard of seven years before, but in the spring of 1927 it was no longer a question of revolt; it was a matter of survival.

Chapter 10

The End of the One Big Union

The One Big Union carried on—a living fossil—for twenty-nine more years. After 1927, without the steady flow of *Bulletin* gambling receipts, its money dried up rapidly. When OBU member William Young was dismissed from his job at the Transcona Shops in 1927, the OBU sponsored a suit against Canadian National Railways to force Young's reinstatement. The case dragged through two years of appeals before the Judicial Committee of the Privy Council finally upheld the dismissal in 1929; the OBU had spent $17 000 in vain and was now broke. In August, 1929, the union's last permanent organizer was dismissed.[1]

Russell continued to work for the OBU as secretary to the Winnipeg central labour council. He was organizer, mediator, negotiator and business agent. Most of his work was in Winnipeg amongst the remaining OBU members in the transit system, and the hotel, restaurant and bakery industries. He made an occasional foray to other areas—the Estevan/Bienfait coal fields in southern Saskatchewan in the late 'thirties, for example—but this kind of organizing was too expensive and yielded almost nothing. During the second World War he served briefly on the Manitoba War Labour Board and with the federal Unemployment Insurance Commission. He left Winnipeg in 1941 to work in an Ontario war plant, but returned to take up his old OBU post in the spring of 1944.

Russell and the other OBU stalwarts refused to wind up the affairs of their union or to submerge its identity in an organization such as the All Canadian Congress of Labour. Their fierce independence was an obstacle to smooth relations with the new partner. When the OBU failed to pay its share of dues to the ACCL in 1928, it was expelled. The following year it pleaded poverty and was granted re-admission. In 1936, after intriguing against the ACCL's leadership and attempting to block the Congress' annual convention, it was expelled again. This time the OBU joined the newly re-created Canadian Federation of Labour which was, in reality, a small collection of ACCL dissidents. Even this "marriage" only lasted three years.[2]

In 1940 the All Canadian Congress of Labour linked up with Canadian branches of the new United States-based Congress of Industrial Organizations to form the Canadian Congress of Labour. The CCL had more autonomy than the older Trades and Labour Congress (affiliated to the American Federation of Labor) and was organized with one union for each industry. When it entered the Winnipeg area to begin organizing steel and packing house workers shortly after its birth, it was supported by the One Big Union. Merger discussions began. Canadian Congress leaders insisted that the OBU dissolve after affiliation and its members find places in existing Congress unions. This was not acceptable and the talks collapsed in February, 1943.[3]

In 1955 the American Federation of Labor and the Congress of Industrial Organizations in the United States joined in permanent union. This set the stage for a similar merger of the Trades Congress and the Canadian Congress of Labour in Canada, and a national merger committee was established by the two organizations to pave the way for a new, united Canadian Labour Congress. Provincial and local affiliates were instructed to establish similar bodies. In Winnipeg, the OBU central labour council decided to examine the possibility of joining the Canadian Labour Congress and approached the Winnipeg and District labour council (TLC) and the Winnipeg labour council (CCL) to find out what the terms of such a union might be. They were invited to participate in discussions between the two international councils and were urged to make application to the national merger committee in Ottawa. In early December, 1955, they sent representatives to the local talks and the following March applied to affiliate as a "national union" with the guarantee that they be allowed to keep their structural integrity in the same way that "the integrity of the respective members of the two congresses has been guaranteed." They were advised their application would be considered by the Canadian Labour Congress after it was officially launched and its executive council chosen at the forthcoming unity meeting.[4]

The Canadian Labour Congress' founding convention opened at Toronto April 23, 1956. Bob Russell and two other OBU delegates were in attendance though they had no assurance their application would be accepted, and were informed that it would not be acted on until the last day of the convention. They were invited to the platform and introduced to the 1600 delegates by president-elect Claude Jodoin where they were given a rousing welcome—testimony to the respect now held for Russell by his onetime bitter foes. But the affiliation did not proceed smoothly. The OBU's insistence on maintaining its identity was clearly not acceptable to a number of unions whose jurisdictions conflicted with some of the surviving OBU units, particularly the transit workers and machinists. The same problem faced the CLC in its efforts to woo the 100 000 members of the Quebec-based Canadian and Catholic Confederation of Labour, a bitter rival of the international and national Canadian unions for many decades. But the Quebec unions had the power of numbers and were clearly dynamic and growing institutions—the OBU was a relic. Many delegates were willing to let the touchy issue of CCCL affiliation rest with the incoming executive, but the OBU difficulties never got to the convention floor.

In a closed meeting between the OBU delegates and the leaders of the Canadian Labour Congress, the issue was settled and the fate of the One Big Union sealed. The application was changed from a national to a provincial organization, allowing the CLC to absorb the OBU. After the agreement was struck, the three Winnipeg councils moved a resolution on the convention floor recommending that the incoming Canadian Labour Congress executive council accept the OBU's application "on the understanding that the various units of the One Big Union . . . endeavour to secure membership in the national or international organizations affiliated with the Canadian Labour Congress holding jurisdiction in the fields." It passed unanimously. OBU members were given two years to find new affiliations.[5] These terms were later accepted by the OBU executive.

The End of the One Big Union

At 8:00 p.m. Tuesday, June 6, 1956, OBU central labour council vice-president Curtis called the last OBU meeting to order in Winnipeg. The regular business was taken care of quickly. Russell then handed out copies of the report of the merger committee of the three Winnipeg councils and the draft constitution and bylaws of the soon-to-be united Winnipeg and District Labour Council. The OBU was allotted three positions on the executive and Russell was to be the executive secretary. The merger formula was adopted, the constitution endorsed and representatives elected to fill the OBU positions. It was then moved and seconded that the meeting adjourn.

But this was their last session. Reg Slocombe took the floor; something had to be said. The council was closing a chapter in the history of labour but "opening a new one with a larger horizon." It was recognized all over that the OBU was small but had made history and a great contribution. It had been "one of the principle driving forces in the labour movement of Canada." He thanked Bob Russell who had been general secretary through the years and who had turned down better positions to carry on the struggle for the OBU; the whole labour movement owed him its gratitude for the service he had contributed.

Russell stood. He had never been a man for public sentimentality. What thoughts went through his mind? Perhaps he remembered his passage to Canada before the Great War, or his climb through the ranks of the machinists union. More likely he recalled the impassioned speeches, the fervour, the religious faith that marked the Western Labor Conference in Calgary more than thirty-seven years before; and his jail cell at Stony Mountain penitentiary. Did he recall the bitterness he must have felt when attacked at the founding meeting of the Workers Party in Toronto in February, 1922? Or the despair born in futile moments trudging through a

251

cold spring rain in Calgary, nailing wet posters to telephone poles for a meeting no one came to? If these
memories clouded his thoughts, he said nothing of
them. He thanked Slocombe and expressed the hope
that the One Big Union membership would continue to
be active in the new organization. Curtis then banged
his gavel and the One Big Union passed into history.[6]

The One Big Union had been intended by its founders to be the vehicle of revolt against capitalism and the
craft union system, while offering a more effective trade
union for the daily struggle. It was one product of the
labour radicalism which developed in the Canadian west
prior to 1920 and of a broad radical coalition, with an
ill-defined philosophy, which emerged by the end of the
First World War. It took in the skilled craftsmen of the
cities and the semi-skilled coal miners, hardrock miners
and loggers on the frontiers. It included syndicalists,
political socialists and social democrats, industrial unionists and amalgamationists. It was radical because it
aimed to accomplish two specific objectives at the same
time: fundamental and revolutionary change in society
and the creation of a system of trade unions that would
greatly increase the economic and political power of the
workers. Every one of these objectives commanded considerable support at the 1919 conventions of the Alberta
and British Columbia Federations of Labor and District
18 of the United Mine Workers. The Western Labor
Conference of March, 1919 was an even truer reflection
of them.

The radical character of the western labour movement was a reflection of the shifting patterns of immigration, industrial development, class polarization, political alignment and broad economic conditions that
affected the west in its early years. All western workers
were not radicals. Those who were radical became so for
different reasons and at different times. They always
depended upon the support of others for their power.

The radical labour movement was no different from movements everywhere in that there were committed and hard-working leaders commanding the support of less committed followers who were probably in the majority. Bob Russell changed little from 1914 to 1919. What changed was the willingness of others to support him. Radical leaders emerged to take control—or seriously challenge for control—because thousands of less radical workers turned to them for direction in the closing years of the war.

Miners turned to radicalism and radical leadership before city workers. The coal miners of Vancouver Island, the Crows Nest Pass and Alberta and the hardrock miners of British Columbia rejected mere reform early and swung behind Marxist political organizations such as the Socialist Party of Canada. They provided fertile ground for doctrines of radical industrial unionism and syndicalism and were among the strongest supporters of the Industrial Workers of the World. The miners formed a large and cohesive group in British Columbia and greatly influenced the urban crafts and railroad lodges. The provincial federation, created in 1910, became a vehicle by which the entire provincial labour movement could be radicalized. The miners' influence was strong when exercised at provincial federation conventions, at political organization meetings and through executive committees. This is one reason why radicals were more influential in Vancouver prior to 1914 than in other western cities. In Alberta the craft unions formed a provincial federation partly to offset the coal miners' influence, but it too was soon a miners' sounding board.

Radicalism emerged first and was strongest among the miners because of the nature of their work and the condition of the communities in which they lived. In the company camps, workers with a common employer and common interests were grouped into a single community. Their struggle with the boss did not begin with the morning whistle and end when the shift was over, because the entire area was company property. They lived with the company every hour of the day and night. They were grouped together to face a common enemy above ground and kept together to face the common dangers of gas, coal dust, rockfall, below ground. They were isolated in their lives, in their work and in their too often violent deaths.

Those who lived in open towns such as Sandon or Rossland in the British Columbia hardrock mining country were only slightly better off. These towns were cut off from the outside by the high mountains and thick forests of the Kootenay range and were dominated by the mining companies and smelter operators. Prices were high, variety restricted. Hotel operators plied expensive liquor, prostitutes joyless sex. These towns offered more services with a variety of outfitters, tobacconists, assayers and laundries, but were small and closed in. Life was raw, opportunity severely limited, and the workers who drank together and dug quartz together made common cause through their tightly knit unions. In each community, the miners' hall was a main centre of recreation, political debate and discussion; almost as important as the town hall itself.

The miners were almost all immigrants. They had come to the Canadian west to build new lives, to live in freedom, to get rich, to escape oppression or grinding poverty, to find relief from societies of squires, lords and industrial masters. It did not take long for many to realize that the mining frontier of western Canada was as bad a place as any in the world: its mines as deadly, its towns as filthy and disease-ridden, its society as closed and polarized. Freedom, opportunity, wealth were too often illusions. Those who came from societies where bare survival was the normal order of things probably considered the Canadian west a fulfillment of their dreams. Work was steady, wages adequate, starvation unknown. But those who came from societies with higher living standards, a broad franchise, traditions of dissent—such as the United States, Great Britain, even central and eastern Canada—saw things differently. For these men, particularly those with backgrounds in trade unionism, or socialism, the first response was trade union organization. They flocked into unions and battled operators with militancy and resolve. Sometimes they won, more often they were beaten. But the basic structure of society remained unchanged. Clearly trade unionism was not enough and the very bastions of capitalism had to be stormed if they were to be liberated. Thus they became radical or supported radical leadership.

Radicalism took longer to dominate the urban labour movement even though it was always present. City workers fought for the radicals' right to preach their cause, but did not endorse their aims. In part this was because they had few clear objectives in common. But it was mainly true because their environment was less dangerous, less polarized, less isolated than the mining communities or logging camps. In the cities there were churches, social clubs, choirs, bars, whorehouses. There were women. There were priests, teachers, doctors, clerks, small shopkeepers. There even appeared, at first, to be opportunity. Skilled workers formed strong unions, bought small pieces of property, built houses and even opened businesses. There were radicals, but there was little concerted radical purpose.

The war created conditions which allowed radicals to capture the support of the city workers. Inflation and manpower shortages prompted the unions to drive for increased organization, union recognition and higher wages. But they were often stopped by court injunctions, orders-in-council and the indifference or hostility of the federal cabinet and the Imperial Munitions

Board. Many otherwise economic and industrial issues, such as higher wages for railway shopcraft workers, became political, as worker hostility towards the war itself became a major issue. The domestic war experience brought to many the reality that opportunity was an illusion and that the elites would not sacrifice or share their privileges, even in the sacred cause of "saving the world for democracy." Many thousands who went overseas realized, as did George Sherston, autobiographical hero of English novelist Siegfried Sassoon's *Memoirs of an Infantry Officer*, that "life, for the majority of the population, [was] an unlovely struggle against unfair odds, culminating in a cheap funeral." The sight of a dead English soldier brought Sherston to the conclusion that war was "simply a continuation of 'life' by other means."[7] Thus the urban workers also began to turn to radicalism. By the fall of 1918 they were ready to unite with the miners in a revolt against capitalism and the trade union system they accused of being its servant.

The American Federation of Labor, moulded and interpreted by Samuel Gompers, came to the west before the dawn of the twentieth century. By 1914 most western union members were tied to it because it offered easy access to established unions with ample treasuries and experienced leaders. It was built on a philosophy—often referred to as Gompersism—of strict organization by craft with tightly defined rules of jurisdiction. It rejected partisan political action, accepted the basic tenets of capitalism and shared the general North American faith in opportunity. It held that workers could improve their lot and their position if they were properly organized. Its aim was simple—to sell labour and skill at the highest possible price and create conditions through organization, strikes and boycotts which would increase the workers' power to influence the labour market. This would bring better wages, and improved working conditions, and earn a greater share of the wealth of modern capitalism. It was an austere code. The workers of western Canada were uncomfortable with it from the beginning even though it was the creed of their leaders in central Canada and the United States. But these westerners were pragmatists. They shared Gompers' belief in strong business unionism to help win the daily struggles and they fought for union recognition, contracts and checkoffs to help them sell their labour at the best possible price. This marked them off from some radicals in Europe, Great Britain, and even the IWW in the United States, who scorned formal dealings with the boss. But western radicals also believed these tactics only won temporary victories and would not achieve the justice and emancipation they so passionately sought. The broader objectives demanded socialism, syndicalism, revolution. Their radicalism was marked, therefore, by the development of a second, political level of activity and agitation. Thus the 1914 District 18, United Mine Workers convention not only elected a scale committee to bargain with the coal operators, it also endorsed the Socialist Party of Canada, while the 1919 convention denounced the contract system, although it refused to chart a course leading to its abolition.

In September, 1918, these workers, radicals or supporters of radicalism, went to Quebec City to change the Trades and Labor Congress from the slave of Gompersism that it was, to an organization capable of fighting for fundamental social and political changes. They had concluded that political and industrial battles were part of the same struggle. They had been uncomfortable with craft unionism for years because the craft unions that existed were few and they were isolated in the west. These workers believed they needed amalgamation of the different crafts in each industry to make fewer, larger, industrial unions in place of many, fragmented crafts. Now they were ready to weld their faith in industrial unions to a program of action for the overthrow of capitalism. They were not quite sure how the latter, perhaps more important, goal was to be achieved, and there were many differences of opinion among them, but they knew that the Trades Congress was useless to them as it stood. They soon found that change was hopeless. There were radicals in Ontario, Quebec and the Maritimes, but not enough to enable the westerners to prevail. Secession was the only solution if the movement was to forge ahead.

After their defeat at Quebec, a new form of trade unionism, based on the needs and ideas of western workers, was possible. This should have been based on a philosophy of vigorous action, organized in a practical manner along industrial lines and capable of holding and protecting its membership against the onslaughts that were sure to come. But the initiative was seized, at this point, by members of the Socialist Party of Canada who placed themselves at the head of the secessionist movement and were able to impose their own concepts on the 1919 conventions and the OBU which grew from them. The One Big Union which emerged was little more than a reflection of their own narrow views.

Western workers demanded organization by industry. The main leadership of the OBU—Midgley, Pritchard, Russell, Kavanagh—believed this was as obsolete as craft unionism. They wanted to bring all workers into one union with no internal divisions except those based on area. For a time they had to put up with separate departments for the loggers, hardrock miners and coal miners, but this was to be only temporary. Their struggle with Winch, not to mention their speeches, pamphlets and other public and private expressions of opinion, leaves no doubt they wanted to dissolve even these divisions as soon as possible. But this concept was itself outmoded. It was very much like the structure of the old Knights of Labor and the Grand National Consolidated Trades Union. Few understood the concept or saw its necessity. Organization by district was fine for a union dedicated to general strikes but awkward for other purposes. The preoccupation with the general strike, not as a means to revolution but as a way of pressuring governments and employers, was as much a product of their own experience as anything else. But regardless of where it came from, it was impractical and was recognized as such after the failure of the general strike in Winnipeg. Many thousands of workers were probably interested in industrial unionism for no other reason than the desire for a more effective organization to fight the boss. They were not revolutionaries and saw the OBU as a larger, better union to serve their needs. But they were soon disappointed and discovered that the OBU was actually less effective than the craft unions.

Other western workers demanded action to destroy or fundamentally change capitalism. But the leaders of the One Big Union not only rejected electoral political action, they also saw no need to lay down a definite program for radical or revolutionary change. They believed the OBU was constructed in such a way that it offered a more effective vehicle for advancing and protecting the workers' interests than any political party. They also held that the inevitability of revolution—as forecast by Marx—made revolutionary planning unnecessary. Those who demanded a definite and vigorous program, who were not content to sit and wait, had to look elsewhere. This is why Knight, Wells, Kavanagh and others defected to the Communist Party.

At first the internal weaknesses and shortcomings were not apparent to most OBU supporters. Not until early 1920 did the true character of the One Big Union emerge because up to this point it was engaged in a battle just to establish itself. The general and sympathetic strikes of May and June, 1919 hurt the fledgling organization in every large city in the west except Winnipeg. In Vancouver, Edmonton, Calgary and elsewhere, radical leaders, who were usually the foremost OBU men in each locality, called on their followers to launch sympathetic strikes to back up the Winnipeg strikers. In most cases the rank and file showed enough faith in their leaders to make a good effort. But this was not their battle even though they sympathized with their fellows in Winnipeg. The strikes were poorly planned and had no clear objectives. When they collapsed, as they all did sooner or later, the radicals fell into disfavour.

The men representing the American Federation of Labor and the Trades Congress—Rigg, Varley, Farmilo—rushed into the breach. They kept cool and refused to be sidetracked by useless public debates. They knew that if they could shore up the crumbling international union structure, safeguard its property and keep hold of its charters, they might have a chance to defeat the OBU. Their tactics were very effective in cities where unsuccessful sympathetic strikes had split the labour leadership and brought OBU supporters into disfavour. In Winnipeg, where the general strike was not a partisan issue to split OBU and international, they were less effective but did assure, nonetheless, that a continuing international union presence would challenge the stronger OBU at every turn.

In Winnipeg, the general strike probably helped the OBU despite the loss of Russell and Johns to federal prison. Here the strike grew out of local issues grounded on a bedrock of class polarization and hatred that stretched back for more than a decade. The leaders of trade unionism in Winnipeg—secessionists and internationalists—were united in their support of the general strike and never quarreled over it afterwards. Nonetheless, the OBU was clearly the descendent of the strike in the minds of many, particularly the strike's enemies. In inheriting the strike's mantle, the OBU gained a legitimacy for itself amongst the city's workers that it did not appear to have in any other urban centre.

The craft union counterattack was strongly supported by business and government. The main weapon of this tripartite coalition was nonrecognition. In every major city, in the railway shops, in the coal fields and in the hardrock mines, the tactic changed little. It never mattered how many workers defected from their international to the OBU, enough could always be found for the bosses to deal with under government protection and with government encouragement and assistance. The OBU was always frozen out. The bitterest of enemies in more normal times bedded down and kept the OBU in the cold. It was the internationals who won wage increases, signed contracts, policed grievance procedures—and always for their own members only. Workers were forced to rejoin their old unions to avoid isolation. Many thousands probably carried two membership cards as long as possible, until the burden of paying two sets of dues and risking dismissal became too great. Recognition would have allowed the OBU to service the needs of its membership and without it the OBU was kept ostracized and isolated. In the coal fields and hardrock mines, OBU leaders fought for recognition but made fatal errors. The 1919 coal strike in District 18 was a wasted effort. Christophers and Browne moved too quickly and tied up the collieries at the worst possible time—just as the warm weather was arriving. If they had held their fire until fall the result might have been different. In the hardrock mining country, Roberts' campaign against the Slocan operators in 1920 dragged on too long. Even Midgley questioned the wisdom of a lengthy strike against a falling market. After the long general strike in Winnipeg, an OBU strike for recognition in the railway shops was out of the question.

The state of the metals market was only one sign of

the depression which began to affect almost every sector of the Canadian economy by the autumn of 1920. The better established trade unions began to fall back everywhere as the gains of the war years were eaten away. Thousands of union members simply stopped paying dues and were dropped from membership roles. The One Big Union was too young and its treasury too empty to withstand pressures that larger, older unions succumbed to. Perhaps if there had been more dues money coming in to OBU headquarters, some help could have been extended to the coal and hardrock miners.

The OBU might have survived these troubles if it had been a truer reflection of the needs and desires of western workers. Certainly the loggers could have been kept within the OBU fold if Midgley and his supporters were not so insistent on imposing their peculiar brand of organization on Winch and the leadership of the Lumber Workers Industrial Unit. The loggers were one of the fastest growing and best organized unions in the western extractive industries and were enthusiastic supporters of the OBU until the summer of 1920. They were beginning to expand to other fields and were adding to their numbers almost daily when the dispute with the OBU head office arose. When they were forced out of the OBU on rather flimsy pretexts, the OBU not only lost a large number of dues-paying members, it lost a vigorous presence on the west coast and in northern Ontario. Here is direct evidence that one large and important group of workers had no use for the peculiarities of the One Big Union.

The OBU's history can be divided into the periods before and after the Port Arthur convention of September, 1920. From this point on, for the next thirty-six years, the OBU did little other than survive. It is always tempting to declare that the birth or death of a person or institution was a turning point in history. One dramatic conclusion would be that the OBU could have developed into a powerful and vigorous trade union movement offering Canadian workers a more national, industrial unionism. Perhaps this OBU would have brought about a new class consciousness or exerted a strong leftward pull on existing trade union institutions. More likely, the forms of trade unionism adopted by a particular group of workers are themselves an indication of deeper economic and political motives. It is true, however, that the labour movement in the Canadian west was at a juncture in 1919 when class consciousness and radicalism were at peaks never before attained. The One Big Union could have shaken Canadian society to its very roots if it had given further form and direction to that awareness.

The decline of the OBU and labour radicalism in the west went together. Followers grew disillusioned and abandoned radical leaders to return to more traditional paths. The leaders also went in several directions—to Communism, to traditional politics, back to the craft unions, out of the movement altogether. Only Russell, from the original group, kept the faith. But radicalism did not die. It had been dealt a heavy blow by the collapse of the sympathetic strikes, the Red Scare, the depression, the failure of the One Big Union. But few of the basic conditions which caused its development changed. In the 1920s the torch was passed, or rather grabbed away, by the Communists whose influence among miners and loggers was particularly strong. In the logging camps and the small coal towns of Alberta, Communists inherited the mantle of radical leadership and became prominent in the unions. Both the Lumber Workers Industrial Union and the Mine Workers Union of Canada joined the Communist-led Workers Unity League in 1930 while Communists continued to hold the allegiance of workers in the hardrock mines, smelters, and coastal logging industry well into the 1940s.

The fall of the One Big Union marked the close of an

era in the history of Canadian workers. Radicalism survived, in the west as elsewhere, and there were other challenges to the established order, particularly in the desperate years of the Great Depression. But the period of boom and expansion, in the cities and on the mining and logging frontier, that had accompanied and created the basic conditions for western labour radicalism, never returned. The unique vitality and experimentation that was so much a part of the western labour movement prior to 1920 was lost. When the One Big Union finally dissolved itself in the Canadian Labour Congress in 1956, it was nothing more than a curious echo of a revolt long since ended.

Footnotes

CHAPTER 1

1. *Calgary Daily Herald,* June 19, 1914 & June 20, 1914; Anderson, *Hillcrest Mine Disaster.*
2. Canada, Sessional Papers, 1915, *Summary Report of the Mines Branch . . . 1914.*
3. British Columbia, *Special Reports on Coal Mine Explosions,* 1918, pp. 529-530; United Mine Workers of America, District 18, Papers (Henceforth cited as District 18 Papers), "List of Fatalities in Coal Mines in Alberta, 1904-1964."
4. *Special Reports on Coal Mine Explosions,* 1918, pp. 529-530.
5. *Ibid.*
6. British Columbia, *Annual Report of the Minister of Mines for the Year ending December 31, 1915* (Henceforth cited as *B.C. Mines,* 1915), pp. 328-334.
7. Macmillan, "Trade Unionism in District 18," pp. 78 *et passim.*
8. District 18 Papers, Box 5, "Proceedings of the Special Convention, 1921," pp. 101-123.
9. *Ibid.,* "Inquiry Re: Mining Conditions, Crows Nest Pass," pp. 215-219; 230-233.
10. *Ibid.*
11. Coal Operators Association of Western Canada Papers (Henceforth cited as Coal Operators Papers), Box 9, file 55.
12. District 18 Papers, Box 5, "Proceedings of the Special Convention, 1921," pp. 101-103.
13. *Ibid.,* p. 105.
14. *Ibid.,* p. 112.
15. Canada, "Evidence Presented to the Royal Commission on Industrial Relations" (Henceforth cited as Mathers Commission Evidence), pp. 141-149.
16. Alberta, "Report of Alberta Coal Mining Industry Commission, 1919" (Henceforth cited as Coal Commission), pp. 278-282. Most of the information on coal towns is from this source. See also in District 18 Papers, Alberta, "Inquiry Re: Mining Conditions, Crows Nest Pass . . . ," pp. 146-154.
17. Coal Commission, pp. 428-429.
18. *Ibid.,* p. 464.
19. *B.C. Mines,* 1914, pp. 371-374, 417.
20. *Ibid.,* 1913, p. 317.
21. Mine Mill Papers, Box 156, file 1, Shilland to Eckstein & McTaggart, n.d.
22. Lingenfelter, *The Hardrock Miners,* pp. 12-26, tells of conditions in United States hardrock mines in the period 1863-1896. Many of these conditions also existed in British Columbia. See Orchard Interviews, Box 2, William Byers, pp. 7-10. Byers worked

in the Phoenix and Rossland area. See also "By Laws and Sketch of Sandon Miners' Union Hospital" in UBC, pamphlets, HD 6521, S1.

23. Mine Mill Papers, Box 156, file 2, MacNeil to Secretary, District 6, Western Federation of Miners, December 17, 1912.
24. *Ibid.*, "Finding of the Arbitrator in Antonio Cervio, Applicant, and the Granby Consolidated Mining, Smelting and Power Company, Respondent," March 26, 1910.
25. *Ibid.*, MacNeil to Secretary, District 6, WFM, December 17, 1912.
26. Most of the correspondence in Mine Mill Papers, Box 156, files 1 and 2, relate to compensation suits.
27. *Ibid.*, file 4, Consolidated Mining and Smelting Company circular to its shift, timber and mucker bosses, October 5, 1912.
28. Mine Mill Papers, Box 156, file 1, Eckstein to Laughlin, May 25, 1911.
29. Mathers Commission Evidence, pp. 395-399, 401-404; Mine Mill Papers, Box 156, file 2, union circular of August 31, 1912.
30. Lingenfelter, pp. 19-20; see also "Account of the Labour Troubles at Rossland," August 20, 1901. UBC pamphlet, HD 6521, W2R61.
31. "Account of the Labour Troubles . . ."
32. Consolidated Mining and Smelting Company Papers (Henceforth Cominco Papers), Vol. 8, file 8-3. "St. Eugene Arbitration," pp. 118-120, 135-138.
33. *Ibid.*, file 8-1, Anon. to Labarthe, February 15, 1905.
34. *Ibid.*, Vol. 9, file 9-2, pp. 72-79
35. Mathers Commission Evidence, pp. 393-395, 405-407.
36. Bergren, *Tough Timber*, pp. 15-17.
37. Orchard Interviews, Box 2, J. E. L. Muir, p. 10.
38. *Ibid.*, George R. Copley, p. 21. Most of this information concerning logging camps comes from the Orchard interviews. Particularly revealing are Ray Elford, Charles R. Mills, George R. Copley (all of Box 2) and Tom Elliott (Box 1).
39. *Ibid.*, Box 2, George R. Copley, p. 8.
40. Bradwin, *The Bunkhouse Man*, pp. 54-62; British Columbia, *Report of the Royal Commission on Labour*, p. M4.
41. Orchard Interviews, Box 1, Tom Elliott, pp. 4-5.
42. *The Voice*, September 13, 1913.
43. Taraska, "The Calgary Craft Union Movement," p. 6.
44. For Winnipeg see Bercuson, *Confrontation*, pp. 22-27. For Edmonton see Taylor, "The Urban West . . . ," pp. 298-301.
45. Ormsby, *British Columbia*, pp. 349-351. See also Robin, *Radical Politics*, pp. 26-27, and Patricia Roy's introduction to Glynn-Ward, *The Writing on the Wall*, p. xiii.
46. Orlikow Interviews, R. B. Russell, Tape 5, p. 1.
47. Artibise, *Winnipeg*, pp. 223-245.
48. Careless, "Aspects of Urban Life . . . ," pp. 32-35.

49. Artibise, p. 25.
50. *Ibid.*, p. 38.
51. *The Voice,* January 9, January 16, October 9, 1914.
52. Canada, Sessional Papers, 1904, Vol. 13, *Evidence Taken Before the Royal Commission to Inquire into Industrial Disputes in the Province of British Columbia,* p. 240.
53. Mathers Commission Evidence, p. 286.
54. *Ibid.*, p. 357.

CHAPTER 2

1. Phillips, *No Power Greater,* pp. 4-9.
2. Bercuson, pp. 11-14.
3. Taraska, pp. 38-40.
4. Cherwinski, "Organized Labour in Saskatchewan ...," pp. 10-13, 15-17.
5. *Ibid.*, pp. 3-4.
6. Pelling, *British Trade Unionism,* pp. 94-97.
7. *Ibid.*, pp. 97-100.
8. Jefferys, *The Engineers,* pp. 162-163.
9. Pelling, p. 139.
10. Levine, *Syndicalism in France,* pp. 133-137; Snowden, *Socialism and Syndicalism,* pp. 214-232; Foner, *The Industrial Workers of the World,* pp. 19-22.
11. Cole, *Attempts at General Union,* pp. 122-136; Harrison, *Robert Owen and the Owenites,* pp. 210-216.
12. See Protherow, "William Benbow ..."
13. Mann, *Memoirs,* pp. 203-207.
14. Macmillan, pp. 85-86.
15. Jensen, *Heritage of Conflict,* has the most comprehensive treatment of these labour wars, especially chapters 3, 4 and 5. Chapter 6 tells the story of the Western Federation of Miners in its early years. Lingenfelter, pp. 196-218, examines the Couer d'Alene strike and discusses the founding of the WFM in pp. 219-228.
16. "Account of the Labour Troubles at Rossland," p. 11.
17. McCormack, "The Origins and Extent of Western Labour Radicalism," pp. 18-19.
18. Orlikow Interviews, R. B. Russell, Tape 5, p. 10.
19. McCormack, pp. 31-90.
20. Foner, pp. 147-172, discusses the tactics and ideology of the IWW; Conlin, *Bread and Roses,* presents a different view of the extent of the IWW's syndicalism, pp. 8-40.
21. Foner, pp. 190-191, 206-207, 228-231; McCormack, "The Industrial Workers of the World," pp. 13-21.
22. Avery, "Foreign Workers and Labour Radicalism ...," pp. 19-21.

23. A translated leaflet is included in Provincial Archives of British Columbia, British Columbia Police Papers, Vol. III, Campbell to Cox, April 9, 1912. I am grateful to A. W. Rasporich for showing me this source.
24. Artibise, p. 163.
25. Rocker, *The London Years,* pp. 234-235.
26. Orlikow Interviews, R. B. Russell, Tape 4, p. 3.
27. *Ibid.,* F. J. Tipping, Tape 7, p. 3. Tipping repeated this story in his speech to the Interdisciplinary Conference on the Social Gospel, University of Regina, March, 1973.
28. Millar Interviews, Alex Shepherd, p. 13.
29. Orlikow Interviews, F. J. Tipping, Tape 7, pp. 2-3.
30. H. Pryde, "Is The Industrial Union in Sight?" in *Souvenir Program and Trade Union Directory,* Calgary Trades and Labor Council Correspondence and Minutes (Henceforth cited as Calgary Council Minutes); *British Columbia Federationist* (Henceforth cited as *BC Federationist*), December 23, 1911 and October 12, 1912.
31. Trades and Labor Congress of Canada. *Reports of the Annual Convention of the Trades and Labor Congress of Canada* (Henceforth cited as *TLC Proceedings*), 1911, pp. 73-74.
32. *BC Federationist.* Vancouver report in September 28, 1912 issue; Winnipeg report in October 12, 1912 issue.
33. McCormack, "Origins and Extent . . . ," p. 321; *BC Federationist,* November 22, 1912.
34. McCormack, "Origins and Extent . . . ," pp. 163-174, 180. See also Robin, pp. 92-103. These attitudes persisted. See *BC Federationist,* April 20, 1912.
35. *Red Flag,* June 7, 1919.
36. Phillips, p. 44.
37. District 18 Papers, "Verbatim Report Twelfth Annual Convention (1915)," pp. 64-76. See also Box 15, file 138, *Constitution of District 18,* p. 2.
38. Robin, p. 95.
39. McCormack, "Origins and Extent . . . ," pp. 315-319.
40. *BC Federationist,* September 12, 1913. Sivertz letter.
41. Morrison, "Community and Conflict . . . ," pp. 239-248.
42. Phillips, pp. 55-61; McCormack, "Origins and Extent . . . ," pp. 301-322; Kavanagh, *The Vancouver Island Strike;* Canada, *Report of the Royal Commission on Coal Mining Disputes on Vancouver Island.*
43. District 18 Papers, "Verbatim Report Twelfth Annual Convention," pp. 237-251, 264-268. There was extensive discussion of the strike, and the role of international officers in it, at this convention.
44. *BC Federationist,* July 17, 1914; McCormack, "Origins and Extent . . . ," p. 314.
45. Phillips, p. 60; McCormack, "Origins and Extent . . . ," p. 314.

CHAPTER 3

1. Flavelle Papers, file 1915-1917. "Report on Labour Conditions in the City of Winnipeg and the Province of Manitoba." March 7, 1917.
2. Borden Papers, file OC 557, "Memorandum re Cost of Living Matters, etc." n.d.; Canada, *Wages and Hours of Labour in Canada, 1901-1920;* Bercuson, pp. 32-34.
3. Brown and Cook, *Canada: 1896-1921,* pp. 234-249.
4. *Annual Report on Labour Organization in Canada* (Henceforth cited as *Labour Organization in Canada*), 1917, pp. 38-39.
5. *TLC Proceedings,* 1916, p. 19.
6. *Ibid.,* pp. 24-28.
7. *Ibid.,* 1917, pp. 31-34.
8. International Brotherhood of Electrical Workers Collection (Henceforth cited as Calgary IBEW Papers). Rigg circular to "Officers and members of Trades and Labor Councils and Local Unions," July 2, 1917; *TLC Proceedings,* 1917, pp. 102-107.
9. Robin, pp. 119-132; Bercuson, pp. 40-43; *Labour Organization in Canada,* 1916, pp. 36-42; *TLC Proceedings,* 1917, pp. 34, 36-39, 142-143.
10. *BC Federationist,* December 14, 1917.
11. Logan, *Trade Unions in Canada,* p. 148; *Bulletin,* October 1918; *Manitoba Free Press,* July 20, 1918.
12. *Labour Gazette,* August 1918, pp. 614-615; *Western Labor News,* August 2, 1918; *BC Federationist,* July 26, 1918.
13. Rigg/Rees Papers, Murray to Rigg, May 28, 1918.
14. *Bulletin,* June 1918.
15. *Labour Gazette,* June 1918, pp. 409-413; *BC Federationist,* May 31, 1918 and June 7, 1918.
16. *Labour Gazette,* August 1918, pp. 604-611; Bercuson, pp. 76-77.
17. District 18 Papers, "Verbatim Report Twelfth Annual Convention (1915)." pp. 64-76.
18. Macmillan, pp. 124-136.
19. Coal Operators Papers, Box 13, file 80, Order in Council P.C. 1725; Macmillan, pp. 135-136.
20. District 18 Papers, "Verbatim Report of the Special Convention, 1917," pp. 18-20.
21. *Western Labor News,* October 4, 1918.
22. *Ibid.,* November 29, 1918, "Vancouver Calls for Convention;" Calgary IBEW Papers, "Western Inter-Provincial Convention" circular issued by Midgley, November 4, 1918.
23. *TLC Proceedings,* 1919, pp. 24-28.
24. Taraska, pp. 68-71; *Western Labor News,* October 18, 1918 and October 25, 1918.
25. *Western Labor News,* December 6, 1918.
26. One Big Union Papers and Correspondence (Henceforth cited as OBU Papers), Midgley to Robinson, October 9, 1918.

27. *Ibid.*, Rees circular of November 16, 1918; Calgary IBEW Papers, Smitten circular of November 25, 1918.
28. OBU Papers, Rees to Midgley, November 18, 1918.
29. *Calgary Daily Herald*, December 19, 1918, "Alberta Labour Men Wanted to Strengthen Western Conference . . ."; Calgary Council Minutes, November 22, 1918 and December 6, 1918.
30. OBU Papers, Young to Midgley, December 21, 1918.
31. *Ibid.*, Robinson to Midgley, November 22, 1918.
32. *Ibid.*, Rees to Midgley, November 24, 1918.
33. *Western Labor News,* December 6, 1918; OBU Papers, Johns to Midgley, December 10, 1918, Robinson to Midgley, December 14, 1918.
34. Manitoba, Court Records—King's Bench, "The King vs William Ivens," trial evidence (Henceforth cited as Ivens Trial Records), Box 3, Russell to Stephenson, January 30, 1919.
35. Russell Collection, MG 10, A14-1, Box 3 (Henceforth cited as Trial Records), Stephenson to Russell, January 18, 1919.
36. *Western Labor News*, November 15, 1918.
37. Tom Walsh, *What Is This Shop Stewards Movement* (London, 1920) and W. Gallagher and J. R. Campbell, *Direct Action* (Glasgow, n.d.).
38. Bedford, *Initiative and Organization,* p. 18.
39. Harris, *The Bitter Fight,* p. 274.
40. *Western Labor News,* September 13, 1918.
41. *Proceedings of the Second Annual Convention of District Lodge No. 2,* p. 14.
42. Russell Collection, Trial Records, Russell to Knight, November 29, 1918.
43. *Proceedings of the Sixth Annual Convention of the Alberta Federation of Labor* (1919), pp. 32, 40-41.
44. Russell Collection, Trial Records, Sarah Knight to Russell, January 13, 1919.
45. Ivens Trial Records, Box 3, Russell to Stephenson, February 18, 1919.
46. *Calgary Daily Herald,* February 18, 1919.
47. *Ibid.*, February 19, 20, 22, 26, 27; *The Morning Albertan,* February 18, 20, 24; District 18 Papers, "Verbatim Report, Sixteenth Annual Convention, District 18 (1919)."
48. *Calgary Daily Herald,* February 19, 20, 1919; *The Morning Albertan,* February 20, 1919.
49. *Calgary Daily Herald,* February 24, 1919.
50. *Proceedings of the Ninth Annual Convention of the British Columbia Federation of Labor* (1919). Discussion throughout the meeting. See especially pp. 2-9, 19-24, 41-52.
51. *Ibid.*, pp. 23-24.
52. *Ibid.*, p. 49.
53. *Ibid.*, p. 8.
54. *Western Labor News,* March 7, 1919.

55. *The Origin of the One Big Union, A Verbatim Report of the Calgary Conference, 1919,* pp. 10-11.
56. *Ibid.,* pp. 42, 57.
57. *Ibid.,* pp. 71-72.
58. *Ibid.,* p. 75.
59. *Ibid.,* pp. 15, 46-50.

CHAPTER 4

1. See Murray, *Red Scare.*
2. Canada, Sessional Papers, 1918, *Report of the Royal North West Mounted Police for 1917,* pp. 8-9.
3. Department of National Defence Papers (Henceforth cited as DND Papers), file C3686, Volume 1, Campbell to General Officer Commanding (GOC) Military District (MD) 10, July 6, 1917.
4. Borden Papers, file RLB 2413, Flavelle to Borden, May 16, 1918.
5. *Ibid.,* Borden to Robertson, April 18, 1918.
6. *Calgary Daily Herald,* January 11, 1919, "Menace of Bolshevism."
7. *Vancouver Daily World,* January 29, 1919.
8. *Calgary Daily Herald,* January 11, 1919, "Bolshevism."
9. *Vancouver Daily World,* February 13, 1919.
10. *Calgary Daily Herald,* January 14, 1919.
11. *Ibid.,* January 18, 1919.
12. DND Papers, file C2051, Cahan to Minister of Justice, January 8, 1919.
13. *Vancouver Daily World,* January 27, 1919; *Manitoba Free Press,* January 27, 1919.
14. *Calgary Daily Herald,* January 17, 1919.
15. DND Papers, file C2051, Horrigan to Perry, January 30, 1919.
16. *Ibid.,* Perry to Comptroller, RNWMP, February 5, 1919.
17. DND Papers, file NSC 1055-2-21, Vol. 1, Perry to Controller, contained in Gwatkin to Stephens, April 12, 1919.
18. *Ibid.,* "Memorandum on Revolutionary Tendencies in Western Canada."
19. *Ibid.,* "Report Re The Russian Socialist Anarchist Party," April 24, 1919.
20. *Ibid.,* "General Strike," April 29, 1919.
21. Royal Canadian Mounted Police Papers (Henceforth cited as RCMP Papers), Vol. 2169, Perry to Primrose, February 20, 1919.
22. For Robertson's views see Borden Papers, file OC 564, Robertson to Marshall, May 26, 1919. For Borden's views see Brown and Cook, p. 313.

Fools and Wise Men

23. Bercuson, pp. 110-114, 120.
24. Borden Papers, file OC 559, White to Borden, April 16, 1919.
25. *Ibid.*, Borden to White, April 29, 1919.
26. *The Globe,* May 19, 1919.
27. *Edmonton Journal,* May 28, 1919.
28. *Calgary Daily Herald,* June 5, 1919.
29. *Vancouver Daily Sun,* June 14, 1919.
30. *Saskatchewan Cooperative Elevator Company Limited News,* June 1919.
31. McNaught, *Prophet,* p. 102.
32. *Calgary Daily Herald,* June 21, 1919.
33. *Ibid.*, June 16, 1919.
34. *Ibid.*, June 17, 1919.
35. *Ibid.*, June 20, 1919.
36. Mathers Commission Evidence, pp. 279-280.
37. White Papers, Vol. 21, Allan to Borden, June 30, 1919.
38. Frontier College Papers, Vol. 31, Fitzpatrick to Calder, February 11, 1919.
39. *Ibid.*, Vol. 32, Playfair to Fitzpatrick, June 16, 1919.
40. *Ibid.*, Anon. to Fitzpatrick, November 14, 1919.
41. Borden Papers, file OC 564, Biggar Memorandum of May 20, 1919.
42. *Ibid.*, file OC 559, "Troopers" to Ottawa, June 6, 1919.
43. *Ibid.*, Milner to Borden, July 3, 1919.
44. *Ibid.*, Borden to Lloyd, June 25, 1919.
45. *Ibid.*, Memorandum of July 8, 1919.
46. *Labour Gazette,* August 1920, p. 14.
47. Borden Papers, file OC 559, Mahoney to Foster, February 10, 1919.
48. *Ibid.*, file OC 564, Borden to Cahan, May 31, 1919.
49. Bercuson, p. 164.
50. Borden Papers, file OC 564, Robertson to Ackland, June 14, 1919.
51. Morton, "Sir William Otter . . . ," pp. 56-58.
52. Avery, "The Radical Alien . . . ," p. 224.
53. Department of Immigration and Colonization Papers, Vol. 627, Blair to Egan, March 7, 1925.
54. Rex vs. Almazoff, *Western Weekly Reports 1919,* Vol. 3, pp. 281-285.
55. Bercuson, p. 155.
56. Brown and Cook, p. 314.
57. Rex vs. Russell, *Western Weekly Reports 1920,* Vol. 1, pp. 624-657; McNaught, "Political Trials . . . ," pp. 146-151.
58. Bercuson, pp. 168-169.
59. DND Papers, file HQS 5678, Adjutant General to GOC, MD 10, April 23, 1920 and to GOC, MD 1, April 16, 1920.
60. *Ibid.*, file NSC 1055-2-21, Director, Flying Operations to Secre-

tary, Air Board, May 3, 1921; GOC, MD 11 to Militia Council, Ottawa, April 12, 1921.
61. *Ibid.*, file HQS 3568, Circular from Adjutant General to General Officers Commanding Military Districts, April 29, 1921.
62. Department of Justice Papers, file 1847, Robertson to Meighen, September 3, 1920.
63. American Federation of Labor Papers, Samuel L. Gompers Correspondence (Henceforth cited as Gompers correspondence), Box 38, White to Gompers, May 7, 1919.
64. Samuel Gompers Letterbooks, Vol. 255, Robertson to Gompers, May 23, 1919.
65. Canada, *House of Commons Debates*, June 9, 1919, p. 3241.

CHAPTER 5

1. Vancouver Trades and Labor Council, Executive Board Minutes (Henceforth cited as Vancouver Executive Minutes), Volume 1913-1920, May 15, 1919.
2. Russell Collection, Trial Records, Pritchard to Executive Members, March 25, 1919.
3. OBU Papers, Russell to Midgley, March 28, 1919.
4. Russell Collection, Trial Records, Russell to Berg, March 31, 1919.
5. *Bulletin,* May 1919.
6. OBU Papers, Johns to Midgley, May 7, 1919.
7. *BC Federationist,* March 28, 1919.
8. Edmonton Trades and Labor Council Minutes (Henceforth cited as Edmonton Council Minutes), March 17, 1919; OBU Papers, S. Knight to Midgley, March 18, 1919; *Edmonton Journal,* March 18, 1919.
9. OBU Papers, J. Knight to Midgley, March 24, 1919.
10. Edmonton Council Minutes, April 21, 1919; *Edmonton Journal,* April 22, 1919.
11. Russell Collection, Trial Records, Berg to Russell, April 22, 1919.
12. *Western Labor News,* May 2, 1919.
13. OBU Papers, Berg to Midgley, May 5, 1919.
14. Edmonton Council Minutes, May 19, 1919.
15. *Calgary Daily Herald,* March 18, 1919.
16. *Ibid.,* March 29, 1919.
17. *Ibid.,* April 12, 1919.
18. OBU Papers, Midgley to Young, April 24, 1919.
19. *Calgary Daily Herald,* April 12, 1919.
20. *Western Labor News,* April 11, 1919.
21. OBU Papers, Mill to Midgley, May 19, 1919.

22. *Victoria Daily Times,* March 21, 1919.
23. *BC Federationist,* March 21, 1919; Vancouver Executive Minutes, March 20, 1919.
24. OBU Papers, Russell to Midgley, April 11, 1919.
25. *Ibid.,* Russell to Midgley, May 1, 1919.
26. *Ibid.,* Berg to Midgley, April 9, 1919; Russell Collection, Trial Records, Berg to Russell, March 24, 1919 and Midgley to Russell, April 10, 1919.
27. OBU Papers, Midgley to Lawson, April 7, 1919.
28. *Ibid.,* Midgley to Lawson, April 19, 1919.
29. *Ibid.,* Midgley to Dickie, April 3, 1919.
30. *Ibid.,* Russell to Midgley, May 1, 1919; Russell Collection, Trial Records, Russell to Manchee, April 30, 1919.
31. OBU Papers, Midgley to Hazeltine, May 5, 1919.
32. *Ontario Labor News,* May 1, 1919.
33. OBU Papers, Johns to Midgley, May 17, 1919.
34. *Ibid.,* Kerrigan to Johns, May 17, 1919.
35. Ivens Trial Records, Box 3, Henderson to Russell, n.d.
36. OBU Papers, Johns to Midgley, May 17, 1919.
37. See Forbes, pp. 88-91.
38. Borden Papers, file OC 564, Report of Horrigan to Commissioner, May 7, 1919.
39. Russell Collection, Trial Records, Roberts to Stephenson, May 9, 1919.
40. *Calgary Daily Herald,* April 4, 1919.
41. Gompers Letterbooks, Vol. 255, Robertson to Gompers, May 23, 1919.
42. *Industrial Canada,* June 1919.
43. Ivens Trial Records, Trades Congress circular of April 19, 1919.
44. *American Federationist,* April 1919.
45. Morrison Letterbooks, Vol. 504, p. 719, Morrison to Moore, March 22, 1919.
46. *Ibid.,* Vol. 508, p. 536, Morrison to Farmilo, April 10, 1919.
47. *Ibid.,* Vol. 508, pp. 593-594, Morrison to Toblin, April 14, 1919.
48. *Ibid.,* Vol. 509, pp. 629-632, Varley to Morrison, May 14, 1919.
49. *Calgary Daily Herald,* April 12, 1919.
50. Edmonton Council Minutes, April 7, 1919.
51. *Morning Albertan,* February 28, 1919.
52. Rigg/Rees Papers, clipping, "OBU or UBO"; *Calgary Daily Herald,* April 19, 1919.
53. *Calgary Daily Herald,* April 15, 1919.
54. OBU Papers, Midgley to McMillan, May 3, 1919.
55. *Ibid.,* Midgley to Smith, May 12, 1919.
56. *BC Federationist,* April 4, 1919.
57. Ivens Trial Records, Box 3, Stephenson to Cassidy, March 21, 1919.

58. Russell Collection, Trial Records, Russell to Midgley, April 17, 1919.
59. *Western Labor News,* April 25, 1919.
60. OBU Papers, Russell to Midgley, April 24, 1919.
61. Ivens Trial Records, Box 3, Midgley to Russell, April 28, 1919.
62. Russell Collection, Trial Records, Berg to Kollings, May 2, 1919.
63. *Ibid.*
64. One Big Union Vertical File #213. "Appendix II" is a tally sheet recording votes of individual lodges on the two questions.
65. Borden Papers, file OC 563, clipping (no title, no date), Vancouver, June 13, 1919.
66. *Calgary Daily Herald,* June 10, 1919.
67. *Constitution and Laws of the One Big Union* as contained in *Labour Organization in Canada,* 1919.
68. Russell Collection, Trial Records, Berg to Kollings, June 24, 1919.

CHAPTER 6

1. Bercuson, pp. 189-194.
2. Phillips, p. 81.
3. *Vancouver Province,* June 30, 1919; *Calgary Daily Herald,* July 4, 1919.
4. Askin, "Labour Unrest in Edmonton . . . ," pp. 85-87; *Calgary Daily Herald,* May 22 and 27, 1919.
5. Askin, p. 96.
6. Russell Collection, Trial Records, Berg to Kollings, June 25, 1919.
7. OBU Papers, J. Knight to Midgley, n.d. (probably mid-June 1919).
8. *Calgary Daily Herald,* May 26, 1919.
9. *Ibid.,* May 28, 29 and June 12, 1919; Taraska, pp. 79-80.
10. Taraska, p. 80; *Morning Albertan,* July 5 and 11, 1919.
11. OBU Papers, Midgley to Knight, June 25, 1919.
12. *BC Federationist,* April 4, 1919.
13. Steeves, *The Compassionate Rebel,* pp. 44-46.
14. Orchard Interviews, L. C. Rogers.
15. *BC Federationist,* May 16, 1919.
16. *The Camp Worker,* June 28, 1919.
17. *BC Federationist,* May 16 and July 11, 1919.
18. *One Big Union Bulletin* (Henceforth cited as OBU Bulletin), November 13, 1919; *BC Federationist,* January 9, 1920.
19. OBU Papers, Berg to Midgley, April 1, 1919.
20. *Ibid.,* J. Knight to Midgley, April 2, 1919.
21. Coal Operators Papers, Box 7, file 43, Biggs and Browne to Armstrong, February 27, 1919.

22. Russell Collection, MG 10, A14-2 (Henceforth cited as Russell Collection II), Box 10, file 57, "Order No. 116" issued March 6, 1919.
23. Coal Operators Papers, Box 7, file 43, Christophers to Armstrong, April 4, 1919.
24. *Ibid.*, Box 14, file 82, Anon. to Oliver, June 12, 1919.
25. *Ibid.*, Box 7, file 43, Robertson to Armstrong, April 28, 1919.
26. Russell Collection II, Box 10, file 57, Armstrong to Christophers, May 20, 1919.
27. *Ibid.*, Christophers and Browne to Armstrong, May 20, 1919.
28. Department of Labour Papers (Henceforth cited as Labour Papers), Vol. 314, file 176 III, Mounted Police report "Re Threatened General Strike of District No. 18 U.M.W. of America," May 22, 1919.
29. *Ibid.*, May 25, 1919.
30. OBU Papers, Midgley to J. Knight, April 15, 1919.
31. Russell Collection II, Box 10, file 57, Browne to Sullivan, June 17, 1919.
32. Coal Operators Papers, Box 14, file 84, Lewis to Armstrong, June 27, 1919.
33. *Ibid.*, Browne to Harrison, July 2, 1919.
34. *Ibid.*, McNeil to Harrison, July 3, 1919; Armstrong to Harrison, July 4, 1919.
35. *Ibid.*, Browne to Harrison, July 7, 1919.
36. Labour Papers, Vol. 314, file 176 III, Mounted Police report "Re General Strike of Dist. 18 U.M.W. of A. Conditions at Fernie, B.C.," July 10, 1919.
37. *Ibid.*, Mounted Police report, "Personal History File Re Ed Browne—Agitator," July 10, 1919.
38. *Calgary Daily Herald,* July 17, 1919.
39. Coal Operators Papers, Box 14, file 84, Browne to OBU Gladstone Local 2314, n.d.
40. Coal Operators Papers, Box 14, file 84, Armstrong to Wilson, July 25, 1919; Ballantyne, Cady, and Dalrymple to Lewis, July 26, 1919.
41. Russell Collection II, Box 10, file 57, Christopher, McFagan, Browne circular letter of July 28, 1919.
42. *Ibid.*, Browne to Sullivan, July 29, 1919.
43. Brinkley, "The Western Federation of Miners," pp. 176, 178; *OBU Bulletin,* August 12, 1919.
44. On the union's troubles see Jensen, pp. 452-466; for employment conditions, *Labour Gazette,* January 1919, p. 108; February 1919, p. 238; March 1919, pp. 387, 396.
45. *Miners Magazine,* May 1919.
46. *BC Federationist,* July 11, 1919.
47. *Miners Magazine,* August 1919.
48. *Calgary Daily Herald,* July 16, 1920, "Advances Money to Defeat OBU."

49. *Western Labor News,* July 18, 1919; Rigg/Rees Papers, Rigg to Draper, July 21, 1919.
50. Rigg/Rees Papers, Rigg to Draper, July 21, 1919.
51. *Ibid.,* Rigg to Moore, August 9, 1919.
52. *Western Labor News,* August 1, 1919.
53. Rigg/Rees Papers, Rigg to Moore, August 9, 1919.
54. *Ibid.,* Rigg to Winning, July 30, 1919.
55. *Ibid.,* Rigg to Moore, August 9, 1919; *OBU Bulletin,* August 12, 1919.
56. *OBU Bulletin,* August 12, 1919.
57. *Ibid.,* November 15, 1919.
58. Russell Collection II, Box 4, file 15, Winnipeg Central Labor Council Minutes (Henceforth cited as Winnipeg CLC Minutes), January 6, 1920.
59. *Ibid.,* November 4, 1919.
60. *Labour Gazette,* December 1919, p. 1489 *et passim; OBU Bulletin,* December 13, 1919.
61. *OBU Bulletin,* September 13, 1919.
62. See, for example, *ibid.,* November 1, 1919 and July 24, 1920.
63. *OBU Bulletin,* November 8, 1919, "Bolshevism and the Vested Interests in America."
64. *OBU Bulletin,* February 14, 1920.
65. *Ibid.,* December 13, 1920; Russell Collection II, Box 4, file 15, Winnipeg CLC Minutes, December 2, 1919.
66. *OBU Bulletin,* May 22, 1920.
67. *Ibid.,* June 5 and 12, 1920.
68. *Ibid.,* May 22, 1920.
69. See, for example, DND Papers, file HQS 5678, Ketchen to Militia Council, April 19, 1920 and Elmsley to General Officer Commanding Military District 1 (London, Ontario), April 16, 1920.
70. Millar Interviews, John Bruce.
71. *OBU Bulletin,* October 4, 1919; Borden Papers, file OC 559, "Notes of the Work of the C.I.B. for the week ending 29th January [1920]."
72. *TLC Proceedings,* 1919, pp. 180-181, 215-216, 219, 221.
73. Friesen, "Yours in Revolt," pp. 153-154.
74. *Vancouver Sun,* August 10, 1919.
75. *Labour Gazette,* October 1919, p. 1200.
76. MacInnis Collection, Box 60, Wells circular letter of October 6, 1919.
77. *Proceedings of the Tenth Annual Convention of the British Columbia Federation of Labor (1920),* p. 9.
78. *Canadian Annual Review,* 1919, p. 490.
79. Rigg/Rees Papers, Rigg to Moore, August 22, 1919.
80. Cherwinski, pp. 75-76.
81. *TLC Proceedings,* 1919, p. 172.
82. Edmonton Council Minutes, October 20, 1919.

83. One Big Union Vertical File #213, "Report of Proceedings, First Semi-Annual Convention of the One Big Union," Winnipeg, January 26-29, 1920. Report of J. R. Knight.
84. Full accounts of many of the meetings of this unit are found in DND Papers, file 20-1-44.
85. One Big Union Vertical File #213, "Report of Proceedings, First Semi-Annual Convention of the One Big Union."
86. *OBU Bulletin,* September 6, 1919.
87. *Bulletin,* September 1919.
88. *Ibid.,* April 1920; Trades and Labor Congress, Executive Council Minutes (Henceforth cited as TLC Exeutive Minutes), January 3, 1920.
89. *Western Labor News,* April 9, 1920.
90. Canadian Brotherhood of Railway, Transport and General Workers Papers, Vol. 23, "Synopsis of Proceedings of Meeting of Canadian Representatives of Organizations Affiliated to the TLC. . . ."
91. Gompers Papers, Box 41, Flett to Morrison, May 17, 1920.
92. Borden Papers, file OC 559, "Notes of the Work of the C.I.B. for the week ending 29th January [1920]"; Macinnis Collection, Box 55, folder 16, *Report of Investigation Committee and Replies of Those Concerned.*
93. This was reported in Sifton Papers, "Notes of the Work of the C.I.B. Division for the Week Ending 9th September [1920]."
94. *BC Federationist,* July 23, 1920.
95. See Sifton Papers, "Notes of the Work of the C.I.B. . . . August 12 [1920]."
96. *Ibid.,* "Notes of the Work of the C.I.B. . . . September 2 [1920]."
97. One Big Union Vertical File #213, "Report of the Second Convention of the One Big Union," General Secretary's Report, Port Arthur, September 20-24, 1920.
98. Sifton Papers, "Notes of the Work of the C.I.B. . . . October 14 [1920]."
99. One Big Union Vertical File #231, "Report of the Second Convention of the One Big Union."
100. Sifton Papers, "Notes of the Work of the C.I.B. . . . August 12 [1920]."
101. Farmilo Papers, Item 56B, no title. This document is the proceedings of the Lumber, Camp and Agricultural Workers Unit Convention held at Vancouver, January 17, 1920.
102. OBU Papers, Midgley circular letter, February 2, 1921.
103. TLC Executive Minutes, November 29, 1924.

CHAPTER 7

1. OBU Papers, Midgley to Goulde, May 3, 1919 (#428).
2. Friedheim, *The Seattle General Strike,* pp. 139-140, 152-154.

3. *Ibid.,* pp. 48-49.
4. *BC Federationist,* April 25, 1919.
5. *Seattle Union Record,* April 18, 1919.
6. *Ibid.,* May 5, 1919.
7. Ivens Trial Records, Midgley to Russell, April 21, 1919.
8. King County Central Labor Council Minutes (Henceforth cited as Seattle Council Minutes), May 7, 1919.
9. Ivens Trial Records, Box 7, ILA circular, n.d.
10. Seattle Council Minutes, May 28, 1919.
11. *Seattle Union Record,* June 14, 1919.
12. *Ibid.,* June 19, 1919.
13. Washington State Federation of Labor Papers (Henceforth cited as Washington Fed. Papers), Box 41, Short to Guard, July 29, 1919.
14. *Seattle Union Record,* June 23, 1919.
15. *Ibid.,* July 31, 1919, "One Big Union."
16. *Ibid.,* August 1, 1919, "One Big Union."
17. *Ibid.,* August 5, 1919.
18. *Ibid.,* August 9, 1919, "Head of Mine Workers Opposes One Big Union."
19. *Ibid.,* July 24, 1919.
20. The Correspondence, including votes and communications from Executive Council members, is found in Morrison Letterbooks, Volume 511, p. 462 *et passim.* F. Morrison to AFL Executive Council, August 20, 1919.
21. Morrison Letterbooks, Volume 510, pp. 298-300, Morrison to Taylor, August 2, 1919.
22. *Seattle Union Record,* August 11, 1919.
23. *Ibid.,* August 14, 1919; Seattle Council Minutes, August 13, 1919.
24. Washington Fed. Papers, Box 60, "Executive Board Minutes." Minutes of August 14, 1919; *Seattle Union Record,* August 15, 1919.
25. Papers on Industrial Espionage report of Agent 106, August 20, 1919.
26. Washington Fed. Papers, Box 10, Morrison to Short, August 27, 1919.
27. *OBU Bulletin,* October 25, 1919.
28. One Big Union Vertical File #213, "Report of Proceedings First Semi-Annual Convention of the One Big Union," Winnipeg, January 26-28, 1919.
29. Mine Mill Papers, Box 160, file 1, report of Tom Cassidy, May 10, 1920.
30. MacInnis Collection, Box 33, file 7, *First Issue of the O.B.U. Bulletin of Oakland.*
31. *Red Flag,* May 28, 1920.
32. *One Big Union Monthly* (Chicago, IWW), May 1919.
33. *Ibid.,* July 1920.
34. *Ibid.,* December 1920.

35. One Big Union Vertical File #213, "Report of the Second Convention of the One Big Union," Port Arthur, September 20-24, 1920, p. 4.
36. *BC Federationist,* July 16, 1920; *OBU Bulletin,* July 10, 1920.
37. Morrison Letterbooks, Volume 517, p. 295, Morrison to Flett, July 19, 1920.
38. Mine Mill Papers, Box 160, file 1, Midgley circular to General Executive Board (GEB), August 24, 1920.
39. Russell Collection II, Box 4, file 18, General Executive Board (GEB) Minutes, December 7, 1923 and January 30, 1924.
40. *OBU Bulletin,* February 19, 1921.
41. *BC Federationist,* March 11, 1921.
42. Mine Mill Papers, Box 160, file 1, Mace to all OBU Units, April 22, 1922.
43. Russell Collection II, Box 4, file 18, GEB Minutes, January 30, 1924.
44. Mine Mill Papers, Box 160, file 2, Emsley to Russell, April 18, 1924.
45. *Ibid.,* Emsley to Doyle, April 17, 1924.
46. Russell Collection II, Box 4, file 18, GEB Minutes, April 28, 1924.

CHAPTER 8

1. *Labour Gazette,* 1919, p. 1134; Macinnis Collection, Box 60, Roberts and Harvey circular, October 1, 1919.
2. *BC Federationist,* October 17, 1919.
3. *Ibid.*
4. *Labour Gazette,* 1919, pp. 1387-88.
5. *Ibid.,* 1920, p. 417.
6. *Miners Magazine,* March 1920.
7. *OBU Bulletin,* May 29, 1920.
8. *Miners Magazine,* June 1920.
9. See Sifton Papers, RCMP Report, "Notes of the Work of the C.I.B. . . . August 19, 1919," p. 3; Mine Mill Papers, Box 156, file 6, "Happie" to Roberts, May 23, 1920.
10. *BC Federationist,* July 9, 1920.
11. Justice Papers, file 1847, Starkey to Robertson, July 31, 1920.
12. *Ibid.*
13. Reprinted in *Miners Magazine,* October 1920.
14. *Ibid.*
15. Sifton Papers, CIB Report of September 23, 1920, p. 8.
16. For mineral price statistics see *B.C. Mines,* 1922, pp. N12-N16.
17. See *Labour Gazette,* 1921, pp. 20, 144-145, 311, 654, 866, 1245.
18. Mine Mill Papers, Box 160, file 1, Midgley to Roberts, November 4, 1920.

Footnotes

19. *Ibid.*, Roberts to Wells, January 20, 1921.
20. *Ibid.*, Mace to Roberts, April 14, 1921.
21. Coal Operators Papers, Box 14, file 85, McNeil to Wilson, July 30, 1919.
22. *Calgary Daily Herald,* August 4, 1919.
23. Coal Operators Papers, Box 14, file 84, Secretary to Ballantyne, August 6, 1919.
24. RCMP Papers, Vol. 582, file 518-566, Rowell to McLean, June 5, 1919.
25. Labour Papers, Vol. 314, file 176 III, RNWMP Report, Calgary Sub-District, August 7, 1919.
26. Labour Papers, Vol. 314, file 176 III, RNWMP Report, Drumheller Detachment, August 7, 1919.
27. The events of August 9 to 12 were reconstructed from: Anne B. Woywitka, "Drumheller Strike," pp. 3-7; *Calgary Daily Herald,* August 11 and August 14, 1919; Labour Papers, Vol. 314, file 176 111, RNWMP Report, Drumheller Detachment, August 13, 1919.
28. *Calgary Daily Herald,* August 14, 1919, "Veterans Act."
29. *Fernie Free Press,* August 15, 1919.
30. Labour Papers, Vol. 314, file 176 III, RNWMP Report, "Re One Big Union at Lethbridge," August 18, 1919.
31. *Ibid.*
32. Labour Papers, Vol. 314, file 176 III, RNWMP Report, "Re General Strike of District 18, U.M.W. of A. Conditions at Canmore and Bankhead," August 23, 1919; Coal Operators Papers, Box 14, file 82, Whiteside to McNeill, August 15, 1919.
33. Coal Operators Papers, Box 14, file 82, McNeill to Wilson, August 26, 1919.
34. *Ibid.*, Wilson to McNeill, August 27, 1919.
35. Coal Operators Papers, Box 14, file 82, McNeill to Drinnan, October 14, 1919.
36. *Ibid.*, "Notes of a meeting held . . . September 6th, 1919 . . . regarding the application for employment of Samuel Whitehouse. . . ."
37. Coal Operators Papers, Box 14, file 83, McNeill to Wilson, December 6, 1919.
38. *Ibid.*, Browne to McNeill, December 2, 1919.
39. See *ibid.* for various resolutions, December 7 to 23, 1919.
40. Various drafts of the agreement are in Coal Operators Papers, Box 7, file 44. The Order 141 is in Coal Operators Papers, Box 10, file 62.
41. *The Searchlight,* December 26, 1919.
42. Coal Operators Papers, Box 14, file 83, Brindley to McNeill, December 25, 1919.
43. *Ibid.*, McNeill to Wilson, December 29, 1919.
44. RCMP Papers, Vol. 593, file 1122, Robertson to Perry, February

6, 1920 and accompanying report, showing proportion of men in the UMWA.

45. Coal Operators Papers, Box 7, file 43, Browne to Armstrong, January 3, 1920.

46. *The Searchlight,* January 23, 1920; *Morning Albertan,* March 24, 1920.

47. Coal Operators Papers, Box 14, file 83, Armstrong to Beard, March 5, 1920.

48. MacMillan, p. 151; *The Searchlight,* March 12, 1920.

49. *Morning Albertan,* March 24, 1919.

50. *Ibid.,* April 8, 1920.

51. *Ibid.,* April 20, 1920; *Labour Organization in Canada,* 1920, p. 25.

52. *BC Federationist,* May 7, 1920.

53. District 18 Papers, Agreement, 1920-1922.

54. MacMillan, p. 152; *The Searchlight,* June 25, 1920.

55. *The Searchlight,* June 25, 1920.

56. The events of the Christophers kidnapping are reconstructed from Martin Papers, file "Re Kidnapping of P. M. Christophers" which contains trial reports. No. 35338-35345.

57. *Ibid.*

58. Cherwinski, pp. 162-163.

59. Sifton Papers, "Memorandum" (n.d., concerns RCMP forecast of a fall coal strike).

60. Sifton Papers, "Notes of the Work of the C.I.B. . . . 26th August," pp. 4-5; *Ibid.,* Perry to Sifton, September 1, 1920.

61. *Morning Albertan,* September 13 and 20, 1920.

62. *Ottawa Journal,* September 24, 1920.

63. Sifton Papers, "Notes of the Work of the C.I.B. . . . 16th September," pp. 15-19.

64. Karas, "Labour and Coal . . .," various statistics.

65. *Calgary Daily Herald,* September 30, 1919; Sifton Papers, "Notes of Work of the C.I.B. . . . 7th October," p. 13.

66. *Morning Albertan,* October 1, 1920; *Ottawa Journal,* October 1, 1920.

67. Strike statistics are found in Coal Operators Papers, Box 17, file 108, "List of strikes in District 18 April 1, 1920 to March 31, 1921."

68. Labour Papers, Vol. 323, file 357, "Extract from the Report of the Lethbridge Correspondent for October, 1920"; *Ibid.,* "Extract from the R.C.M.P. report for week ending October 14, 1920."

69. Labour Papers, Vol. 323, file 357, "Extract from the R.C.M.P. report for week ending October 14, 1920."

70. *Ibid.,* "The Situation Elsewhere"; *Morning Albertan,* October 6, 1920.

71. Sifton Papers, "Notes of the Work of the C.I.B. . . . 28th October," p. 12.

72. Coal Operators Papers, Box 7, file 43, UMW Circular, October 6, 1920.

73. *Morning Albertan,* October 4, 1920.
74. Labour Papers, Vol. 323, file 357, "Extract from the R.C.M.P. report for week ending October 14, 1920."
75. *Toronto World,* October 11, 1920.
76. *Lethbridge Herald,* October 15, 1920.
77. *Ottawa Citizen,* October 25, 1920.
78. *Calgary Daily Herald,* June 14, 1921; see also District 18 Papers, Box 5, "Proceedings of The 1921 Special Convention."

CHAPTER 9

1. Refinery Oil Workers Union Minutes, Midgley circular, December 1, 1920; *OBU Bulletin,* December 25, 1920.
2. Dennison, *Canada's First Bank,* p. 342.
3. *Labour Gazette* presents statistical data on unemployment, prices, etc. See especially March 1921, pp. 402-410; June 1921, p. 753; July 1921, pp. 964-968.
4. *Labour Organizations in Canada,* 1921, p. 7.
5. Morrison Letterbooks, Vol. 523, p. 985, Morrison to Farmilo, October 13, 1921.
6. Vancouver Council Minutes, November 21, 1921.
7. Mine Mill Papers, Box 160, file 1, Mace to Roberts, May 13, 1921.
8. Russell Collection II, Box 5, file 15, Winnipeg CLC Minutes, December 2, 1921.
9. Russell Collection II, Box 4, file 16, One Big Union Bulletin financial statement from February 1st to September 30th, 1922.
10. Gray, *The Roar of the Twenties,* pp. 10-14, for this and other lottery details.
11. Bercuson Interviews, Alex Shepherd. Personal interview with J. H. Gray, June 29, 1976.
12. This is the figure given in Gray.
13. Russell Collection II, Box 4, file 16, One Big Union Bulletin financial statement from February 1st to September 30th, 1922.
14. Discussion of these projects can be found in Russell Collection II, Box 4, file 17, Winnipeg CLC Minutes, March 20, 1923; *Ibid.,* Box 5, file 22, Joint Exec. Board Minutes, March 23, 1926; *Ibid.,* Winnipeg CLC Minutes, July 13, 1926; *Ibid.,* Winnipeg CLC Minutes, May 8, 1926; Orlokow Interview, R. B. Russell, tape 6.
15. Avakumovic, *The Communist Party,* pp. 18-21.
16. Rodney, *Soldiers of the International,* pp. 28-36, 45.
17. *Ibid.,* p. 37; Avakumovic, p. 24.
18. Sobolen, *et al, Outline History of the Comintern,* pp. 133-4.
19. Accounts of the meeting are found in Rodney, pp. 37-39 and Avakumovic, p. 21.

20. Mine Mill Papers, Box 160, file 1, "Proceedings of the Third Annual Convention of the OBU. Winnipeg, September 26, 1921."
21. Mine Mill Papers, Box 160, file 1, "Report of the Red International of Labor Unions Congress opened in Moscow July 3, 1921. Delegate J. R. Knight." January 13, 1922.
22. Avakumovic, p. 29.
23. Russell Collection II, Box 4, file 17, Winnipeg CLC Minutes, February 14, 1922.
24. *BC Federationist,* January 20, 1922.
25. *The Worker,* March 15, 1922.
26. *OBU Bulletin,* February 23, 1922, "Letter Box"; *Ibid.,* May 18, 1922.
27. *OBU Bulletin,* May 18, 1922; Orlikow Interviews, R. B. Russell, tape 6; Russell Collection II, Box 4, file 17, Winnipeg CLC Minutes, March 12, 1922.
28. *OBU Bulletin,* March 23, 1922.
29. *Ibid.,* May 4, 1922.
30. *Ibid.,* May 18, 1922.
31. *The Worker,* August 1, 1922.
32. Russell Collection II, Box 4, file 17, Winnipeg CLC Minutes, November 28, 1922.
33. Alberta, Attorney General Papers, AC 75 126, Box 232, file "Strike Reports," Report of Detective F. Lesley, April 9, 1923.
34. Mine Mill Papers, Box 160, file 1, Russell to Rose, May 24, 1923.
35. *Ibid.,* May 26, 1923.
36. Mine Mill Papers, Box 160, file 1, "Minutes of the Fourth General Convention of the One Big Union, Winnipeg, August 3, 1923."
37. Mine Mill Papers, Box 160, file 1, Legere to General Executive Board, October 4, 1923.
38. Russell Collection II, Box 5, file 20, Winnipeg CLC Exec. Minutes, February 26, 1924.
39. *Ibid.,* Box 4, file 18, Executive circular to Winnipeg Central labor Council, n.d.
40. *Ibid.,* Box 4, file 19, Winnipeg CLC Exec. Minutes, September 26, 1923.
41. *Ibid.,* Box 4, file 18, Executive circular to Winnipeg CLC, n.d.
42. *Ibid.,* Box 4, file 17, Winnipeg CLC Minutes, October 2, 1923.
43. *Ibid.,* Box 5, file 20, Winnipeg CLC Minutes, January 8, 1924.
44. *OBU Bulletin,* February 21, 1924.
45. Frank, "Class Conflict . . .," pp. 172-178; MacEwan, *Miners and Steelworkers,* pp. 78-89.
46. MacEwan, pp. 91-110.
47. *Ibid.,* p. 113ff.
48. Mine Mill Papers, Box 160, file 1, Russell to Roberts, December 10, 1923.

49. MacEwan, pp. 123-126.

50. Mine Mill Papers, Box 160, file 2, Russell to Roberts, April 9, 1924.

51. Derber, "The Idea of Industrial Democracy . . .," pp. 8-9.

52. *OBU Bulletin*, April 10, 1924.

53. *Ibid.*, June 19 and 26, 1924; *The Worker*, July 12, 1924.

54. Russell Collection II, Box 4, file 18, Joint Executive Minutes, July 18, 1924.

55. *OBU Bulletin*, August 21, 1924.

56. *Ibid.*, September 25, 1924.

57. *Ibid.;* Russell Collection II, Box 4, file 18, Special GEB Meeting, September 29, 1924.

58. *OBU Bulletin*, September 25, 1924.

59. Reprinted in *OBU Bulletin*, October 9, 1924.

60. Russell Collection II, Box 4, file 18, Joint Executive Board Minutes, October 11, 1924.

61. Orlikow Interviews, R. B. Russell, tape 6.

62. MacEwan, pp. 127-128.

63. *The Worker*, November 15, 1924; *OBU Bulletin*, October 9, 1924.

64. *Ibid.*, pp. 129-134.

65. See MacEwan, pp. 135-147.

66. See, for example, *OBU Bulletin*, February 12, April 16, April 23, 1925.

67. *The Worker*, June 13, 1925.

68. *OBU Bulletin*, July 23, 1925.

69. Russell Collection II, Box 5, file 20, Joint Executive Board Meeting, September 8, 1926.

70. Russell Collection II, Box 5, file 22, Joint Executive Board Minutes, July 10, 1926.

71. *Halifax Chronicle*, July 30, 1926; *Labour Organization in Canada*, 1926, p. 50; *Montreal Gazette*, August 7, 1926.

72. *Labour Organization in Canada*, 1926, p. 50; *Halifax Herald*, August 26, 1926; *Globe*, August 28, 1926.

73. Russell Collection II, Box 10, file 5, Pamphlet "The New Conspiracy"; Russell Collection II, Box 5, file 23, Winnipeg CLC Minutes, January 4, 1927.

74. See, for example, Russell Collection II, Box 5, file 21, Winnipeg CLC Minutes, November 23, 1926.

75. Mine Mill Papers, Box 160, file 2, Roberts to Dunn, July 26, 1926.

76. Jordan, *Survival*, p. 219.

77. Russell Collection II, Box 5, file 22, GEB Minutes, May 3, 1926.

78. Russell Collection II, Box 5, file 21, Winnipeg CLC Minutes, June 15, 1926.

79. *Labour Organization in Canada*, 1927, p. 49.

80. March 17, 1927.

81. *Labour Organization in Canada,* 1927, p. 52, gives ACCL membership; p. 60 gives claimed OBU membership; membership on which per capita was based is in Russell Collection II, Box 5, file 23, Joint Executive Minutes, March 29, 1927.
82. *Labour Organization in Canada,* 1927, p. 50.
83. "Minutes of the Fifth General Convention of the One Big Union, Winnipeg, May 2, 1927" in Canada Department of Labour Library.

CHAPTER 10

1. Russell Collection II, Box 6, file 26, Joint Executive Board Minutes, August 27, 1929.
2. Logan, pp. 382-385; *Canada Year Book,* 1938, p. 755.
3. Jordan, p. 249.
4. Russell Collection II, Box 9, file 46, Winnipeg CLC Minutes, December 6, 1955; May 1, 1956.
5. *Ibid.,* Winnipeg CLC Minutes, May 1, 1956; *Labour Gazette,* June 1956, pp. 650-651.
6. *Ibid.,* June 6, 1956.
7. See Fussell, *The Great War,* pp. 90ff for a discussion of Sassoon's work.

Bibliography

PRIVATE PAPERS AND CORRESPONDENCE

American Federation of Labor Papers, Samuel L. Gompers Correspondence. State Historical Society of Wisconsin.

Bengough Papers. Public Archives of Canada (PAC).

Borden Papers. PAC.

Canadian Brotherhood of Railway, Transport and General Workers Papers. PAC.

Canadian Pacific Railway, Colonization Papers. Glenbow Alberta Institute (GAI).

Coal Operators Association of Western Canada Papers. GAI.

Consolidated Mining and Smelting Corporation Papers. Provincial Archives of British Columbia.

Farmilo Papers. Provincial Museum and Archives of Alberta (PMAA).

Flavelle Papers. PAC.

Frontier College Papers. PAC.

Gompers, Samuel, Letterbooks (microfilm). University of North Carolina Library.

International Brotherhood of Electrical Workers #348 and #410 (Calgary) Collection. GAI.

MacInnis Collection. University of British Columbia Special Collections (UBC).

Manning Papers. Provincial Archives of Manitoba (PAM).

Martin Papers. Saskatchewan Archives.

Meighen Papers. PAC.

Mine Mill Papers. UBC.

Montcrieff Papers. PAM.

Moore Papers. PAC.

Morrison, Frank, Letterbooks. William R. Perkins Library, Duke University.

One Big Union Vertical File #213. UBC.

One Big Union Papers and Correspondence. PAM.

Rigg/Rees Papers. PAM.

Russell Collection. (This is in two parts: MG 10 A14-1 acquired in 1972 and MG 10 A14-2 acquired in 1975). PAM.

Sifton, A. L., Papers, PAC.

United Mine Workers of America, District 18, Papers. GAI.

Washington State Federation of Labor Papers. University of Washington Library (UWL).

White, Sir Thomas, Papers. PAC.

UNPUBLISHED GOVERNMENT RECORDS AND DOCUMENTS

Canada, Department of Immigration and Colonization Papers. PAC.

Canada, Department of Justice Papers. PAC.

Canada, Department of Labour Papers. PAC.

Canada, Department of Labour, "Evidence Taken Before the Royal Commission on Industrial Relations, Justice T. G. Mathers, Commissioner." Department of Labour Library (DLL).

Canada, Department of National Defence Papers. PAC.

Canada, Royal Canadian Mounted Police Papers. PAC.

Alberta, Attorney General Papers. PMAA.

Alberta, "Report of Alberta Coal Mining Industry Commission, December 23, 1919." GAI.

Alberta, "Inquiry Re: Mining Conditions, Crows Nest Pass, n.d." in United Mine Workers, District 18 Papers. GAI.

Manitoba, Court Records—King's Bench, "The King vs William Ivens" trial evidence. PAM.

Manitoba, Legislative Assembly, Sessional Paper #46, March 1923, "Report: The Council of Industry for the Province of Manitoba, May 1920—November 1922. PAM.

PUBLISHED GOVERNMENT MATERIAL

Canada, Dominion Bureau of Statistics. *Canada Year Book 1920*. Ottawa: King's Printer, 1922.

Canada, Department of Labour. *Labour Gazette*.

Canada, Department of Labour. *Annual Report on Labour Organization in Canada*.

Canada, Department of Labour. *Report of the Royal Commission on Coal Mining Disputes on Vancouver Island*. Samuel Price, Commissioner. Ottawa: King's Printer, 1913.

Canada, Department of Labour. *Wages and Hours of Labour in Canada, 1901-1920*.

Canada, House of Commons. Sessional Papers: 36a, 1903, Vol. 13, *Report of the Royal Commission on Industrial Disputes in the Province of British Columbia;* 36a, 1904, Vol. 13, *Evidence Taken Before the Royal Commission to Inquire into Industrial Disputes in British Columbia;* 36a, 1914, Vol. 27, *Sixth Report of the Registrar of Boards of Conciliation and Investigation of the Proceedings under "The Industrial Disputes Investigation Act 1907" for Fiscal Year Ending March 31, 1913;* 26a, 1915, *Summary Report of the Mines Branch of the Department of Mines for 1914;* 28, 1918, *Report of the Royal North West Mounted Police for 1917.*

Bibliography

Alberta, Department of Public Works. *Annual Report of the Department of Public Works of Alberta 1916.* Edmonton: King's Printer, 1917.

British Columbia. *Report of the Royal Commission on Labour, 1914.*

British Columbia, Department of Labour. *The Logging Labour Force in Coastal British Columbia.* n.p., 1969.

British Columbia, Department of Mines. *Annual Report of the Minister of Mines.*

British Columbia, Bureau of Mines. *Special Reports on Coal Mine Explosions.* Victoria: King's Printer, 1918.

Nova Scotia, Department of Mines. *Annual Report on Mines 1940.* Halifax: King's Printer, 1941.

UNPUBLISHED PROCEEDINGS AND REPORTS

Boilermakers Lodge 126 (Winnipeg) Minutes. PAM.

Brotherhood of Railway Carmen of America (Calgary) Lodge 145 Minutes. GAI.

Calgary Labor Temple Company Minutes. GAI.

Calgary Trades and Labour Council Correspondence and Minutes. GAI.

Edmonton Trades and Labor Council, Minutes of General Meetings. PMAA.

King County Central Labor Council (Seattle) Minutes. UWL.

Painters, Decorators and Paperhangers Local 1016 Minutes. PMAA.

Refinery Oil Workers Union Minutes (IOCO, B.C.). UBC.

Trades and Labor Congress of Canada, Executive Council Minutes. PAC.

United Brotherhood of Carpenters and Joiners of America (Seattle) Locals 131 and 1289 Minutes. UWL.

United Brotherhood of Carpenters and Joiners of America (Edmonton) Minutes. PMAA.

Vancouver Labor Temple Company Minutes. UBC.

Vancouver Labor Temple Company Directors Minutes. UBC.

Vancouver Trades and Labor Council Regular Minutes. UBC.

Vancouver Trades and Labor Council Executive Board Minutes. UBC.

PUBLISHED PROCEEDINGS AND PAPERS

Alberta Federation of Labour. *Proceedings of the Annual Conventions of the Alberta Federation of Labor.*

British Columbia Federation of Labor. *Report of the Proceedings of the Annual Conventions of the British Columbia Federation of Labor.*

Fools and Wise Men

International Association of Machinists. *Proceedings of the Second Annual Convention of District Lodge No. 2, Winnipeg, Manitoba, December 12-15, 1918.*

One Big Union. *The Origin of the One Big Union: A Verbatim Report of the Calgary Conference, 1919* (Winnipeg, n.d.).

Trades and Labor Congress of Canada. *Reports of the Annual Convention of the Trades and Labor Congress of Canada.*

BOOKS, ARTICLES AND DISSERTATIONS

Anderson, Frank W. *Hillcrest Mine Disaster.* Frontier Books, 1969.

Arnott, R. Page. *South Wales Miners.* London: George Allen & Unwin, Ltd., 1967.

Artibise, A. F. J. *Winnipeg: A Social History of Urban Growth, 1874-1914.* Montreal: McGill-Queen's University Press, 1975.

Askin, W. R. "Labour Unrest in Edmonton and District and its Coverage by the Edmonton Press: 1918-1919." Unpublished M.A. thesis, University of Alberta, 1973.

Avakumovic, I. *The Communist Party in Canada: A History.* Toronto: McClelland & Stewart, 1975.

Avery, D. "Foreign Workers and Labour Radicalism in the Western Canadian Mining Industry: 1900-1919." Paper presented to the Western Canadian Urban History Conference, University of Winnipeg, October 1974.

———. "The Radical Alien and the Winnipeg General Strike." In Berger, C. and Cook, R., eds. *The West and the Nation.* Toronto: McClelland & Stewart, 1976.

Beattie, Bill. "Memoirs of the I.W.W." *Labour History* (Canberra, Australia), November 1967.

Bedford, Ian. "The One Big Union, 1918-1923." In Bedford, I. and Curnow, R. *Initiative and Organization.* Sydney, Australia: F. W. Chesire, 1963.

———. "The Industrial Workers of the World in Australia." *Labour History* (Canberra, Australia), November 1967.

Bercuson, David J. *Confrontation at Winnipeg.* Montreal: McGill-Queen's University Press, 1974.

Bergren, Myrtle. *Tough Timber.* Toronto: Progress Books, 1967.

Bradwin, Edmund. *The Bunkhouse Man.* Toronto: University of Toronto Press (Reprint Edition), 1972.

Brinkley, J. E. "The Western Federation of Miners." Unpublished Ph.D. thesis, University of Utah, 1972.

Brooks, John G. *American Syndicalism: The IWW.* New York: Macmillan, 1972.

Brown, R. C. and Cook, G. R. *Canada: 1896-1921, A Nation Transformed.* Toronto: McClelland & Stewart, 1974.

Campbell, E. W. *History of the Australian Labor Movement, A Marxist Interpretation.* Sydney, Australia: Current Book Distributors, 1945.

290

Bibliography

Careless, J. M. S. "Aspects of Urban Life in the West, 1870-1914." In Rasporich, A. W. and Klassen, H. C., eds. *Prairie Perspectives 2*. Toronto: Holt, Rhinehart & Winston, 1973.

Cherwinski, W. J. C. "Organized Labour in Saskatchewan: The TLC Years, 1905-1945." Unpublished Ph.D. thesis, University of Alberta, 1972.

Childe, V. G. *How Labour Governs*. London: The Labour Publishing Company, 1973.

Cole, G. D. H. *The World of Labour*. London: G. Bell and Sons Ltd., 1915.

_____. *Attempts at General Union*. London: Macmillan, 1953.

Conlin, J. R. *Bread and Roses Too: Studies of the Wobblies*. Westport, Connecticut: Greenwood Publishing Corporation, 1969.

Denison, Merrill. *Canada's First Bank: A History of the Bank of Montreal*. Volume II. Toronto: McClelland & Stewart, 1967.

den Otter, A. A. "A Social History of the Alberta Coal Branch." Unpublished M.A. thesis, University of Alberta, 1967.

Derber, M. "The Idea of Industrial Democracy in America: 1915-1935." *Labor History* (New York), Vol. 8, No. 1.

Dubofsky, Melvyn. "The Origins of Western Working Class Radicalism, 1890-1905." *Labor History* (New York), Spring 1966.

Foner, P. S. *History of the Labor Movement in the United States*. Volume IV. *The Industrial Workers of the World, 1905-1917*. New York: International Publishers, 1965.

Forbes, E. R. "The Maritime Rights Movement of the 1920s." Unpublished Ph.D. thesis, Queen's University, 1975.

Frank, David. "Class Conflict in the Coal Industry: Cape Breton, 1922." In Kealey, G. S. and Warrian, P., eds., *Essays in Canadian Working Class History*. Toronto: McClelland & Stewart, 1976.

Friesen, G. "Yours in Revolt." *Labour/Le Travailleur*, 1976.

Fussell, Paul. *The Great War and Modern Memory*. New York: Oxford University Press, 1975.

Glynn-Ward, Hilda. *The Writing on the Wall*. Toronto: University of Toronto Press (Reprint Edition), 1974.

Gollan, R. A. "The Historical Perspective." In Matthews, P. W. D. and Ford, G. W., eds., *Australian Trade Unions*. Melbourne: Sun Books, 1968.

Gutman, H. G. "Work, Culture, and Society in Industrializing America, 1815-1919." *American Historical Review*, June 1973.

Hardy, George. *Those Stormy Years*. London: Lawrence & Wishart, 1956.

Harris, Joe. *The Bitter Fight*. Brisbane: University of Queensland Press, 1970.

Harrison, J. F. C. *Robert Owen and the Owenites in Britain and America*. London: Routledge and Kegan Paul, 1969.

Hopkins, G. C. *Canadian Annual Review of Public Affairs*. Toronto: The Annual Review Publishing Company.

Jamieson, S. *Times of Trouble*. Ottawa: Information Canada, 1971.

Fools and Wise Men

Jefferys, J. B. *The Story of the Engineers: 1800-1945.* London: Lawrence & Wishart Ltd., 1945.

Jensen, V. H. *Heritage of Conflict: Labor Relations in the Nonferrous Metals Industry up to 1930.* New York: Cornell University Press, 1950.

Jordan, Mary V. *Survival: Labour's Trials and Tribulations in Canada.* Toronto: McDonald House, 1975.

Karas, F. P. "Labour and Coal in the Crows Nest Pass, 1925-1935." Unpublished M.A. thesis, University of Calgary, 1972.

Kavanagh, Jack. *The Vancouver Island Strike.* Vancouver: B.C. Miners Liberation League.

Larmour, C. "The 'Y Club' and the One Big Union." *Labour History* (Canberra), November 1970.

Levine (Lorwin) L. *Syndicalism in France.* New York: Columbia University Press, 1914.

Lingenfelter, Richard E. *The Hardrock Miners: A History of the Mining Labor Movement in the American West, 1863-1893.* Los Angeles: University of California Press, 1974.

Lipton, C. *The Trade Union Movement of Canada, 1827-1959.* Montreal: Les Presses Sociales, 1968.

Logan, H. A. *Trade Unions in Canada.* Toronto: Macmillan, 1948.

McCormack, A. R. "The Origins and Extent of Western Labour Radicalism: 1896-1919." Unpublished Ph.D. thesis, University of Western Ontario, 1973.

————. "The Industrial Workers of the World in Western Canada: 1905-1914." *Historical Papers,* 1975.

MacEwan, Paul. *Miners and Steelworkers.* Toronto: Samuel Stevens Hakkert & Co., 1976.

Macmillan, C. J. "Trade Unionism in District 18, 1900-1925: A Case Study." Unpublished M.A. thesis, University of Alberta, 1968.

McNaught, K. "Political Trials and the Canadian Political Tradition." In Friedland, M. L. *Courts and Trials.* Toronto: University of Toronto Press, 1975.

Mann, Tom. *Tom Mann's Memoirs.* London: MacGibbon & Kee Ltd., 1967.

Masters, D. C. *The Winnipeg General Strike.* Toronto: University of Toronto Press, 1950.

Morrison, Jean F. "Community and Conflict: A Study of the Working Class and Its Relationships at the Canadian Lakehead, 1903-1913." Unpublished M.A. thesis, Lakehead University, 1974.

Morton, Desmond. "Sir William Otter and Internment Operations in Canada during the First World War." *Canadian Historical Review,* March 1974.

Murray, R. K. *Red Scare: A Study of National Hysteria, 1919-1920.* New York: McGraw Hill, 1964.

Ormsby, M. A. *British Columbia: A History.* Toronto: Macmillan, 1958.

Bibliography

Pelling, H. *A History of British Trade Unionism*. London: Macmillan, 1963.

Phillips, Paul. *No Power Greater*. Vancouver: British Columbia Federation of Labour, 1967.

_____. "The National Policy and the Development of the Western Canadian Labour Movement." In Rasporich, A. W. and Klassen, H. C., eds., *Prairie Perspective 2*. Toronto: Holt, Rhinehart & Winston, 1973.

Prothero, I. "William Benbow and the Concept of the General Strike." *Past and Present*, May 1974, pp. 132-171.

Robin, Martin. *Radical Politics and Canadian Labour*. Kingston: Queen's University Centre for Industrial Relations, 1968.

Rocker, R. *The London Years* (Translated by J. Leftwich). London: Robert Anscombe & Co. Ltd., 1956.

Rodney, W. *Soldiers of the International: A History of the Communist Party of Canada, 1919-1929*. Toronto: University of Toronto Press, 1968.

Snowden, P. *Socialism and Syndicalism*. London: Collins Clear Type Press, 1915.

Sobolev, A. I. *et al. Outline History of the Communist International*. Moscow: Progress Publishers, 1971.

Steeves, D. G. *The Compassionate Rebel*. Vancouver: Boag Foundation, 1960.

Sutcliffe, J. T. *A History of Trade Unionism in Australia*. Melbourne: Macmillan, 1967.

Taraska, E. "The Calgary Craft Union Movement, 1900-1920." Unpublished M.A. thesis, University of Calgary, 1975.

Taylor, J. "The Urban West: Public Welfare and a Theory of Urban Development." In McCormack, R. and Macpherson, I., eds., *Cities in the West*. Ottawa: National Museum of Man, 1975.

Torr, D. *Tom Mann and His Times*. London: Lawrence & Wishart Ltd., 1956.

Walsh, Tom. *What is this Shop Stewards Movement?* London: 1920.

Warrian, Peter. "The One Big Union in Canada, 1919-1922." Unpublished M.A. thesis, University of Waterloo, 1971.

Woywitka, A. B. "Drumheller Strike of 1919." *Alberta Historical Review*, Winter 1973.

INTERVIEWS

Bercuson Collection, Public Archives of Canada.

Millar Collection, Public Archives of Canada.

Chauncey D. Orchard Collection, University of British Columbia Special Collections.

Stubbs, C. "Reminiscences On Early Union Efforts Among Coal Miners In Alberta." Glenbow Alberta Institute.

Index

Alberta, and Trade union movement, 31; and Western Labor Conference, 86; and socialism, 51; and coal miners, 214; and OBU, 229.

Alberta Federation of Labor, 72, 79, 112

Alberta Labor News, 220

All Canadian Congress of Labour, 246, 248

Allen, E. J. B., 35

Amalgamated Association of Iron, Steel and Tin Workers, 235

Amalgamated Clothing Workers of America, and OBU, 118

Amalgamated Society of Engineers (British), 34

Americans, influence of, on mining, 16, 17, 37, 255; and growth of unions, 31, 37, 40, 255; and development of Canadian unions, 45, 246; and labour radicalism, 32, 38, 40, 255

American Federation of Labor, 38, 172, 245, 256, 260; disenchantment with, 45, 78, 257; and Western Labor Conference, 120; and "Duncan Plan", 122; and OBU, 217; in Winnipeg, 145-155; in Vancouver, 155-157; in Saskatchewan, 158; in Montana, 179; and communism, 221, 226; and CIO, 249

American Labor Union and syndicalism, 40; and OBU, 120

American Railway Union, 120

Anarchism, 33, 35, 42

Appeal to Reason, 40

Armstrong, E. H., 235

Armstrong, George (SPC organizer) 44, 123, 154; and Winnipeg General Strike, 100

Armstrong, W. H. (Director of Coal Operations for Western Canada), 67, 136-142, 196, 197, 202, 204-206

Ault, Harry, 177, 180

Australia, 76, 77, 124, 125

Australian Workers Union, 77

Baltimore and Ohio Plan, 237, 238

Barker, Allen E., 145, 146

Barrett brothers, 27

Barrett, Silby, 235, 236

Barretts, Moses, 43

Bartholomew, H. M., 225, 227

Beard, Henry, 204, 206, 213

Bellamy, Edward and nationalism, 31, 47

Bengough, Percy, 116

Berg, Carl, 51, 78, 85, 132; and OBU, 106-111, 116, 125-128, 159, 169

Blaylock, Selwyn Gwillyn, 189-191

Bloor, Ella Reeve, 220

Boards of Trade, 25

Bolshevism, 88-91, 95, 97, 99, 103, 104; and OBU, 115, 149, 150, 160; *see also* "Red Scare"

Borden, Prime Minister Robert Laird, and organized labour, 60, 63, 104; and "Red Scare," 94, 98, 99

Bowser, W. J., 54

Brandon, Manitoba, 231

Bray, R. E., 100

British Columbia, x; and immigration, 22; and growth of unions, 30, 39, 253; I.W.W. in, 41; socialism in, 51; and OBU, 189-196, 216

British Columbia Federation of Labour, 46, 54, 72, 82; and Victor Midgley, 105, 106; and OBU, 114, 127, 156, 252

British Columbia Federationist, 37, 107, 112, 155, 156, 157, 162, 209, 220

British Columbia Loggers Union, 135

British Columbia Sugar Refinery, 27

British Empire Steel and Coal Corporation (BESCO), 234, 235, 236, 238, 241, 242, 243, 244

British Triple Alliance, 80, 81, 123

Broatch, A. G., 66, 111, 112, 133, 205, 230

Browne, Ed, 80; and OBU, 113, 114, 136, 137; and 1919 strike, 138, 139, 140, 141, 142, 143, 197, 199, 200, 201, 204, 261

Bruce, John, 153, 157

Buhay, Michael, 224

Buhay, Rebecca, 161, 233

Burke, Frank, 119

Burns, Pat, 27

Business, attitudes of, 26, 27; power of, 23; and unions, 60, 261

Cahan, C. H., 90, 99

Calder, J. A., 97

Calgary, ix; and depression, 22; and working conditions, 24; and unions, 31, 65, 66; and strikes, 71, 95, 132, 133; and 1919 UMW convention, 79; and OBU, 111, 112, 158, 159, 165, 206, 211, 216, 229, 230, 260

Calgary Central Labour Council, 162

Fort William, Ontario, and radicalism, 42; and strikes, 53; and OBU, 228
Frontier College, 97, 98

General Federation of Trade Unions (British), 34
general strike, in Britain, 36; in syndicalism, 35, 40; growing support for, 45, 53, 259; early attempts at, 54, 55, 64, 71; and TLC 78; and UMW, 80, 81; and BCFL, 82, 83; and Western Labor Conference, 85; 1918 Vancouver, 91, 106; 1919 Winnipeg, 94, 95, 96, 100-102, 129; leaders of, 215; and OBU, 150, 151, 156
George, Henry, and Single Tax, 31, 47
Glace Bay, Nova Scotia, and 1925 strike, 241-244
Gompers, Samuel, 38, 104, 154, 256; and conscription, 63; and TLC, 69, 70; and UMW local, 80; and general strikes, 120; and "Duncan Plan", 122; and OBU in Montana, 179
Goodwin, Albert, 91; and general strike, 106
Graham, Thomas, 5, 6
Granby Consolidated Mining Co., 19
Grand National Consolidated Trades Union, 258
Great Britain, and labour radicalism, 32, 33, 35; and union movement, 34, 35, 36, 37, 76; and "Red Scare," 98; immigrants from and Canadian labour movement, 255
Great War Veterans Association, and "Red Scare," 91, 92; and OBU, 119; and B.C. loggers, 135; and 1919 coal strike, 198, 199
Great West Saddlery Co., 27
Gunn, J. T., 121
Gutteridge, Helena, 135

Haggerty, Father Thomas, and IWW, 124
Hardie, Kier, 37
Halifax Herald, 239, 240
hardrock mining, hazards of, 13, 14; and contract system, 16, 17, 80, 144; and growth of unions, 30, 144, 253, 254; and Americans, 37; and Western Federation of Miners, 38; and OBU, 119, 143, 144, 189-195, 216, 261, 262; and communism, 263
Hardy, George, 77
Harrison, F. E., and coal mining, 141, 142, 202
Hay, A. C., 74
Haywood, William, and IWW, 41
Hazeltine, R., 85
Heaps, A. A., 100, 102

Henderson, Rose, 118, 125
Hillcrest mine disaster, 1, 2
Hillman, Sydney, 118
Hobson, S. G., and guild socialism, 35
Hooley, J., 112, 113, 132, 133, 159
Hoop, William, 66, 74
Horrigan, F. J., 119
Houston, John, 118, 233
Houston, William, 236, 238, 239

immigration, worker reaction to, 22, 23; and Saskatchewan labour movement, 32; and radicalism, 32, 252; and "Red Scare," 99, 100
immigrants, xii, xiii; East Indian, 22; oriental, 22; and organized labour, 23, 31, 71; living conditions of, 24; Italian, 31, 42, 116, 198; Slavic, 31, 116, 198; British and labour movement, 37; and World War I, 57; European and radicalism, 41, 42, 55; Ukrainian, 41, 42, 90; Jewish, 42, 160, 161; Finnish, 42, 164; Greek, 42; and language restrictions, 70, 71; and "Red Scare," 90, 97, 98, 99, 100; and OBU, 116, 160, 161; and growth of mine unions, 254
Imperial Munitions Board, 61, 65, 255
Industrial Disputes Investigation Act, 60, 61, 207, 213
Industrial Syndicalist Education League, 36
industrial unionism, 80, 82, 253
Industrial Workers of the World (IWW), 35, 112, 121, 124, 125, 128, 144, 149, 162, 165, 209, 257; influence of in western Canada, 40, 41, 51, 52, 115; declared illegal, 71; in Australia, 76, 77; and "Red Scare," 88, 89, 92, 98; and OBU, 166, 184, 245; in U.S.A., 172, 179, 184, 186, 187; and Russia, 221
International Association of Machinists, 50, 116, 117, 237
International Longshoreman's Association, 174
International Union of Mine, Mill and Smelter Workers, 143, 190, 192; *see* also Western Federation of Miners
Irvine, Dave, 79, 80, 140, 142
Ivens, William, and *Western Labor News,* 66; and Winnipeg General Strike, 100, 102, 130, 215; and union schism, 141

Jansen, Carl, and CPC, 223
Johns, R. J., 65, 66, 74, 75, 84, 85; and Winnipeg General Strike, 100, 215; and OBU, 106, 107, 108, 117, 118, 126, 150, 162, 164, 233, 260